SEVENTH EDITION

A Student's Guide
to History

Jules R. Benjamin

Ithaca College

Bedford Books ⋙ **Boston**

For Bedford Books

President and Publisher: Charles H. Christensen
General Manager and Associate Publisher: Joan E. Feinberg
Managing Editor: Elizabeth M. Schaaf
History Editor: Katherine E. Kurzman
Developmental Editor: Charisse M. Kiino
Production Editor: Maureen Murray
Production Assistant: Deborah Baker
Copyeditor: Phil Sbaratta
Cover Design: Ann Gallager
Cover Art: World map from *Novus Atlas* published by Willem Janszoom Blaeu and Iohannem Blaeu, Amsterdam, 1649. Courtesy of the Harvard Map Collection.
Composition: Pine Tree Composition, Inc.
Printing and Binding: Haddon Craftsmen, Inc.

Library of Congress Catalog Card Number: 97–72369

Manufactured in the United States of America.
2   1   0   9   8
f   e   d   c   b

For information, write: Bedford Books, 75 Arlington Street, Boston, MA 02116 (617-426-7440)

ISBN: 0–312–14977–8

Acknowledgments

Antiwar Demonstration at the Democratic National Convention (1968). The Bettmann Archive.

Excerpt from *The Limits of Power* by Joyce Kolko and Gabriel Kolko. Copyright © 1972 by Joyce and Gabriel Kolko. Reprinted by permission of HarperCollins Publishers, Inc.

The Marked Men. Copyright © 1969. Éditions du Seuil. Copyright © Aris Fakinos for the Greek text. Reprinted by permission of Georges Borchardt, Inc.

The Massacre in the Main Temple (Codex Duran) from *The Broken Spears* by Miguel Leon-Portilla. © 1962, 1990 by Beacon Press. Expanded and updated edition © 1992 by Miguel Leon-Portilla. Reproduced by permission of Beacon Press, Boston.

Middlesex Company Boarding House Regulations. The American Textile History Museum.

Excerpt from *Narrative of the Life of Frederick Douglass, An American Slave, Written by Himself,* Edited with an Introduction by David W. Blight. Copyright © 1993 by Bedford Books.

Offerings to Cortés. Courtesy of Bancroft Library, University of California, Berkeley.

From *Rise to Globalism* by Stephen E. Ambrose. Copyright © 1971, 1976, 1980, 1983, 1988 by Stephen Ambrose. Used by permission of Viking Penguin, a division of Penguin Books USA Inc.

Rural Life in Ithaca, N.Y. The Dewitt Historical Society.

The World since 1500: A Global History, fourth edition, by Stravianos, © 1982. Reprinted by permission of Prentice Hall, Inc., Upper Saddle River, N.J.

Yahoo! Search. Text and artwork copyright © 1996 by YAHOO!, INC. All rights reserved. YAHOO! and the YAHOO! logo are trademarks of YAHOO!, INC.

A Student's Guide to History

To Elaine, Aaron, and Adam

Preface

I was motivated to write this guide when I discovered, as have so many others, that there was an invisible barrier between my students and the material I was teaching them. This barrier differed from one student to the next, but at its core was the students' need to learn basic skills: study, research, and writing. Although many of my students had little background knowledge in history, the skills barrier was the more serious problem and was very time consuming. If my students could not take concise notes, if they could not understand what an exam question required of them, or if they could not write clearly, then my effort to explain the meaning of the past ran up against a wall of incomprehension.

I sought to attack the skills barrier outside the classroom so that I could devote my class time to teaching history. In this effort I turned to my students — I asked them why the course material seemed so formidable and what they needed to know to demonstrate their understanding of it. The first edition of the *Guide* was a kind of collaboration: the original structure, still discernible in this seventh incarnation, took the form of responses to their needs.

Chapter 1 discusses why people study history and how we, as historians, go about our investigations. It examines the different interpretations of history and the differing directions of research in the discipline. This chapter also describes how the study of history can prepare your students for a variety of careers. Chapters 2 and 3 teach fundamental skills about reading a history assignment, taking notes in class, studying for exams, and writing a book review or essay exam. These chapters include annotated examples guiding students to the main ideas of a text; a sample book review; and a section on reading maps, charts, graphs, tables, and other nonwritten materials. Chapters 4 and 5 deal with more complex tasks — preparing and writing a research paper. These chapters help students choose a research topic, narrow it down to a practical theme, use the library (and the new electronic aids) to gather information, organize their research, and present the results of their work. Chapters 4 and 5 also stress the importance of good writing skills and the dangers of plagiarism. The new full-scale, annotated sample research paper that concludes Chapter 5 illustrates how to put together research findings and how to write footnotes/endnotes and a bibliography.

Appendix A describes the different types of information available for history research and lists hundreds of sources that can lead your students to everything from a short definition of *feudalism* to a series of books on the history of medicine. Also added to this edition is a section on electronic resources available online from most library computers. This broad list of resources will help your students with almost any assignment in almost any history course. Appendix B elaborates on subjects such as local and family research and library organization and offers extended documentation models (including new examples for electronic sources and the Internet).

New to This Edition

This latest edition of the *Guide* is the most extensive revision I have undertaken. Each successive edition, the seventh included, has benefited from the comments and suggestions from some of the hundreds of instructors who have assigned it and from some of the more than a quarter-million students who have read it over the years.

In this edition, I have strengthened the *Guide* in four fundamental areas. First, following the recent changes in the study of history, I have highlighted the latest directions in which the discipline is moving. Second, I have broken down typical assignments into distinct parts to help students feel better equipped to complete each task without feeling overwhelmed by the whole. Third, I have made the *Guide* a more practical and flexible reference tool. The coverage of basic skills is more thorough and up-to-date, and a new design allows students to get in and out of the book more easily. I have added more on the computer and online information and have spent more time taking students step-by-step through the writing process. The resources listed in Appendix A are expanded and updated, and with such additions as a glossary, an index, shaded pages for quick location of documentation models, and annotations on reading and writing examples, students can go directly to the answers to their specific questions. Lastly, I have tried to make students aware of the impact of the electronic revolution on our field and provided instruction on how they can begin their research on the Internet. I have added, expanded, or amended topics in every chapter:

Attention to changes in the discipline.   While retaining explanations of both traditional and new directions of historical research, I have brought the discussion to the present day by emphasizing the recent focus on local, global, and comparative history and on the greater integration of approaches by historians. Also, a new section devoted to historiography helps students grasp the historian's continual reevaluation of the past.

Four new examples for critical reading. In response to users' requests for a better demonstration of how to read for a text's main ideas and synthesize that information for class assignments, I have added new excerpts of primary and secondary sources, an underlined and annotated textbook page, and examples of conflicting evidence in both texts and visuals. For example, two primary documents on the American Revolution help students sift through different accounts to arrive at a more accurate understanding of a specific event in history.

Completely overhauled research and writing sections. In this edition, I have added fuller explanations of online searches and of each stage of the writing process to help students find resources in the library, formulate research topics, outline and draft a paper, cite sources, and revise. The seventh edition has complete descriptions and examples of research and writing outlines, along with additional models of footnotes/endnotes students encounter most often, and an improved definition of and warning against plagiarism.

A new annotated sample paper with endnotes and a bibliography. The new sample student paper, on a topic your students will find interesting — women workers in the Lowell, Massachusetts, textile mills in the mid-1800s — shows them how to draft a research paper. With fuller explanations in the text and new marginal notes, students are led through each step of the writing process, from the writing outline and the incorporation of primary sources (including information from the Internet), to the organization and documentation of the paper.

Guidelines. New boxed guidelines can serve as checklists while your students work on assignments. These helpful hints include pointers for participating in class as well as the key elements students need to include in their exams, book reviews, outlines, and papers.

Updated and expanded reference resources. The more than six hundred basic reference sources and guides in Appendix A, categorized by type and subject, familiarize students with research materials available in the library and online. A new section on electronic sources will help your students navigate the Internet with explanations of search engines, guides, and databases as well as a list of top sites for history resources.

A better reference tool. A new design and added reference aids — a glossary of seventy terms, forty footnote/endnote and bibliography models (in Appendix B), and an index — make it easier for your students to find answers quickly to their most often-asked questions.

I am always looking to improve the *Guide* and would appreciate any suggestions users would like to share. The e-mail address for comments is guide7@ithaca.edu.

Acknowledgments

I wish to thank the many reviewers of the manuscript: Karen Gernant, Southern Oregon State University; Richard Tompson, University of Utah; Stanislao Pugliese, Hofstra University; Thomas Schwartz, Vanderbilt University; Judith Stone, Western Michigan University; Steven Jay White, Lexington Community College of the University of Kentucky; Jack Marietta, University of Arizona; Glenn T. Eskew, Georgia State University; Joseph Patrouch, Florida International University; David Rich; and David Pivar, California State University. I also want to express my great respect for those at Bedford Books who have contributed to this edition of the *Guide*: Charles Christensen, Joan Feinberg, Katherine Kurzman, Charisse Kiino, Elizabeth Schaaf, Maureen Murray, Deborah Baker, Susan Pace, Ann Gallager, and Phil Sbaratta. I am in their debt not only for their editorial skills but for their commitment to this book and its mission.

Jules R. Benjamin
Ithaca College

A Note to Students

This book has been around for a long time. Since I wrote the first edition in 1975, more than a quarter of a million students have read it. Each year, students have written telling me how the book helped them to master some important part of their work in a history course. Many have offered suggestions for improving the book and some of their ideas have been incorporated into the book you are about to read. You can still write to me or the publisher. Now you can also send your comments to me via e-mail. The address is: guide7@ithaca.edu.

I have tried to make this book useful to you regardless of the kind of history course you are taking. You may be taking world history, Western civilization, ancient history, modern history, social history, economic history, or the history of a particular region or nation. This book presents the tools you need to succeed in your history course. It also gives you skills that will open the past to you.

Each section of the book discusses a specific kind of assignment. Clear guidelines, practical examples, and concise explanations guide you through reading, studying, researching, and writing tasks. Care has been taken to organize the book in a way that makes it easy to find the answers to your questions about history assignments.

In addition to its practical purpose, I have also written this book to introduce you to the enormous world that is our heritage. This world is as fascinating as the world you live in today, or as any vision of the future. I hope to convince you that the study of history is not an idle journey into a dead past but a way to understanding and living in the present. You can use these tools to succeed not only in your history courses but in your future career. Finally, you can use them to answer important questions about your own life and your relationship to the world in which you live. This larger use is what makes the study of history really valuable.

Jules R. Benjamin
Ithaca College

Contents

C H A P T E R 1

The Subject of History and How to Use It

What Historians Are Trying to Do

Since the time when human beings invented writing, they have left records of their understanding of the world and of the events in their lives and how they felt about them. By studying the records that previous generations have left, we can find out about the kind of lives they led and how they faced their problems. We can use what we learn about the experiences of people who lived before us to help solve problems we face today. Though the modern world is quite different from the societies in which our ancestors lived, the story of their accomplishments and failures is the only yardstick by which we can measure the quality of our own lives and the success of our social arrangements.

All of us look into the past from time to time. We read historical novels or books about historical events. We gaze at old photographs or listen to the stories our grandparents tell. **Historians,**[1] however, make a serious and systematic study of the past and attempt to use the knowledge they gain to help explain human nature and contemporary affairs. Professional historians spend their lives pursuing the meaning of the past for the present. To amateurs, historical research is like a hobby, but their occasional journeys into the past may contribute to the store of human knowledge and can greatly influence their own lives. Your study and research as a student qualify you as an amateur historian. Your examination of the past is part of the same search for knowledge carried on generation after generation.

[1]Terms in **boldface** are defined in the Glossary.

What History Can Tell You

Everything that exists in the present has come out of the past, and no matter how new and unique it seems to be, it carries some of the past with it. The latest hit by the newest group is the result of the evolution of that group's musical style and of the trends in music and society that have influenced them. Perhaps their style developed from earlier rock styles associated with the Beatles, or perhaps they are taking off from even older folk themes used by Bob Dylan. Well, Dylan was influenced by Woody Guthrie, who wrote his songs in the 1930s and whose music grew out of his contact with the heritage of American folk music from the nineteenth century, which in turn had come in great measure from earlier music in England and Scotland, some of which has its origins in the Middle Ages. Modern jazz, such as the music of Duke Ellington and Billie Holiday or the more recent music of Miles Davis, Chick Corea, and Pat Metheny, evolved from the music of black communities in the United States and the Caribbean. Enslaved black people brought the earlier forms of that music with them from Africa in the eighteenth and nineteenth centuries. So you can see that the house of the present is filled with windows into the past.

The car you ride in, although it may have been designed only a few years ago, carries within it the basic components of the "horseless carriage" of the turn of the century. Your car works because people who knew how to make carriages, bicycles, and engines put their ideas together in a new way. The knowledge necessary to make the carriages and bicycles came, in turn, from earlier inventions. Some, like the wheel, go back into the antiquity of human history.

Everything has a history. At least part of the answer to any question about the contemporary world can come from studying the circumstances that led up to it. The problem is to find those past events, forces, arrangements, ideas, or facts that had the greatest influence on the present subject you have questions about. The more you understand about these past influences, the more you will know about the present subject to which they are related.

History and the Everyday World

Most of us are curious. Children are always asking their parents the "why" of things. When we grow up, we continue to ask questions because we retain our fascination with the mysteriousness and complexity of the world. Because everything has a history, most questions can be answered, at least in part, by historical investigation.

What are some of the things about which you are curious? Have you ever wondered why women's skirts in old movies are so long, or why French men often embrace one another whereas English men almost

never do? Perhaps you have wondered how the Kennedy or Rocke-
feller familes came to be rich, or why the Japanese attacked Pearl Har-
bor. Have you thought about why most of the people of southern Europe are Catholic whereas most northern Europeans are not? Many
Asian peoples bow when they greet one another; we shake hands. The
questions could go on forever; the answers are written somewhere in
the record of the past.

The record of the past is not only contained in musty volumes on library shelves; it is all around us in museums, historical preservations,
and the antique furnishings and utensils contained in almost every
household. Our minds are living museums because the ideas we hold
(for example, democracy, freedom, equality, competitiveness) have
come down to us by way of a long historical journey. Though we are
usually unaware of it, the past is always with us. Because history is literally at our fingertips, we can travel back into it without difficulty.

A Brief Journey into the Past

If you have ever driven any distance, you have probably ridden over
a system of very modern superhighways with high speed limits and no
cross traffic or stoplights. This national highway network, begun in the
1950s, connects all the major cities of the United States and is known
as the interstate system. These roads were planned by the Eisenhower
Administration in 1955, and, though they are the newest highways in
the country, they have a history that is more than four decades long.

Looking for the marks of history in the world around us is something like the task of the geologist or archeologist. However, instead of
digging down into the earth to uncover the past, the historical re-
searcher digs into the visible, everyday elements of society to find the
historical roots from which they sprang. The fact that the interstate
highway system built in the 1960s and 1970s had its origins in the 1950s
is just, so to speak, the uppermost layer of history. If a study of the
newest highways can take us back forty years, what about the historical
roots of the older highways or of the country roads? How far into the
past can we travel on them?

Turn off the eight-lane interstate, past the gleaming Exxon station,
past the drive-up window of Burger King, past the bright signs before
the multistoried Holiday Inn, and onto, say, U.S. Route 51 or 66. These
are older highways, built mostly in the 1940s and 1950s. Being from an
earlier period, like older strata of rock, perhaps they can tell us something of life in an earlier period of America.

When you leave the interstate system for this older road network,
you first notice that the speed limit is lower and that many of the buildings are older. As you ride along at the slower pace, there are no signs
saying "Downtown Freeway ½ mile" or "Indiana Turnpike — Exit 26N."
They say "Lubbock 38 miles," or "Cedar Rapids 14 miles." As you ap-

proach Lubbock or Cedar Rapids, you will see motels less elaborate than the Holiday Inn. They may be small wooden cottages with fading paint and perhaps a sign that says "Star Motor Court" or "Stark's Tourist Cabins." Instead of Burger King or McDonald's, you may pass "Betty's Restaurant" or "Little River Diner." If you pay close attention to these buildings and do not become distracted by the more modern structures between them, you can take a trip into history even as you ride along. All of the older restaurants, stores, and gas stations you see were built before the large shopping centers and parking lots that separate them, and they are clues to the history of the highway on which you are riding. Places like the Star Motor Court and the Little River Diner probably were built when the road was new. Unless they have been modernized, they are relics of a previous historical period — when men named Roosevelt and Truman were president and when the cars that rode by looked like balloons with their big rounded hoods, trunks, and fenders. The diner isn't air-conditioned, and the sign over the tourist cabins proudly proclaims that they are "heated." This is the world of the 1930s and 1940s.

Now turn off the highway at State Route 104 where the sign says "Russell Springs 3 miles" or where it says "Hughesville 6 miles." Again the speed limit drops, and the bright colors fade farther away. You are on a road that may have been built in the 1920s and 1930s or earlier (in older sections of America, the country roads can go back a hundred years or more). Time has removed many of the buildings that once stood along this road, but if you look closely, the past is there ready to speak to you. The gas station here has only one set of pumps, and the station office sells bread, eggs, and kerosene. The faded advertisements on the wall display some products that you may have never heard of — NeHi Orange and Red Man Chewing Tobacco. If you see a restaurant or motel, it may be boarded up because the people who used to stop in on their way to Russell Springs or Hughesville now go another way or may no longer live in the country but in a nearby city. However, many of the homes along Route 104 are still there. They were built when only farmland straddled the road, and they may go back to a time when horses and not internal combustion engines pulled the traffic past the front door. Such relics of early technology as old washing machines and refrigerators may stand on the tilting wooden porches, and a close look behind the tall weeds beside the dirt driveway may reveal the remains of a 1936 La Salle automobile. As you stop before one of the old farmhouses, the past is all around you, and, although the place does not appear in its youthful form, a little imagination can reconstruct what life was like here on the day in 1933 when President Roosevelt closed all the banks or the day in 1918 when the Great War in Europe ended.

The line linking past to present never breaks, and the house itself has a history, as do the people who once lived in it. In this sense, every house is haunted with its own past, and a keen eye can see the signs. Enter the house and you can see the stairway that was rebuilt in 1894, and in the main bedroom upstairs the fireplace, which was put in about 1878, the year the house was built. Perhaps the old Bible on the table near the bed notes the year the family came to the United States, and the dates in the early nineteenth century when the parents of the immigrants who built the house were born.

The story could go on forever, although the evidence would become slimmer and slimmer. You could find out from county records who owned the land before the house was built, going back perhaps to the time when the people who lived on the land were American Indians. In distance you may have traveled only ten or twenty miles from the interstate highway, and it may have taken you less than an hour; but by looking for the signs of the past in the present, you have traveled more than a hundred years into history.

If you think and study about the passage of time between the old farmhouse on the country road and the gleaming service station by the interstate, you may come to understand some of the social, political, and economic forces that moved events away from the old wooden porch and sent them speeding down the interstate highway. The more you know about this process, the more you will learn about the times when the farmhouse was new and the more you will understand how the interstate highway came about, what you are doing riding on it, and into what kind of a future you may be heading.

Historians don't usually wander into history in such a casual fashion. They have to be trained in their methods of investigation and analysis. As an introduction to your own historical research and study, the next section will describe some of the tools employed by historians in their examination of the records of the past.

How Historians Work

Like you, historians are challenged by the complexity of the world, and many want to use their studies of the past to help solve the problems of the present or future. The questions that can come to mind are numberless, and serious historical investigators must choose wisely among them. They do not want to spend a lot of effort pursuing the kind of question to which history has no answer (for example, "What is the purpose of the Universe?" "Am I a lovable person?" "Who is the smartest person in the world?"). Nor do they want to struggle to achieve the solution to a problem that is not of real importance. (Historical investigation can probably tell you who wore the first pair of pants with a zipper in it, but that might not be worth knowing.) The main difficulty facing historians is not eliminating unanswerable or unimportant questions but choosing among the important ones.

A historian's choice among important questions is determined by personal values, by the concerns of those who support the historian's work, by the nature of the time in which the historian lives, or by a combination of all of these. The ways in which these influences operate are very complex, and often historians themselves are unaware of them.

When the historian has chosen his or her subject, many questions still remain. For example, does historical evidence dealing with the subject exist, and if so, where can it be found? If someone wanted to study gypsy music from medieval Europe, and that music was never written down or mentioned in historical accounts of the period, then little or nothing can be found about this subject through historical research. Even if records exist on a particular subject, the historian may be unaware of them or unable to locate them. Perhaps the records are in an unfamiliar language or are in the possession of individuals or governments that deny access to them. Sometimes locating historical evidence can be a problem.

Having determined that records *do* exist and that they can be located and used, the historian faces another and more important problem: What is the credibility or reliability of the evidence? Is it genuine? How accurate are the records, and what biases were held by those who wrote them? If sources of information are in conflict, which is correct? Or is it possible that most of the sources are in error? Historians must pick and choose among the sources they uncover, and that is not always easy to do. The historian's own biases also cloud the picture, making impartial judgment extremely difficult.

Primary and Secondary Sources of Evidence

There are two basic forms of historical **evidence: primary** and **secondary. Primary sources** (see Figures 1.1 and 1.2) record the actual words of someone who participated in or witnessed the events described or of someone who got his or her information from participants. These can be newspaper accounts, diaries, notebooks, letters, minutes, interviews, and any works written by persons who claim firsthand knowledge of an event. Another primary source is official statements by established organizations or significant personages — royal decrees, church edicts, political party platforms, laws, and speeches. Primary sources also include any official records and statistics, such as those concerning births, marriages, deaths, taxes, deeds, and court trials. Recent history has been recorded by photographs, films, and audio- and videotapes. These recordings of events as they actually happened are also primary forms of evidence. Artifacts are another form

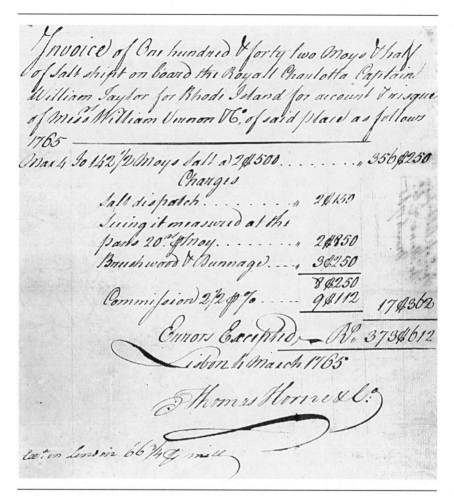

FIGURE 1.1 Example of Primary Evidence (1765)

Primary documents are often handwritten rather than printed and reflect the vocabulary and writing style of the day. Here is an invoice describing a shipment of salt carried from Lisbon, Portugal, to Providence, Rhode Island, in March 1765 "on Board the Royall Charlotta Captain William Taylor for Rhode Island for account & risque of Mr. William Vernon. . . ." The value of the cargo is written in Portuguese escudos. The document was handwritten and signed by Thomas Horne just after the salt was loaded onboard the ship. It brings us as close as we can come to the actual scene on the docks at Lisbon over two hundred years ago.

of primary evidence. These are things made by people in the past: houses, public buildings, tools, clothing, and much more.

Secondary sources (see Figure 1.3) record the findings of someone who did not observe the event but who investigated primary evidence. Most history books and articles fall into this category, although some

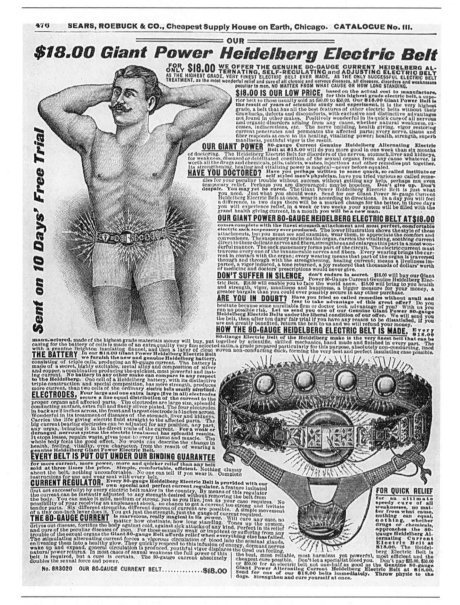

FIGURE 1.2   Example of Primary Evidence (1902)

A more recent primary document is a printed advertisement for a Heidelberg Electric Belt that appeared in the Sears, Roebuck and Company catalog of 1902. If you are doing research on some of the strange medical cures sold at that time, the claims made in this advertisement would be an important piece of primary evidence. What kind of "illness" do you think this belt was supposed to cure?

are actually *tertiary* (third level) evidence because they rely not on primary evidence but are themselves drawn from secondary sources. When your own history **research paper** is finished, it will be secondary or tertiary evidence to anyone who may use it in the future.

Douglass's personal story, like American history itself, is both inspiring and terrible. Few writers have better combined experience with the music of words to make us see the deepest contradictions of American history, the tragedy and necessity of conflict between slavery and freedom in a republic. Douglass exposes the bitterness and absurdity of racism at the same time that he imagines the fullest possibilities of the natural rights tradition, the idea that people are born with equal rights in the eyes of God and that those rights can be protected under human law. Few have written more effectively about the endurance of the human spirit under oppression. And in American letters, we have no better illustration of liberation through the power of language than in Douglass's *Narrative*. With his pen, Douglass was very much a self-conscious artist, and with his voice and his activism, he was a self-conscious prophet.

Readers of the *Narrative* quickly come to realize that language, written and oratorical, had been a fascination and a weapon for Douglass during his years as a slave. When he first spoke before a meeting of New Bedford blacks against African colonization in March 1839, and when he delivered his first public speeches before a gathering of the Massachusetts Anti-Slavery Society on Nantucket Island in August 1841, he was not merely appearing as the spontaneous abolitionist miracle he was often portrayed — and portrayed himself — to be. No doubt the first effort at "speaking to white people" at the Nantucket meeting was a "severe cross," as he describes the experience in the *Narrative*.[4] But Douglass was no stranger to oratory, or to the moral arguments, sentimentalism, and evangelical zeal that characterized the antislavery movement during that era. By 1841 he had been reading abolitionist speeches, editorials, and poetry in William Lloyd Garrison's newspaper, *The Liberator,* for at least two years. And as the *Narrative* tells us in a variety of ways, Douglass had been a practicing abolitionist of a kind — out of self-interest and for his fellow bondsmen —even while he was a slave. He had read the Bible extensively, and he had discovered and modeled his ideas and style on a remarkable 1797 book, *The Columbian Orator,* by Caleb Bingham, a selection from which is reproduced in this volume.

From the earliest period of his public career, Douglass knew that whether in the slave South or in the free North to which he had liberated himself, literacy was power. The nineteenth-century Western world owed much of its values and mores to the eighteenth-century Enlightenment's faith in human reason and its assertion of individual rights. To be judged truly human and a citizen with social and political recognition, therefore, a person had to achieve literacy. For better or worse, civilization itself was equated with cultures that could *write* their history. Hence, writes Henry Louis Gates, Jr., Douglass became an American "Representative Man because he was Rhetorical Man, black master of the verbal arts. Douglass is our clearest example of the will to power as the will to write. The act of writing for the slave constituted the act of creating a public, historical self."[5]

FIGURE 1.3 Example of Secondary Evidence
This example of secondary evidence comes from a book about Frederick Douglass, the escaped slave who became a leader of the movement to end slavery in the United States. It is an essay, published along with Douglass's autobiography (a *primary* source), that explains the significance of the autobiography and sets it in its historical context.

The problem of determining the reliability of evidence is a serious one. Secondary and even primary sources can be fraudulent, inaccurate, or biased. Eyewitness accounts may be purposely distorted in order to avert blame or to bestow praise on a particular individual or group. Without intending to misinform, even on-the-scene judgments can be incorrect. Sometimes, the closer you are to an event, the more emotionally involved you are, and this distorts your understanding of it. We can all recall events in which we completely misunderstood the feelings, actions, and even words of another person. Historians have to weigh evidence carefully to see if those who have participated in an event understood it well enough to accurately describe it, and whether later authors understood the meaning of the primary sources they used. Official statements present another problem — that of propaganda or concealment. A government, group, or institution may make statements that it wishes others to believe but that are not true. What a group says may not be what it does. This is especially true in politics.

To check the reliability of evidence, historians use the tests of consistency and corroboration: Does the evidence contradict itself and does it agree with evidence from other sources? Historical research always involves checking one source against another. For example, Figure 1.4 on pages 11–12 presents two primary documents which both report the fighting at Lexington and Concord, Massachusetts, in 1775 — battles that began the Revolutionary War. As you read them, consider what additional sources would help you decide which report is more accurate. The two accounts agree on some facts but disagree on the responsibility for the fighting. Eyewitness accounts from other English soldiers and from American colonials who were there will help in determining which description is more accurate. It might turn out, for example, that parts of *each* account are correct and other parts are distorted in some way. Sometimes there is no *one* true source for the history of an event. Still, the more primary sources you read, the closer you will come to knowing the event in all its details and meanings.

The bias of a source also presents difficulties. People's attitudes toward the world influence the way they interpret events. For example, you and your parents may have different attitudes toward music, sex, religion, or politics. These differences can cause you to disagree with them about the value of a rock concert, a Sunday sermon, or the president. Historians have their own attitudes toward the subjects they are investigating, and these cause them to draw different conclusions about the character and importance of religious, political, intellectual, and other movements. Later historians must take these biases into account when weighing the reliability of evidence.

Interpreting and Organizing Evidence

In analyzing the evidence, historians must find some way of *organizing* it so that they can make clear its meaning. A mass of facts and opinions concerning a subject is not a historical study. The task of the trained his-

AMERICAN ACCOUNT OF THE BATTLE OF LEXINGTON:
Account by the Provincial Congress
at Watertown, Massachusetts
April 26, 1775

By the clearest depositions relative to this transaction, it will appear that on the night preceding the nineteenth of April instant, a body of the king's troops, under the command of colonel Smith, were secretly landed at Cambridge, with an apparent design to take or destroy the military and other stores, provided for the defence of this colony, and deposited at Concord — that some inhabitants of the colony, on the night aforesaid, whilst travelling peaceably on the road, between Boston and Concord, were seized and greatly abused by armed men, who appeared to be officers of general Gage's army; that the town of Lexington, by these means, was alarmed, and a company of the inhabitants mustered on the occasion — that the regular troops on their way to Concord, marched into the said town of Lexington, and the said company, on their approach, began to disperse — that, notwithstanding this, the regulars rushed on with great violence and first began hostilities, by firing on said Lexington company, whereby they killed eight, and wounded several others — that the regulars continued their fire, until those of said company, who were neither killed nor wounded, had made their escape — that colonel Smith, with the detachment then marched to Concord, where a number of provincials were again fired on by the troops, two of them killed and several wounded, before the provincials fired on them, and provincials were again fired on by the troops, produced an engagement that lasted through the day, in which many of the provincials and more of the regular troops were killed and wounded. . . .

By order,
Joseph Warren, President.

ENGLISH ACCOUNT OF THE BATTLE OF LEXINGTON:
Report of Lieutenant-Colonel Smith to Governor Gage
April 22, 1775

I think it proper to observe, that when I had got some miles on the march from Boston, I detached six light infantry companies to march with all expedition to seize the two bridges on different roads beyond Concord. On these companies' arrival at Lexington, I understand, from the report of Major Pitcairn, who was with them, and from many officers, that they found on a green close to the road a body of the country people drawn up in military order, with arms and accoutrements, and, as appeared after, loaded; and that they had posted some men in a dwelling and Meeting-house. Our troops advanced towards them, without any intention of injuring them, further than to inquire the reason of their being thus assembled, and, if not satisfactory, to have secured their arms; but they in confusion went off, principally to the left, only one of them fired before he went off, and three or four more jumped over a wall and fired from behind it among the soldiers; on which the troops returned it, and killed several of them. They likewise fired on the soldiers from the Meeting and dwelling-houses. . . . While at Concord we saw vast numbers assembling in many parts; at one of the bridges they marched down, with a very considerable body, on the light infantry posted there. On their coming pretty near, one of our men fired on them, which they returned; on which an action ensued, and some few were killed and wounded. . . . On our leaving Concord to return to Boston, they began to fire on us from behind the walls, ditches, trees, &c., which, as we marched, increased to a very great

---

FIGURE 1.4 Two Conflicting Primary Documents

degree, and continued without intermission of five minutes altogether, for, I believe, upwards of eighteen miles; so that I can't think but it must have been a preconcerted scheme in them, to attack the King's troops the first favorable opportunity that offered, otherwise, I think they could not, in so short a time from our marching out, have raised such a numerous body, and for so great a space of ground. . . .

I have the honor, &c.,
F. Smith, Lieutenant-Colonel 10th Foot.

---

torian is to arrange the material so that it supports a particular conclusion. This conclusion may have been in the historian's mind at the outset, or it might be the result of investigation. If the evidence does not appear to support the conclusion, however, then the historian must either change that conclusion or seek other evidence to support it.

Once a historian is satisfied that research has uncovered sufficient evidence to support a particular conclusion, then he or she works to display the evidence in a manner that will clearly show that the conclusion drawn is a proper one. If any evidence that leads to other conclusions is uncovered, the historian has a responsibility to include it. In doing so, he or she must show how the supporting evidence is stronger than the nonsupporting evidence. There are many ways of organizing evidence in support of a conclusion. The historian's arguments in favor of a particular conclusion must be strong and convincing, and the logic of these arguments must not be faulty.

You will confront the issue faced by all historians when you conduct your own historical research, an assignment that is part of all advanced (and some beginning) history courses. (See Chapters 4 and 5.)

Changing Directions of Historical Research

When historians investigate the questions that interest them the most, they are influenced in their approach by their values and experiences, their academic training, and their beliefs about which aspects of human nature and the human environment are most important in understanding those questions. As a result, historians may focus on personal, social, political, intellectual, economic, cultural, diplomatic, ethnic, psychological, or economic aspects of their subject. Again, depending on which approach seems most helpful, they may also combine several of these research directions, and often do. For example, social historians base their research on the development of human communities and their interaction with the larger society. Cultural historians focus on attitudes and behaviors and how they change over time. Intellectual historians examine powerful ideas and how they influence beliefs. Political historians look at issues of power and how they operate in institutions such as governments, political parties, and interest groups. Diplomatic historians deal with relations between governments and nations and how they change over time. Economic historians study developments in technology, production, consumption, and the division of wealth, while historians of science and technology examine the evolution of scientific knowledge, how changes in such knowledge arise, and how its application influences society.

As the interests of historians have shifted, new approaches and questions have become important in recent years. Historians of family and private life examine the structural and emotional development of small, intimate groups and the responses of these groups to powerful forces such as wars, depressions, class and ethnic conflict, and technological change. Another area of growing interest encompasses the history of sports, the media (especially film), and other aspects of popular culture. Environmental historians examine the interaction between human communities and their habitats and the attitudes these communities have toward nature. One of the most rapidly expanding areas of research in recent decades has been women's history, an enormous topic that earlier generations of historians (most of whom were men) had ignored.

While some historians look at personal life and small groups, others, in contrast, study broad stretches of history. The field of world history takes in centuries of change across large areas of the globe. Comparative history seeks to learn the significance of an institution, political system, people, or nation by comparing its history with that of others. You can learn much about Vietnam, for example, by studying the ways in which its culture resembled or diverged from that of China.

Two older areas of historical research are reviving. Genealogy and local history have returned to importance as people in countries undergoing rapid change become concerned with holding on to or rediscovering the past of their family or neighborhood. Genealogy traces the history of a particular family. Local history, pursued with enthusiasm by residents and scholars alike, examines the evolution of a town, community, or neighborhood.

Methods of Historical Research

Certain directions of historical research have been influenced by other disciplines: family history by psychology, demography by sociology, enthnohistory by anthropology, political history by political science, and economic history by economics. While still adhering to the special focus of history — examining and explaining the past — historians welcome ideas and methods of analyzing evidence from other fields. For instance, quantitative history (called cliometrics) uses quantitative data, such as election returns, price levels, and population **statistics** of earlier periods, to re-create a picture of earlier times. Because quantitative data is uniform, it measures the same things — votes, prices, numbers of inhabitants — over time. Thus, comparisons can be made among statistics from different periods. The electoral support of a political party, the price of wheat, or the size of a town can be examined to see if it is rising or falling and at what rate.

If the uniformity of the data can be established (that is, if the numbers really *do* measure the same thing in each period), then they can be subjected to mathematical analysis. Percentages, ratios, averages, the mean, median, and mode can be obtained. If the data set is large, the historian may subject it to more complex analyses that explore patterns within the numbers and among subgroups of them: the frequency distribution, the standard deviation, and the coefficient of variation. The more elaborate kinds of statistical analysis can determine not merely how fast prices are rising or where the majority of a party's voters reside; they also can compare different kinds of changes — party registration with price levels, population decline with employment levels — in an attempt to describe the conditions under which certain changes occur. By noting those categories of numbers (variables) that move together, the historian can begin to explore the causes of the changes under examination.

The Computer and Historical Research

The computer has become an important way of gathering historical data in all fields, not just in quantitative history. Most historians do not use computers to generate *new* data but to gain easier access to existing sources of historical information. Unpublished information residing in **archives** scattered around the world can be made available online to historians (and students) with access to computers that are part of a network like the **Internet.** Primary sources that have been entered into computer databases can be read (and even printed out) by researchers anywhere. Secondary sources that are available only in special libraries can be read in this way also — provided that they have been put into computer-readable form. Already, history **databases,** containing millions of individual historical statistics, are available in many college libraries. The texts of documents, articles, and, in some cases, whole books, can be brought to your computer screen. With more advanced equipment, researchers can gain access to art, photographs, and even films that once resided only in faraway archives. (For information on using computers in your own research, see p. 65 and Appendix A, pp. 173–76.)

Philosophies of History

Historical investigation can lead to very different results depending upon the aspect of human nature or society emphasized and the kind of information obtained. Even greater differences can result from historical investigations that employ different *philosophies* of history.

A philosophy of history is an explanation not only of the most important causes of specific events but of the broadest developments in human affairs. It explains the *forces* of history, what moves them, and in what direction they are headed. The dominant philosophy of history of a particular age is that which most closely reflects the beliefs and values of that age. Most of the historians writing at that time will write from the perspective of that philosophy of history.

Perhaps the oldest philosophy of history is the **cyclical school.** According to this view, events recur periodically. The belief, in short, is that history repeats itself. The essential forces of nature and of human nature are changeless, causing past patterns of events to repeat themselves endlessly. As the saying goes, "There is nothing new under the sun." This view of history was dominant from ancient times until the rise of Christianity. The Aztecs conceived of history this way, as did the Chinese.

A central message of early Christianity was the uniqueness of the life, death, and resurrection of Jesus Christ. In societies influenced by the Christian Church — and especially in Europe in the Middle Ages — the new concept of divine intervention to overthrow the past weakened the cyclical view.[2] The resulting philosophy of history, the **providential school,** held that the course of history was determined by God. The ebb and flow of historical events represent struggles between forces of good and evil. These struggles are protracted, but the eventual victory of good is foreseen.

This particular idea of the providential school — that history is characterized not by ceaseless repetition but by direction and purpose — became an element in the thinking of the more secular age beginning with the eighteenth century. In this new age of scientific inquiry and material advancement, there arose the **progressive school,** whose central belief was that human history illustrates neither endless cycles nor divine intervention but continual progress. According to this school, the situation of humanity is constantly improving. Moreover, this improvement results not from divine providence but from the efforts of human beings themselves. Each generation builds upon the learning and improvements of those preceding it and, in doing so, reaches a higher stage of civilization. This idea of history as continual progress is still very powerful today. Currently, many variations of the progressive philosophy share the field of historical investigation.

Historiography

One final way to approach the study of history — an unusual one — is the field of **historiography,** which is the study of changes in the methods, interpretations, and conclusions of historians over time. As histori-

---

[2]An earlier development of this new view is found in the Old Testament.

ans examine secondary sources, they become aware that earlier studies of the subject they are pursuing often came to surprising conclusions. Here is one example: "Reconstruction" refers to the period in U.S. history just after the Civil War when the defeated South was under the political control of the victorious North. For the first time in U.S. history, black people, many of them former slaves, were allowed to hold and be elected to political office. Almost all the books written on this subject prior to the 1930s (whether by northern or southern historians) concluded that southern politics was corrupted and made ineffective during this post–Civil War period by selfish northerners and ignorant black southerners. Since the 1950s, however, scholars have come to very different conclusions. Most now believe that black people's participation in southern government was a healthy development and that the standard of politics in the South was generally equal to other regions of the nation at that time.

Part of the reason for this new interpretation was due to later historians' more effective use of primary sources; they looked more closely at the primary documents describing the work of the Reconstruction governments of the southern states. In addition, recent historians have compared the Reconstruction record with politics in northern and western states of the period (an example of the use of comparative history). Finally, in looking back over the older literature and by placing it in the context of the race relations that existed at that particular time, most scholars now conclude that an understanding of the racist attitudes toward African Americans does much to explain the negative conclusions of earlier historians. Historiography, then, is an example of historians using the tools of historical research to study themselves.

How You Can Use History

It is said that experience is the best teacher. Still, our learning would be very narrow if we profited only from our own experiences. Through the study of history, we make other people's experiences our own. In this way, we touch other times and places and add to our lifetime's knowledge that gained by others.

If history is the greatest teacher, what can we do with the knowledge we draw from it? In what practical ways does knowledge of the past help us to accomplish the work we do today or will do tomorrow? Perhaps you wait on customers at McDonald's or are the manager of a bank. Will knowledge acquired in history courses be of direct value to you? Probably not. You can serve burgers and fries satisfactorily without knowing that the Safavid empire of the sixteenth century was located in Persia. You can run a bank without knowledge of the philosophy of John Locke. However, while the bank manager can run the bank without *particular* historical knowledge, he or she cannot do so without writing reports explaining changes in the financial transactions of the bank over time. While the bank's computer will record the amount of money flowing into and out of the bank, it is the manager's written reports that will explain the meaning of these transactions. To write such reports, the manager must have mastered the skills of historical research. Though reports to the bank's main office deal only with the past week's or month's transactions at the branch rather than with past years or centuries, the manager must gather evidence, analyze and summarize it, and draw conclusions about it, just as the historian would do whose subject is the hundred-year history of the bank.

History is not merely a course you take in college; it is a way of thinking about the present, one that attempts to make sense of the complexity of contemporary events by examining what lies behind them. Such an examination is intellectual (its goal is to broaden understanding in general), but it can be practical as well. If business at the branch bank falls off sharply in June, what is the manager to do? Does this mean that the branch should be closed? If the manager had no records of the bank's past performance, the question could not be answered. However, all businesses look at themselves over time and employ researchers and analysts to do so. Thus the manager can examine data on the level of business done by the bank in years past. A study of that data (similar to the primary evidence of the historian) makes it clear that business always drops in June because a major depositor, a nearby factory, shuts down then for retooling. The lesson is a simple one: no business can operate intelligently without an understanding of its own history. In a sense, the office workers in business, government, and institutions operate as historical record-producers and record-keepers. When decisions about policy or future production and investment are made, these records are pulled together in research reports that examine the past experience of the firm (or department or institution) in order to judge the likely result of these decisions.

While the ability to re-create the past is an important ingredient in enabling the bank manager to do a good job, there are many careers in which knowledge of historical research techniques is an essential requirement. Government agencies, large corporations, libraries, museums, labor unions, historical parks, monuments, and restorations all take knowledge of the past so seriously that they employ staffs of historians and archivists whose sole task is to conduct research, organize records, re-create historic buildings and events, and write histories. The fields of public and corporate history, museum and archival management, and historic restoration are only some of the areas that *directly* employ the skills you acquire when studying history in school.

When you learn how to read history, how to research the past, and how to write a summary of your findings, you are mastering career skills as surely as if you were taking a course in real-estate law or restaurant management. The ability to see the present in relationship to the past is a skill needed not only by academic and public historians, archivists, historical novelists, and documentary producers; it is an essential preparation for almost any career. Understanding the past can be its own reward, but it pays off in other ways as well. In fact, people who think that history is irrelevant run the risk of history making that judgment of them.

How to Read
a History Assignment
and Take Notes in Class

How to Read a History Assignment

Reading history can be a satisfying experience, but to enjoy the landscape you must first know where you are; that is, you must have a general sense of the subject and of the manner in which it is being presented. If you begin reading before you get your bearings, you may become lost in a forest of unfamiliar facts and interpretations. Before beginning any reading assignment, look over the entire book. Read the preface or introduction. This should tell you something about the author and his or her purpose in writing the work. Then read the table of contents to get a sense of the way in which the author has organized the subject. Next, skim the chapters themselves, reading subheadings and glancing at illustrations and graphed material. If you have the time, preread sections of the book (especially the introductory and concluding chapters) rapidly before reading the full work.

After you have scouted the ground, you will be ready to read. By this time, you should be familiar with the topic of the book (what it is generally all about), the background of the author (politician, journalist, historian, eyewitness, novelist, etc.), when it was written (a hundred-year-old classic, the newest book on the subject), how it is organized (chronologically, topically), and, most important of all, its thesis and conclusions. The thesis of a book is the principal point on the subject that the author wishes to make: that the geography of Spain was a principal factor in that nation's failure to industrialize in the eighteenth and nineteenth centuries; that disagreement on moral issues between J. Robert Oppenheimer and Edward Teller delayed development of the hydrogen bomb. Most authors set out their thesis in a preface or introduction. If you understand the principal point the author is trying to make, then the organization and conclusions of the work will become clear to you. The author will be organizing evidence and drawing conclusions to support the thesis. By the way, if the thesis is not clear or the evidence is not supportive of it, then it is not a good history of its subject no matter how many facts it contains. The ability to spot such weaknesses and describe them is part of learning history too.

Reading a Textbook

The most common history assignment is the reading of a **textbook.** Many students hope to get by with their lecture notes, and they put off reading the text until just before the final exam. Reading the text week by week will give you the background knowledge necessary to understand the lectures and supplementary readings. In most courses the lectures embellish portions of the text, and lecturers assume that students are familiar with it. Sitting through a lecture on the economic aspects of the American Revolution will be confusing if you have not read the textbook discussion of the mercantilist theories behind many of the colonists' grievances.

Read the text chapters in close conjunction with the lectures to which they are related. If you are not sure that you understand the material, read it again. Underline (or highlight) the most prominent factual information. Also underline important generalizations, interpretations, and conclusions. Of course, don't underline most of the book. That would be a sign that you cannot tell the difference between the author's main points and the material he or she uses to tie these points together. In addition to underlining, look for passages emphasized by the author or those which you feel reflect the author's viewpoint or with which you disagree. Write your reaction or a summary of the passages in the margin. All of this will come in handy when you prepare to take a test. You will be able to reread the underlined material and your comments and obtain a quick review of the chapter's contents. Before the final, however, you may need to reread the text itself, especially if you are having difficulty in the course or wish to write an outstanding exam. (An example of an underlined and annotated textbook page is shown in Figure 2.1. on pp. 22–23.)

Reading a Monograph

Another typical reading assignment is a **monograph** (a specialized history work on a particular subject). In addition to the procedures used in reading a textbook, you will need to pay special attention to the theme and point of view of these works. They should be read more carefully because your teacher will expect you to learn not only about the subject they deal with but about the emphasis and methods of the work. Therefore, you will need to determine the author's assumptions and values, and to understand the book's thesis and conclusions. Read this kind of work not only to absorb the facts but also to analyze, question, and criticize. If you own the book, you can do your questioning and criticizing in the margins as I have shown you before in your textbook. If the book is not yours, or if you wish to have an organized set of notes about it, summarize the contents and the author's theme on index cards (4″ × 6″ or 5″ × 8″). You can then review your underlinings or index cards before the exam.

Some courses also include a book of readings. These are usually a series of short essays (excerpts from larger works or from primary documents) that deal with a single subject. All of the suggestions concerning the reading of texts and history books apply here as well, but this type of assignment often calls for a particular kind of reading. Each excerpt usually discusses a different aspect or interpretation of the subject, and some are in serious disagreement. Teachers expect students to be able to assess the arguments of the various writers and on occasion to take a position in the debate. Therefore, you must read this particular kind of book with an eye to analyzing the arguments of the different excerpts or to comparing their different approaches to the subject. A good way to do this is to summarize briefly the argument or approach of each selection.

Reading a Historical Novel

Still another reading assignment is a **historical novel,** a work of fiction based upon actual occurrences and people. It is more dramatic and more personal than a text or monograph and describes the feelings of those caught up in important historical events. Reading such a novel gives you a feel for the times that it conveys and for the historical material it contains, but be cautious not to treat it as historical truth. On the other hand, if the novelist knows the historical period or event well, he or she can make it come alive in ways that scholarly works cannot.

Examples of Reading Assignments

To help you appreciate the differences among the four types of reading assignments, here are passages from each. The subject is the Greek Civil War of the late 1940s and the role of the United States in that war. The textbook passage is from Stephen E. Ambrose, *Rise to Globalism: American Foreign Policy Since 1938* (New York: Penguin, 1971), pp. 148 and 150. The monograph passage is from Joyce and Gabriel Kolko, *The Limits of Power: The World and United States Foreign Policy, 1945–1954* (New York: Harper & Row, 1972), p. 341. The readings passage is from an address delivered by President Harry Truman before a joint session of Congress on March 12, 1947. The final passage is from

Despite the ground Kennedy picked up in the debates, he won only the narrowest of victories, receiving 49.7 percent of the popular vote to Nixon's 49.5 percent (see Map 30.1). Kennedy had successfully appealed to the diverse elements of the Democratic coalition, attracting large numbers of Catholic and black voters and a significant sector of the middle class; the vice-presidential nominee, Lyndon Johnson, brought in southern white Democrats. Yet only 120,000 votes separated the two candidates, and the shift of a few thousand votes in key states such as Illinois (where there were confirmed cases of voting fraud) would have reversed the outcome. The electoral results hardly gave Kennedy a mandate for sweeping change, and the Republicans, though still in the minority in Congress, gained 21 seats in the House.

Kennedy's victory over Nixon in 1960 a very narrow one

Kennedy's activist bent attracted unusually talented and ambitious people—"the best and the brightest" as the journalist David Halberstam called them. A host of corporate and academic leaders flocked to join the new administration, which was christened "Camelot" by the admiring media after the recently opened Broadway musical about King Arthur. Robert S. McNamara, the former president of the Ford Motor Company, came on board as secretary of defense and introduced modern management techniques to that department. The Republican banker C. Douglas Dillon brought a corporate manager's desire for expanded markets and stable economic growth to the Department of the Treasury. The national security adviser McGeorge Bundy, the State Department planner Walt Rostow, and other trusted advisers came from Harvard, MIT, and other leading universities to join the Kennedy foreign policy team.

K. not interested in women's issues

Reflecting the all-male Ivy League world in which Kennedy traveled, the administration was overwhelmingly male. He appointed fewer women to federal positions than had Eisenhower or Truman and made only a token attempt to address women's issues with the establishment of the Presidential Commission on the Status of Women in 1961. Subsequent allegations of Kennedy's womanizing and philandering also hurt his reputation in this area.

Activism Abroad

Kennedy's inaugural address was devoted almost entirely to foreign affairs, reflecting the priorities of his presidency: "Let every nation know, whether it wishes us well or ill, that we shall pay any price, bear any burden, meet any hardship, support any friend, oppose any foe to assure the survival and success of liberty." A resolute cold warrior whose family had supported the red-hunting campaign of Senator Joseph McCarthy, Kennedy took a hard line against communist expansionism. He therefore set out to reverse the fiscal conservatism that had limited military growth under the Eisenhower administration,

K. very interested in combating communism abroad

bringing defense spending to its highest level (as a percentage of total federal expenditures) in the cold war era.

The Military Buildup. During the 1960 presidential campaign Kennedy charged that the Eisenhower administration had permitted the Soviet Union to develop superior nuclear capabilities. Once in office, however, he found that no "missile gap" existed. In fact, Eisenhower had built up the American nuclear arsenal at the expense of conventional weapons. In his first national security message to Congress, Kennedy proposed a new policy of *flexible response*, stating that the nation must be prepared "to deter all wars, general or limited, nuclear or conventional, large or small." Congress quickly granted Kennedy's military requests, boosting the number of combat-ready army divisions from eleven to sixteen and authorizing the construction of ten Polaris nuclear submarines and other warships. The result was a major expansion of the military-industrial complex as thousands of workers were recruited to build more weapons systems and military equipment.

Those measures were designed to deter nuclear or conventional attacks by the Soviet Union. But what about the new kind of warfare, the wars of national liberation that had broken out in many Third World countries when their inhabitants sought to overthrow colonial rulers or unpopular dictatorships? In early 1961 the Soviet premier, Nikita Khrushchev, proclaimed that conflicts in Vietnam, Cuba, and other countries were "wars of national liberation," worthy of Soviet support. To counter that threat, Kennedy adopted the new military doctrine of *counterinsurgency*. U.S. Army Special Forces, called the Green Berets for their distinctive headgear, received intensive training in repelling the random, small-scale attacks typical of guerrilla warfare. Vietnam soon provided a testing ground for counterinsurgency techniques (see Chapter 31).

The Peace Corps and Foreign Aid. The idealism and commitment to public service that characterized the New Frontier were perhaps most evident in the newly established Peace Corps, headed by Kennedy's brother-in-law, Sargent Shriver. The idea, Kennedy explained on March 1, 1961, was to create "a pool of trained American men and women" to be sent "overseas by the United States government or through private organizations and institutions to help foreign countries meet their urgent needs for skilled manpower." Thousands of young Americans, many of them recent college graduates, responded to the call, agreeing to devote two or more years to teaching English to Filipino schoolchildren or helping African villagers obtain adequate supplies of water. Embodying the idealism of the early 1960s, the Peace Corps was also a cold war weapon designed to bring Third World countries into the American orbit and away from communist influence.

*"flexible response"
Being prepared to
fight any kind of
war*

Growth of arms industry

*"counter-
insurgency"
Combating Soviet
influence in Third
World countries*

*Peace Corps as example of New
Frontier idealism*

*Peace Corps combines idealism and
anti-communism*

FIGURE 2.1 Example of Underlined and Annotated Textbook Page

the historical novel *The Marked Men* by Aris Fakinos (New York: Live-right, 1971), pp. 92–93. As you read these passages, note the different manner in which each deals with this subject.

TEXTBOOK   The day before, 6 March, Truman had begun to prepare the ground. In a speech at Baylor University in Texas he explained that freedom was more important than peace and that freedom of worship and speech were dependent on freedom of enterprise. . . .

The State Department, meanwhile, was preparing a message for Truman to deliver to the full Congress. He was unhappy with the early drafts, for "I wanted no hedging in this speech. This was America's answer to the surge of expansion of Communist tyranny. It had to be clear and free of hesitation or double talk." Truman told Acheson to have the speech toughened, simplified, and expanded to cover more than just Greece and Turkey. He then made further revisions in the draft. . . .

At 1 P.M. on 12 March 1947, Truman stepped to the rostrum in the hall of the House of Representatives to address the joint session of the Congress. The speech was also carried on nationwide ratio. He asked for immediate aid for Greece and Turkey, then explained the reasoning. "I believe that it must be the policy of the United States to support free peoples who are resisting attempted subjugation by armed minorities or by outside pressures."

The statement was all-encompassing. In a single sentence, Truman had defined American policy for the next twenty years. Whenever and wherever an anti-Communist government was threatened, by indigenous insurgents, foreign invasion, or even diplomatic pressure (as with Turkey), the United States would supply political, economic, and most of all, military aid. The Truman Doctrine came close to shutting the door against any revolution, since the terms "free peoples" and "anti-Communist" were assumed to be synonymous. All the Greek government, or any dictatorship, had to do to get American aid was to claim that its opponents were Communists. And the aid would be unilateral, as Truman never mentioned the United Nations, whose commission to investigate what was actually happening in Greece had not completed its study or made a report.

MONOGRAPH   What was really on the mind of the president and his advisers was stated less in the Truman Doctrine speech than in private memos and in Truman's March 6 address at Baylor University. Dealing with the world economic structure, the president attacked state-regulated trade, tariffs, and exchange controls — ". . . the direction in which much of the world is headed at the present time." "If this trend is not reversed," he warned, ". . . the United States will be under pressure, sooner or later, to use these same devices in the fight for markets and for raw materials. . . . It is not the American way. It is not the way to peace."[16] . . .

The question of how best to sell the new crusade perplexed the administration, not the least because Greece was a paltry excuse for a vast undertaking of which it "was only a beginning," and in the end it formulated diverse reasons as the need required.[18] The many drafts that were drawn up before

---

[16]DSB, March 16, 1947, 484. See also Acheson, *Present at the Creation*, 219; Jones, *Fifteen Weeks*, 139–42. . . .

[18]Acheson, *Present at the Creation*, 221.

the final Truman Doctrine speech was delivered to Congress on March 12 are interesting in that they reveal more accurately than the speech itself the true concerns of Washington. Members of the cabinet and other top officials who considered the matter before the twelfth understood very clearly that the United States was now defining a strategy and budget appropriate to its new global commitments — interests that the collapse of British power had made even more exclusively American — and that far greater involvement in other countries was now pending, at least on the economic level.

Quite apart from the belligerent tone of the drafts were the references to ". . . a world-wide trend away from the system of free enterprise toward state-controlled economies," which the State Department's speech writers thought "gravely threatened" American interests. No less significant was the mention of the "great natural resources" of the Middle East at stake.

READINGS (EXCERPT FROM SPEECH)   The very existence of the Greek state is today threatened by the terrorist activities of several thousand armed men, led by Communists, who defy the government's authority at a number of points, particularly along the northern boundaries. . . .

Meanwhile, the Greek Government is unable to cope with the situation. The Greek army is small and poorly equipped. It needs supplies and equipment if it is to restore authority to the government throughout Greek territory.

Greece must have assistance if it is to become a self-supporting and self-respecting democracy.

The United States must supply this assistance. . . .

At the present moment in world history nearly every nation must choose between alternative ways of life. The choice is too often not a free one.

One way of life is based upon the will of the majority, and is distinguished by free institutions, representative government, free elections, guarantees of individual liberty, freedom of speech and religion, and freedom from political oppression.

The second way of life is based upon the will of a minority forcibly imposed upon the majority. It relies upon terror and oppression, a controlled press and radio, fixed elections, and the suppression of personal freedoms.

I believe that it must be the policy of the United States to support free peoples who are resisting attempted subjugation by armed minorities or by outside pressures. . . .

It is necessary only to glance at a map to realize that the survival and integrity of the Greek nation are of grave importance in a much wider situation. If Greece should fall under the control of an armed minority, the effect upon its neighbor, Turkey, would be immediate and serious. Confusion and disorder might well spread throughout the entire Middle East.

Moreover, the disappearance of Greece as an independent state would have a profound effect upon those countries in Europe whose peoples are struggling against great difficulties to maintain their freedoms and their independence while they repair the damages of war. . . .

The free peoples of the world look to us for support in maintaining their freedoms.

If we falter in our leadership, we may endanger the peace of the world — and we shall surely endanger the welfare of this Nation.

Great responsibilities have been placed upon us by the swift movement of events.

I am confident that the Congress will face these responsibilities squarely.

HISTORICAL NOVEL   Tzelekis was right: now it was 1949, and war was beautifully organized — things were done in an orderly fashion. Various specialists had come in, trained in "wars of movement": The British, the Americans, with a good deal of experience in such matters. They put things in their places, taught enemies and friends to recognize each other — you over here, them over there. Work with a system, no fooling around! Back in '46, you see, everything was topsy-turvy. The army was an indiscriminate herd, no organization whatever; everyone did as he pleased, everything pell-mell, all mixed up together slaughtering: EAM-ites, EDES-ites, X-ites — you didn't know who was your enemy and who your friend. At night they sent out patrols — in the morning they came back in company with the others and cut up their captains. Other times when they fought at night with knives and bayonets it was like mother losing child and child losing mother: same clothes (all the rags of the world resemble each other), same appearance — you came face to face with the enemy, you went at him with a dagger to rip out his guts, and you saw — if you had time — that he was one of your own men, so you let him go and went for the one beside him. And don't forget, what mixed things up even worse was the language; since they were all spouting Greek, who could tell them apart? . . .

Later when foreign aid began to arrive, the army got new uniforms, munitions, wireless transmitters, codes of recognition. Things were put in order, names were given to the enemy, and the radio blared them out every day, they were written on the walls and in the newspapers; and finally, for the first time in their history, the Greeks began to kill each other systematically. The solution was a very simple one; and a considerable number of people couldn't understand why they had not thought of it before.

Note that the textbook is general in its coverage. It does not use footnotes or quote from primary sources other than Truman's speech. It tries to summarize the content and meaning of the event without too much detail and without extensive proof for its conclusions. The monograph, on the other hand, covers a small portion of the topic, gives more detail, quotes from primary materials, and uses footnotes to record its sources of information. The selection from the book of readings is a primary source — the Truman speech itself. Often these books are composed of the original documents that form the basis of the historical events discussed by textbooks and monographs. Although this particular selection from a book of readings is a primary document, such works, as already noted, may also be collections of short essays or excerpts from monographs.

The section from the historical novel is very different from the first three passages. The author gives us the thoughts of some of the soldiers who fought in the Greek Civil War, far away from the formulation of foreign policy in Washington.

How to "Read" Nonwritten Materials

Maps, Charts, Graphs, and Tables

History is often displayed on maps. The landscape of history is one of its most fundamental settings. The rise and fall of empires, the course of wars, the growth of cities, the development of trade routes, and much more can be traced on maps of large areas. Figure 2.2 indicates the dates on which parts of Africa came under European colonial rule. This map tells you which European countries controlled which parts of Africa and when this control was established. Analyzing the map more closely, you can see that Britain and France had the largest colonial empires in Africa and that most of Africa was free of colonial rule before the 1880s. Figure 2.3 indicates the dates on which the nations of Africa became independent. By comparing this map with Figure 2.2, you can determine which countries changed their names upon achieving independence. Comparing the dates on the two maps, you can figure out how long colonial rule lasted in different countries. Note also that the first wave of independence came in the 1960s and that the date for Namibian independence is 1990 — just a few years ago.

Small area maps can show the layout of villages, the outcome of battles, or the location of mines, canals, and railroads. To read a map, you must learn the *key,* which translates the symbols used on the map. A line on a map may be a road, a river, or a gas pipeline. The key tells you which it is. The *scale* of a map tells you the actual distance of the area the map represents. Maps are an important aid in understanding history because they display the physical relationship between places. Never ignore maps in a text or other reading. It is also wise to put a good map of the area you are studying near your desk so that you can see the location of places mentioned in lectures and readings.

In addition to maps, works in history often include statistical data arranged in **charts, graphs,** or **tables.** These data describe the amounts of something (e.g., warships, marriages, schools, bridges, deaths from smallpox) at a specific time in the past and usually compare these amounts (e.g., the number of marriages in relation to the number of schools) or trace changes in amounts over time (e.g., the number of warships in 1820, 1830, and 1840). Figure 2.4 (on p. 30) shows a typical arrangement of statistical data with explanations as to how to read them.

The table organizes population statistics from different regions of the earth and across more than three hundred years. Reading across the lines allows you to trace the changes in population of a particular region (Europe, Africa, Asia) over time. By doing so, you can follow the population of each region at hundred-year intervals (the population of Latin America in 1650, 1750, 1850, and 1950). You can note the change for each region and the rate of change. For example, the population of the United States and Canada did not increase in the hun-

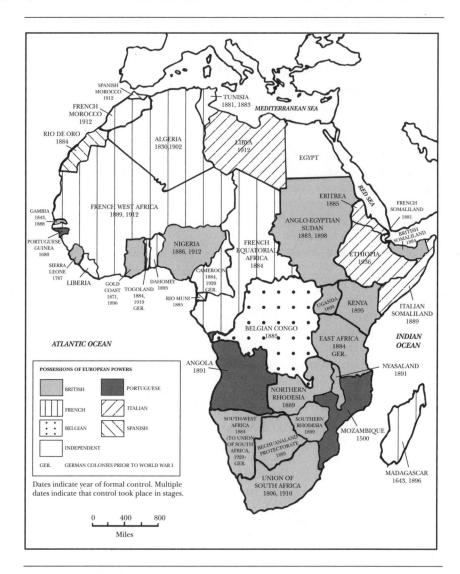

FIGURE 2.2   The March of Colonialism in Africa

dred years between 1650 and 1750, whereas it more than doubled in the fifty years between 1900 and 1950. Reading down the chart, you can examine the population of each region during the same period in time. This allows you to compare the populations of the different regions. In 1650 the populations of Europe and Africa were the same, whereas in 1950 the European population was more than two-and-one-half times that of Africa.

More complex comparisons can be made by combining the differences between regions (reading down) and their rates of growth over

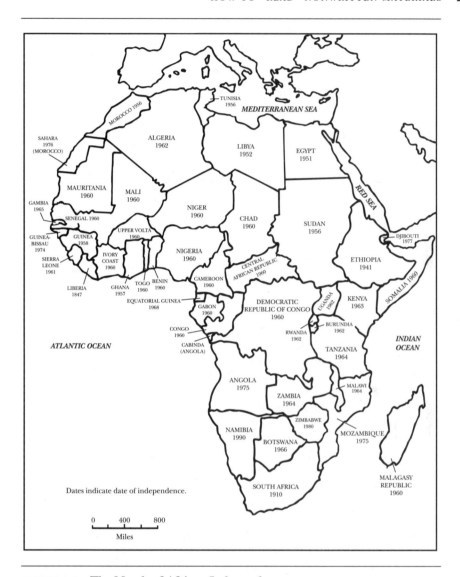

FIGURE 2.3   The March of African Independence

time (reading across). For example, you can discover that whereas the population of Asia has grown more than that of any other region in absolute terms, its *rate* of growth from 1850 to 1980 (750 million to 2600 million, or about 350 percent) was much less than that of Latin America (35 million to 362 million, or around 1,000 percent).

Even the cold statistics of a table can provide images of the great drama of history. The decrease in African population between 1650 and 1850 may tell us something of the impact of the slave trade, and the decrease in population in Latin America between 1650 and 1750

	1650	1750	1850	1900	1950	1980	1996
Europe	100	140	265	400	570	730	800
United States and Canada	2	2	25	80	165	252	295
Latin America	12	10	35	65	165	362	489
Africa	100	95	95	120	220	470	732
Asia	330	480	750	940	1370	2600	3430

FIGURE 2.4   Estimated World Population
Numbers represent millions of persons. These are rough estimates only. The figures for 1650 and 1750 in particular come from a time before it was common to conduct a periodic count (*census*) of populations. There is great debate about the size of the native populations of the Western hemisphere before 1850.

hints at the toll taken among Native Americans by the introduction of European diseases. The large increase in the United States population between 1850 and 1900 tells us something about the history of European immigration.

The information in the table can be presented differently in order to highlight different aspects of the data. In Figure 2.5, the numbers for each region are represented as percentages of the total world population. By changing the numbers from absolute amounts to percentages, the new table facilitates the comparing of populations and population growth.

Another way of presenting these population data is in the form of a graph. Note that Figure 2.6 makes more obvious the differences between numbers and thus makes comparisons easier. However, ease of comparison is traded for a loss in precision; the graph gives less specific numbers (reading along the vertical axis) than the table. A graph also requires more space to convey the same information as a table. Figure 2.6, were it to have included all of the time periods of the table, would have been very large.

The more detailed the data and their arrangement, the more historical information that can be displayed and the more intricate the comparisons that can be made. Figure 2.7 presents a table that lists the percentage of the total vote and the number of deputies elected to the German parliament by each of the major political parties in each election from 1919 to 1933. (Note that in the parliamentary system, elections do not come at regular intervals.)

This table allows you to follow the changing fortunes of each political party. A wealth of information on German political history is contained in these figures. Between the lines one can also find pieces of the social and economic history of Germany. To choose only two

	1650	1750	1850	1900	1950	1980	1996
Europe	18.4	19.3	22.8	25.0	23.2	16.5	13.9
United States and Canada	0.2	0.1	2.3	5.1	6.7	5.7	5.1
Latin America	2.2	1.5	2.8	3.9	6.3	8.2	8.5
Africa	18.4	13.2	8.1	7.4	8.8	10.6	12.7
Asia	60.8	65.9	64.0	58.6	55.0	58.9	59.7

FIGURE 2.5 Estimated World Population
Numbers represent percentages.

examples, the strength of the Communist and Social Democratic (Socialist) parties attests to the deep dissatisfaction of many German workers with the state of the economy during the period known as the Weimar Republic. Even more striking is the tremendous growth of the National Socialist (Nazi) party after 1930. It was this development that brought Adolf Hitler to power in 1933. Eventually the results of that event would reverberate around the world. A table is not just numbers.

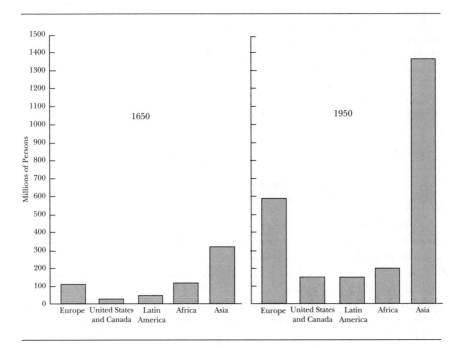

FIGURE 2.6   Estimated World Population

Party	1919	1920	1924	1928	1930	1932	1933
Communist							
No. dep.	0	4	45	54	77	89	81
% vote		2.1	9.0	10.6	13.1	14.6	12.3
Social Democratic							
No. dep.	165	102	131	153	143	133	120
% vote	37.9	21.6	26.0	29.8	24.5	21.6	18.3
Democratic							
No. dep.	75	39	32	25	20	4	5
% vote	18.6	8.3	6.3	4.9	3.8	1.0	.8
Centrum							
No. dep.	91	64	69	62	68	75	74
% vote	19.7	13.6	13.6	12.1	11.8	12.5	11.7
Bavarian People's							
No. dep.	0	21	19	16	19	22	18
% vote		4.4	3.7	3.0	3.0	3.2	2.7
German People's							
No. dep.	19	65	51	45	30	7	2
% vote	4.4	13.9	10.1	8.7	4.5	1.2	1.1
National People's							
No. dep.	44	71	103	73	41	37	52
% vote	10.3	14.9	20.5	14.2	7.0	5.9	8.0
National Socialist							
No. dep.	0	0	14	12	107	230	288
% vote			3.0	2.6	18.3	37.4	43.9

FIGURE 2.7   **Reichstag Elections, 1919–1933 (Number of Deputies and Percentage of Total Votes)**
Under the electoral system provided for in the Weimar Constitution, each party received approximately one representative for every sixty thousand popular votes cast for its candidates. Various small parties, not listed here, were underrepresented in the Reichstag. From L. S. Stavrianos, *The World Since 1500: A Global History,* 4th ed. (Englewood Cliffs, N.J.: Prentice-Hall, 1991), p. 419.

Illustrations and Photographs

Visual material can also present historical information. However, gathering information from old paintings, drawings, and photographs can be more difficult than it may seem. You need to do more than *look* at them. First, you need to recognize the actual information that they present — what Columbus's ships looked like, how Hiroshima appeared after the explosion of the atomic bomb. Then, you need to *interpret them.* This involves an effort to understand what the artist or photographer is "saying" in the work. (This advice applies also to film and to any visual form.) When an artist draws something and when a photographer takes a picture, he or she is not simply recording a visual image but is sending a message to anyone who looks at the work. In this way, artists and photographers are like writers whose written work needs to be interpreted.

Figures 2.8 and 2.9 present two illustrations of the Spanish conquest of Mexico. Look at them and see if you can detect what they are saying. The first of the two is by a European artist and shows Hernán Cortés, who conquered Mexico for Spain, being offered young Indian women by a coastal tribe. The Indians seem happy to greet the Spaniards. The other was drawn by an Aztec Indian and shows Cortés's soldiers (having fought their way from the coast to the Aztec capital) massacring Indians in their main temple. Not all drawings have such obvious (and opposite) messages: the Spanish as friends of the Indians and the Spanish as murderers of the Indians. The interpretation of some visual material requires knowledge about the subject matter, the artist, the style, and the context in which it appeared. Like written descriptions of past events, art does not simply "speak for itself."

FIGURE 2.8 **Indian Offerings to Cortés**

FIGURE 2.9   Massacre of the Aztec Indians

Now turn to Figure 2.10, a photograph of a clash in 1968 between Chicago police and demonstrators opposing the war in Vietnam. Like the illustrations in Figures 2.8 and 2.9, it too has information. Even a casual glance shows confusion and violence. Looking more closely, you can see the kinds of weapons used by the police and the facial expressions of some of the demonstrators. The more difficult part, again, is interpreting the photograph. Is this a scene of provocation by lawless demonstrators or an attack by the police? A careful look at the picture may help you answer this question. In any case, you need more evidence. While an (undoctored) photograph does show something that actually happened, another photograph — even one of the same event — might show something very different. In most cases, the person taking the photograph has made an effort to have it say something, and you need to take this motive into account.

Not all pictures have controversial interpretations. Figure 2.11 is a photograph of a city street in Ithaca, New York, in the 1890s. There is a wealth of information here about nineteenth century town life. Note that at this early date, the town already had electric trolleys. Note also that the horses are not pulling wagons or carriages ("buggies," as they

FIGURE 2.10 **Antiwar Demonstration at the Democratic National Convention (1968)**

FIGURE 2.11   Town Life in Ithaca, New York (1890s)

were called) but sleighs ("cutters"). This simple fact opens up a window to farm life in winter. When roads were covered with snow and especially ice, the flat, smooth wheels of wagons could not navigate while the sharp runners of the cutter dug into the ice and gave it stability.

How to Take Notes

From Class Lectures

The first rule concerning note taking is simple: pay attention. Don't sleep, doodle, talk, stare out the window, or write a letter to a friend. Some lecturers are not exactly spellbinding or fully organized in what they say, but there is no point in going to class if you are not going to listen to the lecture.

Read the text before going to class or you may be taking notes on the material in the book. If everything the instructor says is new to you, you will spend so much time writing that you won't be able to get an understanding of the theme of the lecture. If you have obtained some basic information from outside readings, you will be able to concentrate on noting points in the lecture that are new or different.

An instructor is most likely to prepare exam questions from material that he or she considers most important. It is therefore essential in preparing notes to determine which points in the lecture are given most prominent attention. Some instructors are very open about their preferences and clearly emphasize certain points, often writing them on the blackboard. Never fail to note something that the instructor indicates is important. Other instructors are less explicit about their biases and values, and you will have to try to figure them out. Listen closely, and make note of those interpretations and generalizations that seem to be stressed, especially when they differ from the approach in the text. You should not feel obliged to parrot your instructor's interpretations in an exam, but ignorance of them will work against you.

Your notes should be written legibly and headed by the date and subject of the lecture. They should reflect a general outline of the material covered, with emphasis on major interpretations and important facts not covered by the text. It is often best to write on every other line and to leave a large margin on at least one side of the page. This will allow you to add material later and to underline your notes and write marginal comments without cluttering the page.

If possible, reread your notes later in the day on which they were written. If your handwriting is poor or your notes are disorganized, it is best to rewrite them. Check the spelling and definitions of any unfamiliar words, and be sure that the notes are coherent. Remember, your notes are an important source of information in your studies, and if they don't make sense, you won't either.

Examples of Note Taking

To illustrate some of the essentials of good note taking, here are portions of two sets of class notes taken from the same lecture. The first example illustrates many of the common errors of note takers, and the second is an example of a well-written set of notes. The subject of the lecture was early European contact with Africa.

EXAMPLE OF POOR NOTE TAKING

Colonization of Africa — People were afraid to sail out. Afraid of sea monsters. But they liked the stories about gold in Africa. The Portuguese King Henry sailed south to find the gold mines and built a fort at Elmina.

England and France want to trade with Africa. They begin trading. Competing with Portugal. These countries got into wars. They wanted to control Africa.

China had spices. They traded with Cairo and Venice. The Asians wanted gold, but the Islams stopped all trade. They fought wars about religion for hundreds of years. Fought over Jerusalem. The Pope called for a crusade. This was in the Middle Ages.

Spices came from Asia. In Europe they were valuable because the kings used them to become rich. They also ate them.

The Portuguese wanted to explore Africa and make a way to India. Their boats couldn't get around until Bartholomew Diaz discovered the Cape of Good Hope in 1487.

Most of all, the Portuguese wanted slaves. They shipped them back from Africa. Columbus took them after he discovered America (1492). The Pope made a line in the Atlantic Ocean so the Catholics wouldn't fight. The colonies needed slaves. They sent 15 million from 1502 to the 19th century. Slaves did the hard work. They got free later after the Civil War.

Immigrants go to Africa from Europe but they don't like the hot weather and they catch diseases. The Dutch set up their own country at the Cape. Then the English conquer them.

EXAMPLE OF GOOD NOTE TAKING

Early European Contact with Africa   History 200

Why Did Europeans Come to Africa?   10/22/97

1. Desire for gold
   — Medieval legends about gold in Africa.
   — Prince Henry (Portuguese navigator) sent men down coast of Africa to find source of gold. (Also to gain direct access to gold trade controlled by Muslims.)
   — Portuguese built forts along the coast. Their ships carried gold and ivory back to Portugal (16th century).
   — Then the other European states came (England, Holland, France, Spain) to set up their own trading posts.
   — Competed with each other for African trade. (Will talk about rivalry next week.)
2. Wanted to trade with Asia and weaken the Muslims
   (The Muslims had created a large empire based on the religion of Islam.)
   — Religious conflict between Christianity and Islam. Fought a religious war in the 11th–12th centuries — the Crusades.
   — The Muslims had expanded their empire when Europe was weak. In 15th century they controlled North Africa and they dominated trade in the Mediterranean. They controlled the spices coming from Asia, which were in great demand in Europe. In Europe they were used to preserve meat. So valuable, sometimes used as money.
   — Portugal and Spain were ruled by Catholic monarchs. Very religious. The Catholic monarchs wanted to force the Muslims out of Europe. (They still held part of Spain.) Wanted to convert them to Christianity.

MPORTANT]— The Muslims controlled North Africa and Mediterranean trade. If the Portuguese and Spanish could sail to the Indian Ocean directly, they could get goods from China and the Muslims couldn't stop them. The way to Asia was the sea route around Africa.

3. The Europeans wanted slaves
   — When the Portuguese explored West Africa (15th century), they sent back the first slaves (around 1440).
   — The Spanish conquered the New World (Mexico, Peru, etc.). (Columbus had made several trips for Queen Isabella I of Spain.)
   — In America (the name for the New World), they needed slaves. Most slaves were sent to America.
   — Native Americans died from diseases of white men. They were also killed in the wars. There was nobody to run the mines (gold and silver).

MPORTANT]— Sugar plantations of the Caribbean (and Brazil) needed labor. Cotton plantations in the south of U.S. also. It was hard work and nobody wanted to do it.
   — 15 million (maybe as many as 40 million) slaves were brought to work the plantations starting in 1502 until mid-19th century.

Colonization of Africa

1. Immigration (why white people didn't come)
   — They couldn't take the climate.
   — There were a lot of tropical diseases.
   — The Europeans didn't want to live in Africa, only run it.
   — Only the Dutch settlers came. They set up the Boer states in South Africa. After them came British settlers.
   — Some French settled in Algeria.
   — Some English also moved to Rhodesia.
2. Dividing Africa
   — Whites began exploring into the interior. (Will discuss exploration next week.)

Copying notes during a lecture is difficult, and even a good set of notes can be greatly improved by being rewritten. Following is a rewriting of these notes. Note how much clearer everything becomes.

REWRITTEN GOOD NOTES

Early European Contact with Africa   History 200
What Drew Europeans to Africa?   10/22/97
   Gold
      There were medieval legends that there was a lot of gold in West Africa. Access to the gold was controlled by non-Christian powers (Muslims — believers in Islamic religion). Tales of gold lured the Portuguese (led by Prince Henry) to explore the coast of West Africa in the late 15th century. By the 16th century, the Portuguese had built several trading posts and forts along the West African coast and were bringing back gold, ivory, and pepper.
      By the 17th century, English, Dutch, French, and Spanish ships challenged the Portuguese trading monopoly and set up their own trading

posts. This was the beginning of rivalry between European countries over the wealth of Africa.

Desire to weaken the power of the Islamic Empire (Muslims) and expand trade with Asia

Conflict between Christianity and Islam was an old religious conflict (the Crusades as an example in 11th and 12th centuries). The Muslims controlled North Africa and the Mediterranean. They also controlled the spice trade from Asia. Spices were important in Europe because they were the only known way to preserve meat.

The Catholic states of Portugal and Spain wanted to fight with the Muslims. They wanted to drive them out of Spain and challenge the large Muslim empire in Africa, the Middle East, and Asia. They hoped to convert them to Christianity. *The Muslims were strong in North Africa, but if European powers could discover a way around Africa into the Indian Ocean, they could outflank the Muslims and obtain direct access to the trade with India and Asia.*

Slaves

Portuguese trading posts in Africa had sent a small number of slaves to Europe starting in the late 15th century. With the discovery and conquest of America at the turn of the 16th century, a new and larger slave trade began to European colonies in the New World (America).

The Native Americans died (they were killed in war and by European diseases in great numbers). There was a shortage of labor. In the 17th and 18th centuries, large sugar plantations were set up in the Caribbean and Brazil and cotton plantations in the southern United States. *The need for laborers to do the hard agricultural work led to the importing of millions of slaves from Africa.* Somewhere between 15 and 40 million Africans were sent to America as slaves between 1502 and the mid-19th century. This slave trade made Africa valuable to the European powers.

The Colonization of Africa

Immigration

Because of the unsatisfactory climate and tropical diseases, there was no major European immigration to Africa. The only significant white colony was set up in South Africa by the Boers (Dutch) and later the English. There were smaller European settlements in Rhodesia (English) and Algeria (French).

Dividing up the continent

Exploration

If you reread the poor notes now, you can easily see how little of the lecture material is recorded in them and how confusing and even erroneous a picture you get from them. What is there about the poor notes that makes them inferior?

First, they are not organized. They do not even record the title of the lecture, the course number, or the date. If these notes get out of order, they will be useless. In fact, they are almost useless anyway. They are nothing more than a series of sentences about gold, trade, spices, Portugal, and slaves. The sentences are not in any particular order, and they do not say anything important. Even the factual information does not cover the major points of the lecture. Instead, it is peripheral information about sea monsters, China, Jerusalem, Bartholomew Diaz, and Columbus, most of which the good note taker wisely omitted. By paying too much attention to trivial points, moreover, the poor note taker missed or did not have time to record the principal theme of the lecture — the relationship between European-Asian trade and the religious struggle between Islam and Christianity. The poor note taker also missed another major point — the connection between the enslavement of Africans and the need for plantation labor in the New World. Without these two points, this student cannot write a good exam on this subject.

The good notes, on the other hand, follow the organization of the lecture and touch upon the major points made in class. The notes make sense and can serve as the basis for reviewing the content of the lecture when studying for exams.

These notes have a wide margin for extra comments and the marking of important passages. (Note the sections marked "important.") The instructor had emphasized these points in class, and by making special note of them, the good student will be sure to master them.

The rewritten version, which eliminates certain unimportant or repetitious phrases and smoothes the language into connected sentences, is even better as a study guide. The greatest value of rewriting, however, is that by re-creating the lecture material in essay form, it becomes part of the note taker's own thinking. The mental effort that goes into revising lecture notes serves to impress the material and its meaning upon the mind. This makes it much easier to review the material at exam time.

From Slides and Films

Some instructors present slide lectures or show films or videotapes. Note taking in these instances involves special problems. If a lecture is accompanied by slides, you will need to include in your notes information as to what the slides illustrated (for example, the Pyramid of Cheops, the novels of Willa Cather, the assassination of John F. Kennedy, the dances of Martha Graham) and anything of importance your instructor said about the slides.

Taking notes on films or videotapes presents some unusual problems. The lighting may be dim. The greatest problem may be the film itself. In our culture, films are a medium of entertainment rather than education. Your natural response will be to sit back and relax your mind. You must fight this response and learn to probe a film as you would a lecture. If a film is essentially factual *(Walled Cities of the Middle Ages),* note the major facts and interpretations as you would in a lecture. If a film is dramatic rather than documentary *(Ivan the Terrible, Citizen Kane),* examine the emotional message and artistic content as well as any historical facts it describes (or claims to describe). As with the author of a book, you need to ask: What is the movie director trying to say, and what dramatic and technical devices does he or she use to say it? Your notes should record important narration and dialogue that illustrate the theme of the film. Finally, you will need to take note of pictorial elements (camera angle, sets, lighting, gestures and movements, facial expressions) because the core of a dramatic film and its impact are essentially visual. It takes practice to learn to take notes on slides and films. It will be worth the effort because photographs, films, and videotapes are used increasingly in history courses.

Classroom Participation

Classroom Discussions

Many instructors encourage class participation, and some base a portion of the final grade on it. Here are a few pointers for improving your ability to participate in class discussions.

Guidelines for Speaking in Class

1. Be familiar with the subject under discussion.
2. If a point is made that disagrees with your understanding, or if something in the lecture or discussion is confusing, formulate a clear question or statement in your mind.
3. If you don't get a chance to be recognized in class, bring up your question with the teacher when the session is over.
4. Teachers are not impressed with students who like to hear themselves talk or who ask careless questions, but if you are interested in the subject and have thought about what you want to say, never hesitate to speak up.

Giving an Oral Presentation

If a course involves an oral presentation in class, you must learn something about this type of assignment. Eloquence and effectiveness in public speaking cannot be mastered in a week or two, but you can make a start by taking such an assignment seriously and adequately preparing yourself for it. If allowed the option, reading from a prepared text is often the safest procedure. However, this can lead to a dull presentation. It is usually better to speak from notes. This kind of presentation will be livelier and more enjoyable for the class. To do a good job, you will have to be fully familiar with your subject and pay close attention to getting your points across. You should prepare your presentation outline as you would that of a short paper. (See the section on short papers in Chapter 3.) Be sure that you cover all the important points and that you present them in a logical manner. A dry run before a relative, friend, or roommate is recommended. Be sure that you exhibit a knowledge of your subject because this is most likely to determine your grade. Effective public speaking is one of the most important tools of success in many fields of work, and giving a talk in class is a good opportunity to develop your skills in this area. Here are some tips to help you give your presentation.

Guidelines for Giving an Oral Presentation

1. Use 3″ × 5″ **note cards** each with one or (at most) two major points on it.
2. Write neatly and use phrases, not whole sentences. If you intend to tell the class that: "Before 1848, most of the large landowners of California were Mexicans. In the decades after California was annexed by the United States, these Californios, as they were called, lost most of their lands to migrants from the eastern states." Your notes need only read: (a) Until 1848 big landowners "Californios." (b) Cal. annexed in 1848. (c) Lost land to easterners.
3. Put a number in the corner of each note card so that they will not get out of order.
4. Relax! Speak slowly and clearly and make eye contact with your audience every few sentences. If you have a time limit, rehearse your talk beforehand so that you won't need to rush. Cut down your notes to fit the time needed to present the material clearly.
5. Visual aids (overhead projections, slides, or even videos) can make your presentation much more interesting. Make sure, however, that you have the resources you need well beforehand and that you know how to integrate them easily and smoothly into your verbal remarks. Unless you have the time to prepare adequately as well as the time to include such aids, you should wait for an occasion when such material is a required part of a presentation.

Taking Exams and
Writing Short Papers

How to Study for Exams

When a test is announced, be sure to find out what kind of an exam it will be: essay, short answer, multiple choice, and so forth. Determine what topics will be covered and what portions of the reading material and lectures deal with the topics. If you have not done all of the necessary reading, do so immediately and record the important facts and interpretations as indicated in Chapter 2 in the section on "How to Read a History Assignment." If you have missed any lectures, obtain a copy of the notes from someone who knows the rules of good note taking. Now gather together all the materials to be covered in the exam. Reread the parts of the texts that you underlined (or otherwise noted) as being important. Reread *all* of the relevant lecture notes, paying special attention to any points emphasized by the instructor. Sometimes it helps to do your rereading aloud.

If the test is to be an **essay exam,** compose sample questions based upon the important topics and themes contained in the readings and lectures. (Many textbooks contain sample exam questions or topics for discussion at the end of each chapter). If you do not know how to answer any portion of the sample question, go over your study materials again and look for the information needed. If you are preparing for an **objective exam** — that is, one requiring short answers — you must pay special attention to the important facts (persons, places, events, changes) in your study materials. You must be precise in order to get credit for your answer. Make a list of the outstanding people, events, and historical developments, and be sure that you can adequately identify them and explain their importance. (Again, your text may help you by providing sample short-answer questions.)

Take the time you need to prepare adequately. If tests make you nervous, the best medicine is to go into the exam confident that you know the material. Keep on studying until you have mastered your sample questions and until the material to be covered makes sense to you.

Objective and Short-Answer Exams

Objective exams call for short, factual answers. The three most common objective exams are: (1) **short answer,** (2) **identification,** and (3) **multiple choice** or true/false.

Short Answer and Identification. Read the question carefully and don't jump to conclusions. Answer briefly (there is usually a time and space limit) and directly. Don't put anything in your answer that wastes space or time. If you are asked to identify John F. Kennedy, don't mention how he was killed (unless that is part of the question). Talk about some aspect of his presidency that was stressed in class or in course readings. When you have so little room to show what you know, answers that stray away from the core of the subject are as bad as wrong answers.

Examples of Objective Exams

Example of a Short-Answer Question

QUESTION: What were the motives that caused the European powers to explore Africa beginning in the late fifteenth century?

INCORRECT ANSWER: They wanted to dominate Africa and get all the gold for themselves. Columbus wanted to take slaves from Africa, but the Pope said it would start a war. But the war didn't start and the Europeans dominated Africa anyway because they were stronger. (43 words)

CORRECT ANSWER: The wars between Christianity and Islam were an important factor. The Christian States wanted to weaken the hold of the Muslim religion on Africa and to convert the natives. They also hoped to break Muslim control of trade with Asia by finding a sea route around Africa (47 words)

(Check these two answers against the example of good note taking on pp. 38–39. These notes make clear why the second answer is satisfactory while the first one is not.)

Example of Identification Question

QUESTION: Identify the "progressive" philosophy of historical interpretation.

INCORRECT ANSWER: Historian who believed that our country was always making progress because Americans were very hardworking people.

CORRECT ANSWER: The interpretation of history that holds that human beings and their condition are continually improving as each generation builds on the foundation laid by previous ones.

(See the section on philosophies of history in Chapter 1 to find the basis for the correct answer.)

Example of Multiple-Choice Question

The British monarch at the time of the American Revolution was:

    a. George II
    b. Charles I
    c. James II
    d. George III
    e. Henry I

If you look up the dates of reign of these monarchs, you will discover that George III (who was king from 1760 to 1820) was the ruler of England at the time of the American Revolution. But perhaps you already knew that.

Preparing for Essay Exams — Composing Sample Questions

Of course, the best preparation for an **essay exam** is to be given the question in advance. Some instructors do this (usually in the form of a **take-home exam**), but many give in-class essay exams and hand out in advance a number of possible topics or questions from which they choose in making up the exam. If you face an upcoming essay exam without *any* questions presented in advance, the key to successful preparation is to come up with potential questions on your own.

As your instructor probably will have told you, the essay questions will deal with the major topics covered in the course so far. Using your texts, lecture notes, and other course materials, determine what these topics are. Then compose your own questions. For example, if the material to be covered in the exam is the reasons for the decline of the Roman Empire, list the major explanations for that decline mentioned in the course work. (Among these may be civil war, military insubordination, the cost of defending distant frontiers, declining agricultural output, barbarian invasion, heavy tax burdens on the peasantry, the growth of central bureaucracy, the decline of the Senate, the cult of the Emperor, the rise of Christianity, and the rise of Islam.) Be prepared to write about *each* of these factors and how they relate to one another. If the course has covered the rise of industrialization in New England, study carefully the major social and technological changes

HOW TO STUDY FOR EXAMS **47**

and how people responded to them. Think about the aspects of industrialization that might form the exam questions. One question might ask you to describe the ways in which factory production was different from the workshop production that it displaced. Other questions might be: How did industrialization affect family life? What were the major technological innovations behind early industrialization? How did the rise of the textile industry affect the lives of young women?

Don't prepare for an essay exam by composing questions that are too broad. If you have spent six weeks examining the decline of the Roman Empire, don't expect a broad question such as: "Discuss the decline of the Roman Empire." Don't prepare questions that are too narrow either. For example, "Who owned the biggest textile mill in New England in the 1830s?" That is a question for a short answer or an identification exam.

Writing a Good Essay Exam

Even if you have prepared properly for an essay exam, your problems are not over. You must stay calm enough to remember what you studied, you must understand the questions, you must answer them directly and fully, and you must not run out of time. None of this is easy, but here are a few pointers to follow until you gain the experience to overcome these problems.

Guidelines for Writing a Good Essay Exam

1. When you are given the exam, don't panic. Read the entire exam slowly, including all of the instructions. Gauge the amount of time you will need to answer each question. Then choose the question you know most about to answer first.

2. Don't write the first thing that comes to your mind. Read the question slowly, and be sure you understand it.

3. Determine how you will answer the question and the central points you wish to make.

4. Write these central points or even a full outline in the margin of the exam booklet, and as you compose each sentence of your answer, make sure that it relates to one of these points.

5. Your answer must follow the question. Be as specific or general, as concrete or reflective, as the question suggests. Never allow your answer to wander away from the focus of the question. If the question asks you to "describe" or "trace" or "compare" or "explain," be sure that that is what you do.

6. Don't repeat yourself. Each sentence should add new material or advance a line of argument.
7. Where necessary, refer to the facts that support the points you are making. You must also give evidence that you have thought about the question in broad terms. The mere relation of a series of facts will rarely earn you a high grade.
8. Toward the end of your answer, you may wish to include your own opinion. This is fine, even desirable, but be sure that your answer as a whole supports this opinion.
9. If there is time, always reread and correct an answer after it is finished. The pressure of an exam can often cause you to write sentences that are not clear.
10. Write legibly, or your grader will be in no mood to give you the benefit of any doubts.
11. Don't write cute or plaintive notes on the exam. They seldom raise a grade and may prejudice the grader against you.

Examples of Essay Exams

A well-written essay answer is a combination of (1) adequate knowledge of the subject, (2) clear thinking about the points to be covered, (3) well-structured sentences, and (4) complete understanding of the question. Following are two answers to a sample essay question on modern Chinese history. The first answer is very poor and meets none of these requirements. The second answer is very well written and deals successfully with the four requirements listed.

QUESTION: Explain the origins of the Chinese Civil War of 1945–1949. How did the differing political programs of the two contenders affect the outcome of that conflict?

POOR ANSWER: The Guo Mindang (Kuomintang) had a stronger army than the Communists, but the Communists won the civil war and took over the country. Their political program, communism, was liked by the peasants because they didn't own any land and paid high taxes.

China was based on the Confucian system, which was very rigid and led to the Manchu dynasty being overthrown. The Chinese didn't like being dominated by foreigners, and Sun Zhongshan (Sun Yat-sen) founded the Guo Mindang (Kuomintang) to unite China. He believed in the Three People's Principles. At first he cooperated with the Chinese Communists, but later Jiang Jieshi (Chiang Kai-shek) tried to destroy communism because he was against it. Communism was not in favor of the wealthy people.

The Communists wanted a revolution of the peasants and gave them land. They also killed the landlords. Jiang Jieshi (Chiang Kai-shek) worried more about the Communists than about the Japanese invasion. The Japanese looked to conquer China and make it a part of their empire. Jiang Jieshi (Chiang Kai-shek) wanted to fight the Communists first.

After World War II the Chinese Communists attacked Manchuria and took over a lot of weapons. They fought the Guo Mindang (Kuomintang) army. The Guo Mindang (Kuomintang) army lost the battles, and Jiang Jieshi (Chiang Kai-shek) was chased to Taiwan, where he made a new government. The Communists set up their own country, and their capital was Beijing (Peking). That way the Communists won the Chinese Civil War.

GOOD ANSWER: The origins of the 1945–1949 Civil War can be traced back to the rise of Chinese nationalism in the late nineteenth century. Out of the confusion of the Warlord period that followed the overthrow of the Manchu dynasty in 1911, two powerful nationalist movements arose — one reformist and the other revolutionary. The reformist movement was the Guo Mindang (Kuomintang), founded by Sun Zhongshan (Sun Yat-sen). It was based on a mixture of republican, Christian, and moderate socialist ideals and inspired by opposition to foreign domination. The revolutionary movement was that of the Chinese Communist Party (CCP), founded in 1921, whose goal was a communist society but whose immediate program was to organize the working class to protect its interests and to work for the removal of foreign "imperialist" control.

Although these two movements shared certain immediate goals (suppression of the Warlords and resistance to foreign influence), they eventually fell out over such questions as land reform, relations with the Soviet Union, the role of the working class, and the internal structure of the Guo Mindang (Kuomintang). [The CCP operated within the framework of the more powerful Guo Mindang (Kuomintang) during the 1920s.]

By the 1930s, when Jiang Jieshi (Chiang Kai-shek) succeeded Sun, the CCP was forced out of the Guo Mindang (Kuomintang). By that time the CCP had turned to a program of peasant revolution inspired by Mao Zedong (Mao Tse-tung). A four-year military struggle (1930–1934) between the two movements for control of the peasantry of Jiangxi (Kiangsi) Province ended in the defeat but not destruction of the CCP.

The Japanese invasion of Manchuria (1931) and central China (1936–1938) helped salvage the fortunes of the CCP. By carrying out an active guerrilla resistance against the Japanese, in contrast to the more passive role of the Guo Mindang (Kuomintang), which was saving its army for a future battle with the Communists, the CCP gained the leading position in the nationalist cause.

In the post–World War II period, the CCP's land reform program won strong peasant support, whereas the landlord-backed Guo Mindang (Kuomintang) was faced with runaway corruption and inflation, which eroded its middle-class following. The military struggle between 1945 and 1949 led to the defeat of the demoralized Guo Mindang (Kuomintang) army and the coming to power of the CCP.

Let's see the differences between the poor and the well-written essays in regard to each of the four requirements for a well-written answer.

1. *Adequate knowledge of the subject.* The poor answer fails to indicate adequate knowledge in several ways. It is too brief, omitting many im-

portant facts. It describes the political programs of the two contending
parties in the most vague terms. It refers to the CCP only as the Chinese Communists, leaving the impression that they were a loose group-
ing of like-minded individuals rather than a strong, well-disciplined political organization. It does not even mention the name of the most
famous leader of the CCP — Mao Zedong (Mao Tse-tung). Jiang Jieshi
(Chiang Kai-shek), the leader of the Guo Mindang (Kuomintang), is
mentioned, but there is no mention of his political program or beliefs,
other than that he was opposed to communism. Another serious defect
is the lack of chronology. The answer jumps back and forth between
earlier and later periods, and no dates are given for major events.

The well-written answer illustrates a good knowledge of the subject
matter. The origins, philosophies, leaders, and relationship of the two
contending parties are clearly described. This answer brings in related
issues such as nationalism, Warlords, guerrilla warfare against Japan,
corruption, and inflation, thus indicating a broader knowledge of the
historical context in which the Chinese Civil War developed. The
chronology is very clear, with events proceeding in proper time sequence and with all major events identified by date.

2. *Clear thinking about the points to be covered.* The poor answer is not
organized. Note that the paragraphs do not make separate points and
that each succeeding paragraph does not further develop the theme of
the essay. Paragraph one is a conclusion rather than an introduction.
The second paragraph goes back to the founding of the Guo Mindang
(Kuomintang) but, instead of discussing the origins of the hostility between it and the CCP, merely states that hostility came into existence.
The third paragraph begins by introducing the CCP (though not by
name). However, it does not expand on the CCP's programs and
points of conflict with the Guo Mindang (Kuomintang), but instead
abruptly changes the focus of events and the time frame by introducing the Japanese invasion of China, which the last sentence of the paragraph only vaguely relates to the question. The last paragraph, instead
of drawing conclusions about the causes of the Communist victory in
the Civil War, merely states that it occurred.

The well-written answer, on the other hand, uses each paragraph to
make a separate important point, and each succeeding paragraph further develops the theme of the essay. Paragraph one sets out the political programs of the two groups and the historical context in which the
movements originated. The second paragraph explains the beginning
of the conflict in the 1920s. Paragraph three discusses that conflict in
relation to the Chinese peasantry during the early 1930s. The fourth
paragraph discusses the development of the conflict in relation to the
Japanese invasion of the late 1930s. The final paragraph summarizes
the effects of the conflicts and of postwar developments on the outcome of the Civil War.

3. *Well-structured sentences.* Many sentences in the poor answer are badly constructed either because they are awkward or because what they say adds nothing to the answer. Some of the awkward phrases are "the Communists won the Civil War and *took over* the country"; "communism was *liked by* the peasants"; "China was *based on* the Confucian system"; "communism was not *in favor* of the wealthy people"; "the Japanese *looked* to conquer China"; "the Communists *set up their own country.*" These phrases cause the sentences to be unclear, and they keep the student from getting his or her point across. The other major defect in sentence structure is repetitious or irrelevant sentences and phrases. These are "Jiang Jieshi (Chiang Kai-shek) tried to destroy communism *because he was against it*"; "they *fought the Guo Mindang (Kuomintang) army*"; "that way *the Communists won the Chinese Civil War.*" The sentences of the well-written answer, on the other hand, are clear, and each adds new material to the essay.

4. *Complete understanding of the question.* The poor answer does not deal with the central issue of the question — the political programs of the Guo Mindang (Kuomintang) and the CCP. It notes that the Guo Mindang (Kuomintang) was founded on the Three People's Principles, but it does not explain what these were. Of the CCP, it says that there was a belief in communism (which is obvious) and peasant revolution (which is vague). These are the only references to political programs in the entire answer! It is obvious that the writer of this answer failed to understand that the central focus of the question was on political philosophy.

The well-written answer is directed to the central issue of political programs and begins on that very point. The remainder of the answer makes clear the relationship of political programs to the origins and course of the Chinese Civil War as called for in the first sentence of the question.

Here is another good answer to an essay question. Note how it meets the four requirements set out above.

QUESTION: What were the major features of Russian expansion across Siberia? What factors facilitated this expansion? How did it compare with the expansion of the United States across North America?

GOOD ANSWER: Russian expansion to the east began in the sixteenth century from the area around Moscow, which had become the center of a powerful state under Ivan the Terrible (1533–1584). Eastern expansion was spearheaded by the Cossacks, who were in most instances former peasants who had fled to the frontiers of the Russian state to avoid serfdom. There they became shepherds, hunters, and expert horsemen. Some joined robber bands and preyed on commerce. Eventually they took up arms in service to the Russian nobility and fought against the Siberian Tatars, Moslem peoples who raided Russia from across the Ural Mountains. In a series of wars against the Tatars, Cossack forces fought and marched across northern

Eurasia, covering a distance even greater than that across the United States, and reached the Pacific Ocean before the middle of the seventeenth century.

This vast territory was conquered in a brief period of time because of several favorable conditions. In a wide band of territory stretching eastward, the climate was similar to that of European Russia. Within this forested zone there were no major natural obstacles. The mountains were low and the rivers navigable. The native population was small and no powerful tribes existed. None had armaments equal to those of the Cossacks.

There are several similarities between Russian and United States continental expansion. The great extent of the two expansions is similar, as is the influence of the frontier experience on both cultures. Continental expansion in both cases engulfed (and often destroyed) weaker native peoples and incorporated their lands into the expanding nation rather than holding them as colonies. In both cases an important economic incentive was the fur trade and the ability of trappers to use the extensive river systems to send their pelts to market.

In some respects, however, the expansionist experiences were different. The Russian advance was much more rapid than the American. Cossacks began to push eastward about the same time (late sixteenth century) as the first English settlers came to America. By the mid-seventeenth century, however, the Russians had reached the Pacific Ocean while the settlers in North America had yet to cross the Appalachian Mountains. Although the Russian advance was swift, settlement of the land was sparse compared with the slower American expansion. In 1763, all across the newly conquered expanse of Siberia there were only 400,000 Russians. At about the same date, the much smaller territory of the thirteen English colonies in North America contained about 1.7 million settlers.

The two expansions were similar in scope and in the nature of the native forces encountered. They were, however, different in content. Siberia is to this day a rather backward, isolated, and thinly populated region of Russia, whereas the lands that lie beyond the early eastern settlements of the United States today hold the greater part of the population and economic resources of the nation.

Take-Home Exams

A take-home exam usually consists of one or more short essays that you prepare outside of class. The writing of a short essay should generally follow the rules for writing a short paper (see pp. 56–58). There are, however, a few specific guidelines for this type of assignment.

First, note the length requirements of the exam and the due date. Obviously, you need more time to prepare a six-page essay than to prepare a three-page one. If your instructor allows you access to sources, review all course materials that deal with the question being asked. If you have not yet outlined or taken notes from these readings, do so now. Then list the most important points made in these readings or in your own notes. Try to find anywhere from two to six main points for each essay, depending on the length of the essay. Compose your answer by discussing each of these points in logical order. As with all essays, you should have a clear central theme. Make sure that the theme *directly* addresses the question.

A problem that sometimes arises with take-home exams is **plagiarism.** In such an exam, it is usually permissible to **paraphrase** the sources used in preparing your answer. Be sure, however, that you write in your own words. If you use sentences from a book in your answer, you are **cheating,** whether you mean to or not. Copying from a text or history work is unlikely to get you anywhere. Your instructor knows that experienced historians write quite differently from students, and passages taken from such a source will jump out of the page as your paper is being read. Most instructors penalize students severely for plagiarizing. (See the section on plagiarism later in this chapter.)

Writing Assignments in History and Why They Are Important

One of the most important tasks you will be given in a history course will be a writing assignment. It may be a short **book review,** like the task discussed later in this chapter. On the other hand, it may be a lengthy research paper, like the one described in Chapter 5. Whether you are writing a few paragraphs or an essay, it must be your best work, which requires time and care. Every history instructor has had the experience of reading a bad paper from a good student who did not take the trouble to do his or her best. If you hand in sloppy or thoughtless work, it not only earns you a poor grade, it indicates that you are not aware of the importance of writing. Nothing about writing should be casual or halfhearted. It is a task of great importance, for you may be judged not only by your history instructor but by everyone who ever reads your words. Two years after graduating you may not remember the causes of World War I; but if your history assignment has sharpened your writing, then you have honed a skill that you can use for all of your life.

Good writing requires more than knowing your subject; you must also explain the subject clearly to an audience. Whenever you write, treat it as a step-by-step process in which you move from initial ideas, through many stages of development (in your mind and on paper), and on to a finished, polished product. Begin to write only after having thought about (and taken notes about) your subject. Never accept your first product as anything more than an initial **draft.** Go over it, add or delete, clarify sentences, rearrange paragraphs, correct grammar and spelling. Do this once, twice, perhaps three or more times until you get to the finished piece. Then ask someone else to go over it too. If you follow these steps, you will never hand in written work that is unworthy of you. You will achieve good grades, and you will have developed a skill that is invaluable.

Book Reviews

A common assignment in history courses is writing a review of one of the readings. The most important point to remember about a book (or article or chapter) review is that it is much more than a summary. Unless your instructor specifically asks you to summarize the content, spend most of your review in an *anlaysis* of the author's work. What is the topic, how is it described, what did you learn from it, how does it compare to other course materials? If your assignment is to review two or more works, be sure to *compare* their treatment of the subject. Following are the key elements of a book review:

Guidelines for Writing a Book Review

1. Author, title, and publishing information of the book or other reading at the top of the page (along with your name and the course information).
2. Introductory paragraph stating the thesis or the main points made by the author.
3. Description of the evidence presented to support the thesis.
4. Information about the author's background and viewpoint (if available).
5. Assessment of the arguments and evidence used. (Are they clear or unclear, strong or weak, convincing or unconvincing?)
6. Compare the work under review to any related course material. (Does it agree or disagree? Does it add a new perspective?)
7. Final paragraph summarizing the book's strengths and weaknesses. (Was the thesis clear, was evidence strong, were conclusions sound? Do you agree or disagree with the author's assumptions and conclusions?)

The length and difficulty of the work being reviewed (scholarly book, short article, primary document, etc.) should determine how complex your review needs to be. In any event, be sure to make clear to your instructor that you read and understood the work and that you made the kind of analysis and comparison asked of you.

To provide you with an example of a book review, here is one about the book you are now reading.

John Q. Student
History 100
February 14, 1998

Book Review of:
Jules R. Benjamin
A Student's Guide to History
Bedford Books, 7th ed., 1998

Benjamin's purpose, as stated in the preface, is to introduce students to the subject of history and to provide them with study and research skills. The author includes sections on such matters as "What History Can Tell You," "How to Read a History Assignment," "A Note on Plagiarism," and "Organizing a Bibliography." These subjects and others are presented clearly and succinctly, often with examples. It does seem, however, that Benjamin has only the beginning student in mind and thus explains some topics (such as how to answer an objective-exam question) that seem to be matters of common sense.

The most valuable sections of the book are those entitled "A Brief Journey into the Past," "How to Research Your Family History," and "Sources for History Research on the Internet." In "A Brief Journey . . ." Benjamin makes clear how history surrounds us if we only know how to look for it. The section on family history is very useful to anyone conducting that kind of research. Nevertheless, the author could have given greater attention to this topic, despite the need to cover many other subjects. However, the section on computer research opens a whole new area for students.

Benjamin's point of view is consistently student oriented, attempting to fill study and research needs while still paying some attention to history as an intellectual field. Overall, the book is clearly of the "how to" variety. As a result, the discussion of the philosophy of history is very brief.

Perhaps the most successful part of the book is the long appendix: "Basic Reference Sources for History Study and Research." Here the author lists dozens of different kinds of reference works (dictionaries, encyclopedias, atlases, biography collections, periodical guides) and page after page of bibliographies on specialized periods, areas, or topics in history. The section devoted to bibliographies on "Asian Immigrant and Ethnic History" was very helpful in finding books for a paper on "The Chinese in Nineteenth-Century San Francisco." The list of sources in the appendix is very.broad but seems to be most complete in Benjamin's own area of interest, which, according to the <u>Directory of American Scholars</u>, is in modern United States history.

All in all, Benjamin has created a useful and interesting guide for history students. It enables the student to acquire a better understanding of the purpose of a history course and to get more out of it by using the skills discussed in <u>A Student's Guide to History</u>.

Writing Short Papers

Instructors assign many kinds of short written assignments. These may range from three to as many as ten pages. Some, such as the essay exam or the book review, have already been described. Now let's look at more complex written assignments. A discussion of how to compose short papers will also prepare you for the most complex written assignment — the research paper — to be explained in the next two chapters.

Writing assignments in history sometimes require you to take a position in a controversy, compare the approach to a topic in two or more readings, write about your own life history, or keep a journal — a daily or weekly record of your experiences related to your history assignments and class experiences. As previously pointed out, always take these writing tasks seriously.

Instructors, when assigning a short paper, commonly give out a topic or question. If you are taking a course on the history of journalism in the United States, you might be asked to write a short paper on the relationship between rising literacy and the growth of newspaper circulation in the nineteenth century. The paper is assigned because the relationship between these two factors (literacy and readership) is not a simple one. Don't make the mistake of merely stating in your paper that circulation rose because more people could read. Knowing how to read doesn't automatically give a person the desire (or the money) to buy a newspaper. The course material will inform you that by the late nineteenth century a large part of newspapers was not text but illustrations. This means that even people who knew very few words of English might still want to buy a newspaper. Perhaps you are beginning to see why the question is worth writing about. The relationship between literacy and readership is not a simple one — few things in history are. The key to a good answer is to realize that rising literacy and rising newspaper circulation reinforced one another; neither was the simple cause of the other.

How do you prepare for and how do you execute this assignment?

Guidelines for Writing a Short Paper

1. Understand the topic or question. (Thinking about the question is always the first step.)
2. Determine which materials you will need to answer it.
3. From the relevant materials, take notes on any facts and explanations that have to do with the topic or question.
4. Examine your notes closely and compose a **theme** or **thesis;** that is, a principal idea or conclusion that your paper will support. (If your sources have described the interaction of literacy and readership, your notes should reflect it. Poor note taking can lead to an unsound thesis.)
5. Organize your paper by outlining it, first in your head and then on paper. What evidence do you need to support your thesis? What is the best way to present the evidence? In what order?
6. Begin to flesh out your first draft. Compose a paragraph (or more if necessary) for each of the points you wish to make.

- reasons for the rise in literacy
- evidence that such a rise actually occurred
- reasons for the growing popularity of newspapers
- evidence that circulation increased
- changes in the technology for printing newspapers
- changes in the format and content of newspapers
- how rising literacy interacted with changes in the nature of newspapers

7. Weave together the paragraphs created in step 6 so that each point follows clearly from the one before it and that each adds support to your thesis. This is your **rough draft.**
8. Read and **revise** your draft. Question each sentence and paragraph to be sure that it is supported by your notes and that in turn it supports your thesis. Add, delete, or change your writing where this is not the case. (One exception is counterevidence: material in your notes that could be used to argue against your thesis. You should include some of this material and explain to your reader why you are sticking by your thesis.)
9. Write your introduction and conclusion. (Yes, this step comes toward the end rather than at the beginning.) Your introduction should explain your thesis, why you chose it, and how you plan to support it. Your conclusion is a brief restatement of the thesis and the principal evidence that led to it.

10. If the assignment asks for **documentation** and a **bibliography,** be sure that you know how to create them. (The form for writing **citations** and bibliographies is described in Chapter 5.)
11. Read and revise your draft again. Add any important new material that you have not yet included. Let a friend read the paper and make comments. Check the writing for clarity, grammar, and spelling.
12. Type the final draft neatly, following any instructions concerning form that your instructor has given.

A Note on Plagiarism: A Serious Offense

Whenever you write from your own notes, you run the risk of using the phrases and even sentences in the original works you read. Even if you do this without realizing it, it constitutes *plagiarism.* Unless the phrases or sentences are placed in quotation marks and you identify their source in a **footnote** or **endnote,** you have committed a very serious breach of academic honesty. Plagiarism is severely penalized and can lead to failing a course or even suspension. Turn to the discussion of avoiding plagiarism on page 83 to make sure you know how to avoid this dangerous possibility.

C H A P T E R   4

How to Research a History Topic

In basic history courses, you may be called upon to do historical research. If you take advanced courses, you certainly will be called upon to do research papers. Whether you are preparing a short essay or book review or a long class presentation or term paper, you will need to know how to gather all the necessary materials and how to organize and analyze your information. This chapter will survey sources of historical information and will explain how to use these sources most profitably. The chapter also includes sections on choosing a topic, how to record information, and how to organize your notes.

What Is a Research Paper?

A research paper requires you to gather your own sources of information. It is one of the most creative tasks you will do as a history student. Since you choose your own material and draw your own conclusions, the product is uniquely your own. Because a lot of independent work is involved, research is often the most challenging history assignment. The skills you gain from doing this kind of a project (gathering, organizing, and interpreting evidence) are invaluable. Any professional or business career that you later pursue will call upon one or more of these skills. In years to come, you may not remember the name of the secret research program that produced the atomic bomb during World War II (the Manhattan Project) and about which you wrote a paper. Nevertheless, you strengthened important skills during the research *process* that produced the paper.

Five stages of research are involved in preparing your paper: (1) choosing a topic, (2) finding the best sources of information, (3) determining what you need to record from these sources, (4) organizing your research, and (5) writing the research paper. The last step — writing the paper — is covered in the next chapter. This chapter takes you through the first four steps.

What Should I Write About: Choosing a Topic

Some instructors assign a specific research topic, but most set out a range of possible topics and leave the choice to you. Choose your topic carefully. You will become bored if you have to spend weeks searching out and reading information about a subject that does not interest you. Try to select a topic about which you are genuinely curious. No matter what subject, person, or event you are interested in, it has a history. Every subject can be studied backward in time because every event was caused by events that preceded it. A history research project can be made out of almost anything. Perhaps in the neighborhood where you grew up there was a very old building and you had always wondered about when it was built and what it was used for. Finding out what the neighborhood was like when that building was new can be an exciting search.

An ideal topic is not only one about which you are curious but one about which you already know something. Perhaps you read a book about Socrates and want to know more about why he was condemned to death; or perhaps you saw a movie about the Depression and want to know what it was like to live through it. Instructors are eager to help students who show a real interest in a topic. Your instructor can assist you in selecting a subject related to your interests that also suits the particular course you are taking.

Coming Up with a Theme for Your Paper

A theme is more narrow than a **topic.** A *topic* is the general subject that you will investigate (the influence of Islam on the Kingdom of Mali; the philosophy of Martin Luther King, Jr.). A *theme* is some important point about the topic that you wish to make. For the paper on King, you may want to show that his famous speech at the Lincoln Memorial in 1963 expressed several elements of his religious beliefs. In that case, your theme is the connection between the speech and King's earlier religious development. This connection will be the central point of your paper and making that connection will direct your research and writing. Without a theme, you will not have a clear idea of which sources of information to investigate, what to take from them, or how to organize your paper.

Moving from a topic to a theme is not always easy. The key is to find an aspect of your topic that can serve as the core of your paper, that fits the sources available to you, and that can be satisfactorily researched within the time available to complete the assignment. A topic such as the conquest of the Aztec Empire can produce both workable and unwieldy themes. The theme "The Correspondence of Cortés and King Ferdinand," may be feasible if it is confined to letters from Cortés about the conquest of the Aztecs. The trouble here is access to sources. Unless translations of this correspondence are available in your library (or can be gotten without too much difficulty), you do not have the research material to explore this theme. On the other hand, the theme "The Factors that Enabled the Spanish to Defeat the Aztecs" is workable since you should not have difficulty in finding enough material on this subject. Even if resources are available, make sure that your theme is not too broad. For a topic such as European exploration of Africa, you might come up with the theme "Exploration of the Congo River." As dozens of such explorations were made over many years, this is not a proper theme — it is actually a topic. If you begin to research "Exploration of the Congo River," you will soon discover that there are too many sources and that you do not have time (or space in your paper) to do them justice.

Formulating a theme that is narrow enough and yet not too narrow is tricky. It is often useful in narrowing a theme to compose questions about your topic. If your topic is Native Americans of the Western United States, ask yourself a question you would like to know the answer to. Maybe some aspect of Native American life, such as the thoughts of their medicine men or the conflict of a particular tribe with European settlers, has aroused your curiosity. You might ask yourself: "What did medicine men believe?" or "How did the Indians defend their lands?" These questions might yield themes such as "The Practice of Magic among the Cheyenne," or "Efforts of the Nez Perce to Protect their Native Lands in Oregon." For a topic about Canadian frontier communities in the nineteenth century, again, ask yourself what specific things you would like to know about them. Was the coming of the railroad of great importance to them? This might lead you to a theme: "The Canadian Pacific Railroad Comes to Winnipeg, Manitoba." (By the way, you may have noted that a theme can usually serve as a *title* for your paper.) Although composing questions is usually helpful in arriving at themes, be careful that the questions you ask are not too broad. ("Why did the Roman Empire fall?"). Questions can also be too narrow ("Who was the first person to sign the Declaration of Independence?") or too unimportant ("Why are ping pong tables green?").

If you know very little about your topic, then it is wise to learn more about it before you attempt to narrow it and produce a good theme. If your topic is the Mexican Revolution of 1910, check a brief outline history of the subject in a good historical dictionary or encyclopedia (for example, the *Encyclopaedia Britannica* or the *Encyclopedia of Latin America*). The description of the Mexican Revolution in these works will likely mention its principal leaders — Francisco Madero, Pancho Villa, Emiliano Zapata, and Venustiano Carranza. Perhaps your interest will now be triggered by the recollection of stories concerning Villa's daring raid on a United States border town (Columbus, New Mexico) in 1916 and how the U.S. Army under General Pershing marched into Mexico to capture him — but never did. Or perhaps you have seen the Hollywood movie *Viva Zapata,* which tells the story (not necessarily accurately) of the peasant leader Emiliano Zapata and his fight to preserve the lands of the Indian villages in his native state of Morelos. If you have ever seen photographs of Zapata (and they were popular in poster form among college students in the 1960s), you know his piercing eyes and look of determination. If your interest in the Mexican Revolution is now focusing on Villa or Zapata, you should next turn to a biographical dictionary. Here you will discover that Villa's real name was Doroteo Arango and that he was a cattle thief as well as a brilliant military commander. Zapata, you will learn, led a peasant guerrilla army whose aim was to recapture the land taken from its villages by owners of expanding sugar plantations. To flesh out a paper on Villa's military career or Zapata's land reform program (some elements of which Mexican peasants are still struggling for today), turn to the **subject bibliographies** in Appendix A of this book or to the reference section of your library. Subject bibliographies will lead you to individual historical works on the Mexican Revolution, and from the book and article titles (and the descriptions of their contents if they are annotated) you will be able to determine those which may contain information on the topic you are considering.

Creating a Research Outline

A **research outline** is different from the one you will create when you *write* your paper. (See the section on preparing a writing outline later in this chapter.) A research outline helps you to investigate your theme in an organized way. It tells you which parts of your research should come first. Here is a sample research outline for investigating the topic of agrarian reform in the Mexican Revolution, which, after preliminary research, led to the theme: "The Land Reform Program of Emiliano Zapata."

RESEARCH OUTLINE: Things I need to do before I begin. Take a tour of the library. Find out what kinds of information are kept where. Leave myself enough time to do all of the tasks I list.

Task #1: [Background] Gain a general knowledge of the Mexican Revolution from a good encyclopedia or textbook. Time = 1 day.

Task #2: [Background] Learn about land reform *before* the revolution. An encyclopedia or a general history of Mexico in the 19th century. Time = 1 day.

Task #3: [Information about Zapata] Life in Ananecquilco, Morelos (village and state where Zapata grew up). A **biography** of Zapata, and a book or articles examining the changes in village life in Morelos in the decades before 1910. Time = 3 days.

Task #4: [Information about land reform] Books, articles, and documents about how the villagers lost their lands before 1910. Time = 3 days.

Task #5: [Zapata's role in the effort to regain village lands] Sources that examine Zapata's early career as a village leader. Time = 3 days.

Task #6: [The period of the Revolution, 1910–1920] Sources examining the role of Zapata and his followers in the revolution. Time = 4 days.

Task #7: [Specific land reform programs] Books (maybe old ones on **microfilm** or **microfiche**) that contain **quotations** from or copies of the actual proposals by Zapata. Time = 2 days.

Task #8: [The fate of the programs] Read about the final years of the revolution and of the fate of Zapata (assassinated in 1919). Time = 2 days.

Not all research outlines need to be this specific. The time frame, in particular, is merely for purposes of illustration. It contains twenty-one days of research, assuming that you spend about two or three hours each day conducting research and reading. Your particular assignment may require more or less time, depending on the length of your paper and the importance given to it by your instructor. (Remember this is only time needed for *research*. Writing your paper will, of course, take additional time.) Moreover, the outline is only suggestive. Your own research may move back and forth among the tasks (especially the later ones) on a given day in the library. While you are gathering material on Zapata's early life, you may come across a book about his land program. In fact, the same book may discuss both.

The information in the library will not be neatly divided into the tasks you have laid out. The purpose in organizing your research in a formal way, even if the actual process is much messier, is that your research has a sense of direction that it otherwise would lack. If you don't know what kinds of sources to look for first, which to read first, and which to read later on, you may try to take notes on specific land reform proposals before you even know who Zapata was or how long the revolution lasted. Even if you cannot actually follow an outline like the one above, just making it and having it in mind as you do your research will help you. In short, don't begin serious research until you have a clear idea of what you will be looking for. You may change directions (even change your theme) after some background reading, and you can always adjust your outline. It is better to have a research outline that you can change than none at all.

After conducting preliminary research to help you decide what part of your topic interests you most, narrowing it to manageable size, and formulating a theme and a research outline to direct your research, you will be ready to seek out sources of information. The **library catalog** and the reference works listed in Appendix A will help you create a list of books, articles, and other relevant sources. If these works lead you to specific sources (e.g., the title of a book or the volume of a **periodical**), the next step is to see whether your school library has them. You will also want to know of any other books, articles, and so on that your library possesses on your topic. To find these sources, you will first have to learn how to conduct library research.

Library Research

Finding Information about Your Topic/Theme in Your School Library

A college library can be an intimidating place. Don't begin your research until you are familiar with it. Take the formal library tour and read the handouts that describe the organization of the library's holdings. Libraries have much more than just books. Some library materials are printed and some, like microfilm and microfiche, are in miniaturized form. Libraries have collections of music, art, film, photographs, and other sound and visual material. Some of the books are reference works (like those in Appendix A) that help you find different sources of information. Various parts of the library's collection of materials are found in different places: some (like books and bound copies of journals) are in the stacks,[1] miniaturized material is in its own area because machines (microfilm and microfiche readers) are required to read it, **reference books** are on shelves separate from the stacks. Know the layout of your library and never hesitate to ask a librarian if you can't find what you are looking for.

In addition to knowing the *kind* of material that is in your library and *where* it is kept, you need to know what specific material on your topic (and theme) it possesses. To find the information you need, learn to use all of the library's "finding aids." These are the catalogs and lists that tell you which books, **journals,** magazines, microfiche, videos, etc. the library has and where they are located. The principal finding aid in the library is its main catalog.

---

[1]The *stacks* are the shelves on which most of the library's books and journals are stored. Some stacks are open and you can go through them on your own; others are closed and you need permission to get access to them.

Creating a Research Bibliography.   As you begin to discover useful materials in your library, make sure to copy down *exactly and fully* all of the information on each item. Your goal is to compile a **research bibliography,** a list of the sources you think will give you the information you need to describe your theme and to document the facts you write about it. When you finally write your paper, you may not use some of the items that you list in this phase of your research. At this stage, however, cast your net broadly.

Using the Library Catalogs

The main catalog, now usually in electronic form on computer, is the most important pathway into the materials you need to know about to conduct your research. Once this catalog consisted of row after row of wooden filing cabinets each containing drawer after drawer of cards. The computer-based or **online catalog** that has replaced it is easier and much faster to use. In order to get what you want out of the catalog, however, you will need to know the rules for searching its contents.

Searching the Catalog by Author and Title.   You can search for books in the online catalog by author, title, or subject. The catalog will have a screen or menu (or a printed guide beside the computer) that tells you which commands begin an author search, a title search, a subject search, or **key-word** search. Author and title searches are usually simple as long as you know the proper commands and spell the names or titles correctly. If you enter the author name "Chakspeere, William" (instead of "Shakespeare, William") you will not get very far. The spelling of ancient and foreign names is especially tricky. Check the spelling before you begin your search. If still uncertain, ask the reference librarian. Title searches have a few dangers also. Again spelling is crucial. In addition, titles that begin with "A" or "The" can confuse the computer. The rules for title searching usually tell you which words in titles can cause trouble. Finally, be sure to get the words of the title just right. If you are looking for *A Student's Guide to History* and type in *A Student's Guide to Hysteria,* you are in for a surprise.

While author and title searches are fairly straightforward, they require you to know in advance what person or book you are looking for. This is often not possible, especially when just beginning your research. For the most part, you will need to discover which books by which authors are related to your theme. To do this, you must search the online catalog by subject. This is a little more difficult. Unless you enter the right words, the computer will not list the materials you really need.

Searching the Catalog by Subject.   Most online catalogs allow you to search their contents by subject or by key word or both. Although simi-

lar, subject and key-word searches are not the same. In a library catalog, a **subject heading** is the term that the creator of the catalog thinks
is the best word (or words) to describe the contents of the books (and
other materials) included under that heading. A *key word,* on the other
hand, is a term that *you* choose because it seems to describe the kinds
of sources you think you need.[2] This discussion first takes up subject
headings; an examination of key words follows.

SUBJECT HEADINGS

If you want to do the job of searching by subject heading in the most
complete way, go to the official set of headings compiled by the Library
of Congress. These headings are printed in the volumes, *Library of Congress Subject Headings,* usually kept in the reference section of the library
or near the computer terminals. If you are lucky, the online catalog
will include a list of such headings in menu form. Another way to discover the best subject headings is to look up a book that you already
know about (by author or title), and when you get it on the screen, go
to "long" or "full" display. This display tells you more than the author,
the title, and location; you get the full publication data as well as the
subject heading or headings under which it is placed in the catalog.
Other books on your theme may be listed under this heading, so you
now can use this heading to find them. Since no two computer catalogs
are exactly alike, finding out how to use subject headings may require
the help of a librarian. Don't be shy; a librarian's assistance can save
you a great deal of time. (An introduction to subject headings is contained in Appendix B.)

KEY WORDS

Another way of searching the computer catalog is by key word. Not
all catalogs enable you to search in this way, but if the one in your library does, take advantage of it. Instead of trying to figure out the subject your topic is under, you ask the computer to search its records of
books and other materials for certain words. If your topic is women
workers in early industrial America, and you have narrowed it to the
theme: "Women Workers in the Lowell, Massachusetts, Textile Mills,
1820–1850" (see the sample student paper in Chapter 5), then your
key words are the nouns in your theme — "women," "workers," "Lowell," "textile mills." Don't search by using any of these words by themselves, for they are too general and will generate a long list of sources,
most of which will not be related to your theme. Entering the word
"women," for example, will get you everything in the library that has
anything to do with the topic of women. Some computers allow you to

---

[2]An example of a subject heading is "Textile industry — Massachusetts —, Lowell — History
— 19th Century" while a key word in the same topic area might be "women textile workers."

do complex key-word searches that combine several key words so that you can ask it, for example, to find records that mention "women" *and* "workers" or, better yet, "women workers" *and* "textile mills." (Placing the word "and" between your key words narrows the search accordingly.) When key-word searching is available, the rules are described in the Help (or another) menu on the computer or in a display near the terminal. Again, if you need assistance with key-word searches, ask for it. Using the wrong key words will get you a lot of material that you cannot use. Even the precise key word will turn up unrelated items. The key word "textile mills" may give you a useful title such as *The Textile Mills of Lowell, Massachusetts,* but it might also give you *Textile Mills in Japan During World War II.* Notice that time period is crucial in a history search. A search for "history" *and* "textile mills" or "history" *and* "women workers" should cut out most studies that are about recent developments.[3] Figure 4.1 shows what you are likely to see on the computer screen as you begin to conduct a search.

Don't sit at the computer monitor for long stretches trying to find that one subject heading or key word that will give you everything you want. Once your searches have turned up a number of promising titles, print out or write down (preferably on note cards) *all* of the information on the screen that you will need for your bibliography (see the section on organizing a bibliography in Chapter 5) as well as the **call number** of each book. The call number indicates its location in the library stacks. (See the section on locating materials and using call numbers later in this chapter.) You will probably discover that many of the books you have listed have similar call numbers, that is, they begin with the same letters or numbers. When you get to the appropriate place in the stacks, don't look only for the specific books you found in your computer search; look at *all* of the books on nearby shelves as well. You will likely find some other works that are related to your theme.

A word of caution about using an electronic catalog. You cannot find what is not there. Not everything in the library may be included, or the electronic catalog may include only material received by the library after a certain date. Some libraries have not yet put all of their materials online. Ask the librarian for the starting date for the catalog. Another problem is that an electronic catalog may include material that is *not* in your library but in one very far away. Make sure you find out *whether* the material you want is on campus. Getting material from outside your library can take time. The process is called **interlibrary loan,** where your library borrows the book from another library. Don't

[3]The spelling of place names can make key-word searches difficult. This is especially true for place names that have changed over time. Persia became Iran; Gold Coast became Ghana; New Spain became Mexico. Know the proper name of the place you are looking for *during the period you are focusing on.* Geographical subdivisions present problems as well. Umbria is a region of Italy; if you did not know this, you might not be able to search for it effectively. Always learn the larger geographical or political unit that your own subject is a part of.

```
You searched for the WORD: women textile workers
21 entries found, entries 1-8 are:        LOCATIONS        CALL#
 1 Bare threads: human life in the serv    Main General     HD6073.T4 G76 1991
 2 European women and preindustrial c      Main General     HD6134.W65 1995
 3 Factory girls: women in the thread m    Main General     HD6073.T42 J38
 4 Farm to factory: women's letters, 18    Main General     HD6073.T42 U53
 5 For we are sold, I and my people: w     Main General     HD6073.T42 M63 198
 6 Form of production and women's lab      Main General     HD6189.B38 1992
 7 Hands to the spindle: Texas women       Main General     HD6073.T42 U55
 8 Hard times cotton mill girls: person    Main General     HD6073.T42 A132
Please type the NUMBER of the item you want to see, OR
F > Go FORWARD                   P > PRINT
N > NEW Search                   D > DISPLAY Title and Author
A > ANOTHER Search by WORD       + > ADDITIONAL options
Choose one (1-8,F,N,A,P,D,L,J,E, + )
```

```
Record 4 of 21
TITLE    Farm to factory : women's letters, 1830-1860/edited by Thomas Dublin.
PUBLISHER    New York: Columbia University Press, 1981.
DESCRIPT.    x, 191 p. : ill. ; 24 cm.
SUBJECT    Women--Employment--New England--History.
Women--New England--Correspondence.
Textile workers--New England--Correspondence.
ALT AUTHOR    Dublin, Thomas, 1946-
BIBLIOG.    Includes bibliographical references.
ISBN    0231051182.
 0231051190 (pbk.)
LCCN    80028084.
```

FIGURE 4.1   Sample Computer Search

Here is an example of a computer screen that might appear when you search the library's catalog for sources on "women textile workers." Note that the titles on the initial screen are shortened. Be sure to DISPLAY the *full title* before you decide to seek out the book. In your own library the online search screen may look different but it should be organized along the same lines as this one. This is an example of a search on a Dynix system, quite common in college libraries. The top half shows the results of a search; the lower half gives the details for one book.

wait until it is too late to find out that a book you really need has to be borrowed from another library.

Searching for Articles in Journals, Magazines, and Newspapers.   Students often search for books but skip over other valuable library sources. Books are usually easier to locate. Some computer catalogs don't even include what librarians call "non-book" items. If, for example, you want to know if the library has newspaper articles and documentary films related to your theme, you need to know where to look for them. Sometimes non-book items have their own catalog; in other instances they are part of the main computer catalog. Often non-book items are listed in "databases" contained on **CD-ROM** discs. Different terminals in the library may be dedicated to different databases. Be sure to ask where the finding aids and databases for non-book items are located. (The most useful history databases are described in Appendix A, pp. 175–76.)

Periodical articles are important non-book sources of information. A periodical is any publication that is issued "periodically." This category of publication includes **journals** (which contain articles for students and scholars) and *magazines* and *newspapers* (which contain articles for the general reading public but can sometimes be helpful to students). If you have access to *old* editions of magazines and newspapers, these can sometimes be useful for history research.

JOURNALS

Journals are the best periodical sources for history research. Articles in journals may contain important information related to your topic. For the theme "Women Workers in the Lowell, Massachusetts, Textile Mills, 1820–1850," you could gain useful information from an article "Letters of a Lowell Mill Girl and Friends," published in the journal *Labor History* in 1976. But how would you find out about this article and whether your library has it? In this case you need an index (electronic or printed) that lists journal articles by author, title, and subject.

The journal indexes of your library may be a part of the main computer catalog or may be housed on separate computers with their own databases. Most libraries also have printed copies of journal indexes. Wherever it is located, your library probably has an index such as *America: History and Life* that covers articles in scholarly journals. Check the subject index of this database under women workers, textile mills, and Lowell, Massachusetts. In this way, you should be able to find any journal articles it contains that are related to your topic. What you are doing is searching for journal articles in the same way you searched for books — by subject (or key word). Of course, if you already know the author or title of the article you want, those are also search options. (There are several journal indexes in history. These are listed in Appendix A, pp. 146–47.)

An important advantage in searching for journal articles, especially on a computer, is that the indexes are often annotated, that is, they contain brief descriptions (called "abstracts") of the contents of each article. Annotation helps you to decide whether to read the article. Certain databases allow you to print out the entire article from the computer in your library, even if the library does not have the journal in its collection. In this way, a student at a small library can get articles instead of requesting an interlibrary loan. If you can print out a copy of an article, however, make sure that the title and annotation really sound promising. Your library may charge for such a service. Even if it is free, there is the danger that you will be tempted to print the article mainly because this is easier than going into the stacks to look for articles which you cannot print out. Seek out the articles that are most relevant for your topic, not simply those that are easiest to come by. One final problem in searching for articles in databases is that they rarely include ones that were published prior to the early 1980s. At least that is the situation at this time.

Many academic journals have their own printed indexes. For example, all of the articles in the *Canadian Historical Review* will be printed in the volume *Index to the Canadian Historical Review*. Indexes to specific journals are kept in the stacks next to the bound volumes of the journal. Once you have looked at general journal indexes (ones that cover many journals) you will probably discover that several articles related to your topic come from a small number of journals. If this is the case, it is wise to go into the stacks and seek out the indexes to these journals. Returning to the theme "Women Workers in the Lowell, Massachusetts, Textile Mills, 1820–1850," you may have discovered that the journal *Labor History* has several articles that sound promising. If this is the case, look through the index to that journal. You will probably find other useful articles there.

Another, and quicker, way to find journal articles related to your topic is in the books and articles that you have *already* found. The footnotes (or endnotes) in these sources will include the books and articles that the author relied upon, and many of them will also be relevant to your topic. From the footnotes/endnotes, copy down any articles (and books) whose titles seem close to your topic. In fact, whenever you find a good source, check its notes (and also its bibliography) against the sources you already have and add any promising ones to your research bibliography. Be sure, as always, to copy down *all* of the relevant information for your own notes and bibliography. (See the sections on documenting your paper and organizing a bibliography in Chapter 5.)

MAGAZINES AND NEWSPAPERS

Current issues of popular magazines *(People, Time, National Geographic)* and newspapers rarely contain serious historical studies. However, if your library has printed or electronic copies of magazines and newspapers from the period of your topic, these can be valuable sources. For example, the *Lowell Courier* from the 1830s may very well have *contemporary* articles on women workers in the mills. This is a valuable source because it is also a *primary* source. (See the section on primary and secondary sources of evidence in Chapter 1.) Old issues of magazines and newspapers may be available in your library (usually on microfiche or microfilm) and can be very helpful. When you search for newspapers or magazines in your library's catalog, be sure to note the span of years that are included. If a particular magazine was published in the 1830s and 1840s, it may be useful in a paper on early textile mills. However, your library may not have issues going back that far.

Sources for History Research on the Internet

One or more of the computer terminals in your library may be connected to the Internet. This is a worldwide network of computers that can transfer information back and forth among them. If you can get "on the Net," you can search the databases of an enormous number of computers anywhere in the world. If you know your way around, you can expand your research to include information from any computer that is part of the Net.

There are many problems involved in using the Net for history research. First, let's see what kind of information is available on the Net. At present, the most accessible portion of the Net is the **World Wide Web,** and the best way into the Web is by means of a **Web browser** such as Netscape. Once you have reached the Web via a browser, you have the choice of dozens of **search engines.** These engines act like catalogs to the millions of sites (addresses) on the Net.[4] Some of the most useful engines for research are Lycos, AltaVista, WebCrawler, and Yahoo! (see Figure 4.2). Each allows you to search the web by key word just as you would the computer catalog. From the search engine you can connect to sites that specialize in history topics. At these sites you can read, download, or print the files that interest you. Some of these files will be research sources: books, journal articles, illustrations, photographs, videos, music, almost anything. On the Net you can talk to people as well as computers. Electronic mail (e-mail), news and discussion groups put you in touch with other Net users who are communicating with one another. There are many history-oriented news groups where you can post messages, ask questions, and join conversations about topics in history of interest to you. H-Net is one of the largest history-oriented sites. Some colleges also make Net surfing available in your home or dorm.

Finding what you want on the Net is not easy, but if you have access to a Net connection, spend some time exploring it for information concerning your research project. Even if you don't turn up useful material, you will become familiar with what is likely (some day) to be the principal avenue for finding just about *anything* or *anyone.* Just as computer literacy has become almost essential for living in a modern environment, so Net literacy will soon be essential for finding your way around such an environment.

Now for the bad news: the Internet is a chaotic place. Until you become familiar with it, it will be very frustrating: you won't be able to connect to the computer you want, or you connect but don't end up where you expected to be, or you discover that you "can't get there from here." Perhaps you will end up where you want to be but can't download or print out what is there. Worst of all, you can become lost in cyberspace, following one link after another until you just give up.

Even if you find what you want on the Net, download and print it, you may discover that what you have obtained is, well, junk. Published

---

[4]An alternative to using search engines, which often retrieve vast numbers of undifferentiated sites, is a good directory. A directory is a selective list of sites, usually chosen because they are valuable sources for a particular topic or field of study. The *Argus Clearinghouse* and *World Wide Web Virtual Library* provide collections of such selective subject directories. The *Index of Resources for Historians* is a vast directory of history sites.

Found **1** Category and **12** Site Matches for **Wounded Knee.**

Yahoo! Category Matches (1 - 1 of 1)

Category listing. All of these sites should relate to native American history. —— Arts: Humanities: History: U.S. History: Native American: **Wounded Knee**

Yahoo! Site Matches (1 - 12 of 12)

Specific sites. —— Arts: Humanities: History: U.S. History: Native American: **Wounded Knee**

Note word choice in site titles; some will likely be from a definite point of view.

- ❑ Massacre at **Wounded Knee**
- ❑ **Wounded Knee,** South Dakota - a brief memorial.
- ❑ Butchering at **Wounded Knee,** The
- ❑ **Wounded Knee** - Reiteration?
- ❑ Medals of **Wounded Knee**

Entertainment: Music: Events: Festivals

Some sites are clearly unrelated to the topic.

- ❑ **Wounded Knee** Creek Concert to Mend the Sacred Hoop - outdoor music festival (Aug. 8–12)).

These sites from an images subcategory look interesting.

Arts: Humanities: History: U.S. History: Native American: **Wounded Knee:** Images

- ❑ Ghost Dance Movement and **Wounded Knee**
- ❑ Aftermath of **Wounded Knee**
- ❑ Casualties of **Wounded Knee**

Entertainment: People

- ❑ Fouche, Marie - This page is in regards to Native American Adoptions. It also discusses Lost Bird who was found four days after the **Wounded Knee** Massacre and was adopted into a prominent family soon afterwards.

This is a link to a fictional work rather than a history site. —— Arts: Humanities: Literature: Genres: Web Published: Fiction: Works

- ❑ Godseeker - Meet Roman General Marcus Aurelius, Jewish scholar Moses Maimonides, see the Battle of **Wounded Knee.** Find romance in the land of snow and orchids.

Regional: U.S. States: South Dakota: Entertainment

- ❑ **Wounded Knee** Creek Concert to Mend the Sacred Hoop - outdoor music festival (Aug 8–12)..

FIGURE 4.2   Sample Internet Search

Here is the result of an Internet search for the key words "Wounded Knee" using the search engine Yahoo! The student is researching the Indian wars in the nineteenth-century American West. (Wounded Knee was a creek in South Dakota where over three hundred Sioux were killed by the U.S. Cavalry in 1890.) From this Web page you can connect to the twelve sites that Yahoo! has gathered. Remember, an Internet search will turn up many sites that are not useful for history research. Note that not all of the sites retrieved by this search are history sites.

materials, the kind of materials on your library's shelves, are, for the most part, written by someone who knows the subject well, who had to get the work accepted by a publisher who first submitted the manuscript to other scholars and writers, and later to editors and proofreaders. On the other hand, anyone, smart or dumb, wise or foolish, sane or wacko, can publish on the Net. There is much serious material on the Net, and some of it may be very helpful in your research. But nothing separates the good stuff from the bad, the serious from the silly. You can search the Net by key word (using the search engines), just as you do on the library's online catalog. But Net searching is less organized and selective. Be prepared to get some very strange and often unrelated material, and in huge quantity at that. If you find something on the Net that you want to use, ask your instructor what he or she thinks of it. Knowledge of Net searching and improvements in the search engines that take you around the Net will make things easier, but Net searching is not yet as organized as library research. Do a little surfing, but don't expect to do a serious research assignment entirely this way, at least not yet. (For those who are beginning surfers, Appendix A lists the best sources of historical information on the Net.

Research in Primary Sources

One of the most interesting aspects of historical research is to read what someone who was part of a historical event or period felt and thought about the experience. The diary of a young woman crossing the West by wagon train, a newspaper article describing Babe Ruth hitting a home run, the minutes of a private meeting between President Kennedy and his advisors during the Cuban missile crisis, a recording of Bessie Smith singing the blues — each of these is as close to history as you can get and helps you to imagine what the past was like for those who lived it. If at all possible, include primary material in your research.

If a history archive (a place like a museum or historical society where primary sources are stored) is near you and holds materials related to your topic, or if you can interview someone who lived through the time period you are researching, you have the extraordinary opportunity to do research that puts you in touch (literally) with the past. In many cases, however, primary sources on your topic are not within your reach either in terms of money, time, or expertise. Still, every college library, even small ones, have *copies* of primary materials that you can use. The sample student paper "Women Workers in the Lowell, Massachusetts, Textile Mills, 1820–1850" (see Chapter 5) includes the book *Women of Lowell* (which you might find in your library), a book that *reprints* two primary documents from the 1840s about conditions in the mills. In addition to reprints of old books and pamphlets, many libraries have microfilm or microfiche collections of old documents and newspapers, as well as sound recordings and motion pictures from the early twentieth century. U.S. government documents going back to the early years of the United States are often available. A final source of primary materials is the Internet. Several Internet sites specialize in historical documents. (See Appendix A, pp. 173–76) As you may have noticed by now, it will be difficult to obtain primary documents about the history of non–English speaking nations. Moreover, such documents would need to be available in translation. Of course, if you read another language, you can broaden your search accordingly.

One final point about primary documents: you need to have read a lot about your topic in order to understand them. You won't know why the faces of the Italian family look so bewildered in the old photograph of immigrants arriving in America if you haven't learned about the mixture of confusion, fear, and excitement that was part of coming to the United States in the late nineteenth or early twentieth centuries. You won't know why the letters of Thomas Jefferson on the subject of slavery sound so uncertain unless you know the battle going on in his mind about the place of Africans in a republic. Use primary sources if you can, but save them until you are acquainted with your topic.

Reference Books

As was pointed out before, the old card catalog has been almost completely replaced by the computerized catalog, by computerized databases, and by Net connections. However, these electronic wizards have not yet taken over the job of the reference collection of your library. If it is not yet a time when you can do all your research on the computer, it is also not yet a time when you can dispense with the aid of *printed reference works*. The reference section of your library, usually a series of shelves on the library's main floor, contains dictionaries, **encyclopedias, atlases,** and finding aids to many kinds of information — such as the periodical, magazine, and newspaper indexes that were discussed earlier. The usefulness of different kinds of reference works and the kind of material they contain are described in Appendix A. Each reference work has its own way of organizing its contents. Just as you need to know the rules for searching on a computer, so you need to be familiar with organizational guidelines of a particular reference work. These are printed at the beginning of each work. Again, if you are having trouble using a printed reference book, ask the librarian for help.

Subject Bibliographies. The most important part of the reference collection are its *subject bibliographies*. These comprise a path into the materials of the library that are just as important as the online catalog. In fact, an important part of the book you are reading (see Appendix A, pp. 151–70) is dedicated to helping you find the subject bibliographies that will be most helpful in finding books (and other materials) on your topic.

Subject bibliographies are printed reference materials that list books, articles, and other materials according to subject. Their contents are confined to the subject indicated in their title. To aid you in your research, this book lists several hundred subject bibliographies, separating them by historical period, area, or topic. You should keep in mind, of course, that, like electronic databases, not all of the material listed in these bibliographies will be in your school library. Despite this fact, a subject bibliography that lists books and other material related to your topic is often the best place to begin research. The task is made easier for you because you can start your research in Appendix A of this book. Much of what you need to research your topic may be discovered in this way. For example, if your topic is the use of chemical weapons in the Vietnam War, the subject bibliography *The Wars in Vietnam, Cambodia, and Laos, 1945–1982: A Bibliographic Guide* (listed in Appendix A) may lead you to many sources of information on your topic.

One advantage to using subject bibliographies is that you have already narrowed your search by choosing one that covers your topic. Another advantage is that after you go to the section or sections that seem closest to your topic, you can *browse* through the rest of the volume to see what other headings and subheadings sound promising. This is more difficult to do online. Also, many subject bibliographies are annotated. Finally, a subject bibliography, unlike some online catalogs, will have older sources as well as recent ones. If it has been recently published or updated, it will list very new works as well. Of course, a bibliography compiled in 1965 will not contain material published later. Keep this in mind.

There is no one best way to conduct library research. Each of the paths described in this chapter is useful and has its own strengths and weaknesses. Your research goal should not be to find *enough* information on your topic but the *best* information on your topic. An element of the grade you receive for your history paper will be based upon the quality of your sources.

Locating Materials and Using Call Numbers

After completing your search of the catalogs and subject bibliographies, you will have a list of materials that you want to look at. If some of these are located outside your library, you will have to borrow them. A librarian will have to assist you in this task. If the materials are in your own library, the call number will lead you to them. The call numbers in use in almost all libraries are of one of two types: the Dewey Decimal System or the Library of Congress System. The Dewey call numbers begin with a *number;* the Library of Congress call numbers begin with a *letter.* These are both complex systems of organizing books by subject. However, if you go to the trouble of mastering their principles, you will have an excellent road map to your library's shelves. (An explanation of the Dewey Decimal and the Library of Congress classification systems can be found in Appendix B.)

If the stacks are open to students, pay attention to the signs on the walls and at the ends of rows of shelves that tell you where a particular group of call numbers is to be found. If you get to the place in the shelves where you think the book should be and it is not there, you are facing one of several problems: (1) the book has been taken out by another reader; (2) it has been shelved incorrectly; (3) you have copied down the call number incorrectly; or (4) it has been lost or stolen. Often an online catalog will tell you if a book has been taken out by someone else. This is one of the advantages of a computer search. In any event, the circulation desk librarian can tell you if another reader has checked the book out. If it has not been checked out, go back to the catalog and check the call number. An error of even one number in a call number can make your search all but impossible. Always be sure to copy call numbers letter by letter and number by number just as they appear in the catalog.

Browsing the Library Shelves. Most of the call numbers on the list you have created will be in groups. They will begin with similar letters and numbers. All of the books with similar call numbers will be near one another on the library's shelves. As a result, when you get to the place in the stacks where one book is located it will be surrounded by other books with very similar call numbers. Since the system of filing books by call number is related to their subject, nearby books may also be on your list. Just as important, nearby books that are not on your list may be just as close to your topic as those that are. Read the titles of the books near to the one you are seeking. If the titles seem promising, they should be added to your list.

Mining Information from Your Sources

Once you have a book in your hand, you can now find out if it contains the kind of information on your topic that you are looking for. Up to this point you have been relying on titles. Now you can go through the book's table of contents and the index at the end. These are much better guides to the book's contents. After all, titles can be misleading. *The Election of Woodrow Wilson* may turn out to be about the inner workings of the Democratic Party. If you are preparing a paper on Wilson, this book may not be of much use to you, despite its title. Even when a book deals specifically with your topic, its handling of the subject may make it less than satisfactory. For example, a book that is written for less advanced students, even though it is on your topic, will not make a good source. Its coverage will be too general, and it will also likely gloss over or omit important facts or interpretations that your research should include. You should avoid textbooks or works that seem to be written more for entertainment than information. If the author does not include footnotes and a bibliography, the book may not be a proper source for a research paper. A glance at the introduction should help you determine the kind of reader for whom the book was written. (A primary source, however, is good regardless of its form or intended audience.)

Another problem you may encounter is the author's viewpoint or bias. For example, a history of World War I by a French author is likely to have a different viewpoint from one written by a German author, especially if the books were written close to the time of the war. It is very important for you to understand the point of view from which a book was written. Many historical events and their interpretation are the centers of profound controversy. It is almost impossible for a historian to investigate one of these controversial areas without the involvement of certain biases. A particular attitude toward the topic is not necessarily bad, however. Historical problems are immensely complex, and without a sense of which things are important, the historian will not be able to choose from among those facts that can give some clear meaning to the larger questions involved. In any event, it is important for you to become familiar with the biases of the authors you read so that you will not unknowingly accept their viewpoints. If you agree with an author's bias, it is natural that you will favor his or her work in your research. But unless you understand the biases of the authors you read, and your own as well, you will not know why you agree with some authors more than others. Furthermore, you won't be able to make a logical presentation in your research paper of the varying points of view.

Determining Whether a Book Will Be Useful

The first place to check for determining the usefulness and emphasis of a book is its table of contents. Although some chapter titles are vague, most will give you a clearer picture of the contents than the work's title. If your topic is the Caribbean policy of Theodore Roosevelt, and you have come upon a book entitled *The Era of Theodore Roosevelt,* you will be pleased to find a chapter called "Hemisphere Diplomacy." Though the entire work may be of value to you, it is this chapter that will contain the most material on your topic. On the other hand, if the chapter headings are all concerned with Roosevelt's domestic policies or the cultural, scientific, and intellectual trends of the early 1900s, there may be little in the book on foreign policy.

If the chapter headings are not clear enough for you to determine the book's usefulness, read the index. Not every book has an index, but when one does, it is an invaluable tool. The index lists in alphabetical order the pages on which different persons or subjects are discussed. The index in a book on the Progressive Party in Wisconsin will list each of the pages on which Robert M. LaFollette is mentioned. It may even break this down and tell you which pages discuss LaFollette's early career, which discuss his campaigns for the presidency, and so on. When the scope of a book is very broad, the index is the best guide to finding that portion of it that is closest to your topic. Remember, however, that unless you read more of the book than just those pages that deal with your topic, you will not know the author's biases or conclusions, and these may be of great importance. Although you may want to select only small portions of a book to use in your research, if any of your own conclusions are drawn from a particular work, you will need to know its overall contents.

If the book has no index, or if you wish to get the flavor of the work as a whole before selecting it as a source for your paper, the introduction, conclusion, and bibliography may be of help. Authors often explain some of their purposes and conclusions in the introduction, and a look at the bibliography (if one is included) will give clues as to what sources the author felt were important and how extensive his or her own research was.

Perhaps the best way to gain an overall impression of a work is to skim its contents by reading the introductory paragraph of each chapter and perhaps the introductory sentence to each paragraph in those parts of the book that seem most important. Once you have chosen a book for your research, of course, there is no substitute for careful reading.

How to Read Your Sources

Reading books may sound easy, but, unless you have had experience in reading serious historical studies, you may have problems. First of all, some of the vocabulary may be new to you. A book on the French Revolution will contain such words as "Jacobin," "Thermidor," and "Girondin." A study of the atom bomb will talk about implosion and fission and such places as Tinian and Eniwetok. It is best to have a good dictionary handy. Another problem will be the academic or scholarly style of writing often found in specialized works. You will come across sentences like this:

> Despite the innumerable, and often contradictory, themes reflected in the ideological stance of the right wing of the movement, it nevertheless managed, despite the defection of a small fascist element, to maintain the loyalty of the land-owning peasantry of the Central Highlands as well as the professional and shopowners associations of the capital, not to mention that of several union organizations that still maintained a craft orientation.

The best thing to do is to reread such a sentence slowly and look up any words unfamiliar to you. Don't be intimidated by references to "balkanization," "corporativism," "Hegelianism," "Mandate of Heaven," "negritude," "neomercantilism," "Pan-Slavism," "Pax Romana," "popular front," "primogeniture," "Reconquista," "shogunate," "Trotskyism," "utilitarianism," "White Terror," or "Zoroastrianism." As you become familiar with your topic, you will learn the meanings of the terms used by scholars. The way to get through the complex prose and vocabulary is to have a good command of English grammar and a familiarity with the subject being discussed. It is also best to ease into your topic gradually by reading the least specialized works first.

To summarize the ways of determining the usefulness of a book, following is a short checklist.

Guidelines for Reading Your Sources

1. Check the table of contents
2. Check the index for key terms
3. Read the introduction and conclusion
4. Check the bibliography
5. Skim the introductory paragraph of each chapter

As you become familiar with the style and terminology used in a work, your main task will be to understand the points the author is trying to establish. All good works of history do more than just lay out a series of historical events and then combine them to form an understandable story of what occurred. Good historians want to prove a point, to show that a series of historical events means one thing rather than another. A history of the rise of Adolf Hitler won't merely tell you that the National Socialist Party, which he led, increased the number of its representatives in the German Reichstag (parliament) from 12 to 107 in the election of 1930. It will attempt to describe the conditions that led to such an outcome and to explain the impact of the election on later events. Perhaps the author will discuss unemployment, German nationalism, the cartelization of German industry, the Treaty of Versailles, the growth of the German Communist Party, anti-Semitism, the structure of the German family, the philosophy of Nietzsche, or the insecurity of the lower middle class. The author will probably deal with some of these more extensively than others, and will attempt to show how the emphasized factors offer a better explanation of the subject than any others. Although almost all historians will agree on the number of National Socialist members of the 1930 Reichstag, each will construct the causes and effects of that fact in different ways — sometimes in *very* different ways. If you wish to understand a particular author's interpretation of an event, you must know how the author arrived at that interpretation and what significance he or she believes it to have. Only a careful reading of the entire work and close attention to the book's main arguments can give you such knowledge. Remember, history books are a selection of certain facts and interpretations constructed to explain a particular writer's understanding of a historical subject. If your own research relies heavily on a particular book, you will need to know its theme and bias.

How to Take Notes from Your Sources

The first rule in note taking is to know in advance what you are looking for. In order to avoid either taking note after note that you will never need or failing to note things that you will, you should have a clear understanding of your topic and the kind of evidence you are seeking. This is especially difficult at the outset of your research when your understanding of your topic is still somewhat vague. It is thus important to define the scope and content of your topic as quickly as possible or your research and note taking will wander, and valuable time will be lost.

As you go through a book, you will find portions that you will want to refer to in your own research paper. You will want to note the author's general idea or perhaps even record the actual words used. While overreliance on quotations can be a weakness, if you feel that a quote is necessary, be careful to copy exactly the words in the book. Be sure that the meaning of the words you quote is clear and that you have not altered the author's point by quoting it out of context. If you wish to use a quotation, say, to show that Robert E. Lee was a good military strategist, a quotation such as "Lee was more admired by the average soldier than any other commanding officer" doesn't make that point because it refers to his popularity, not his generalship. Moreover, if the following sentence in the book is "However, his strategic decisions were not usually equal to those of Union army commanders," then you have actually altered the author's point by taking it out of its original context. Make sure you understand the author's meaning before you use a quotation. Again, be sure not to overquote. Do not quote more material than is necessary to convey the desired point clearly and accurately. Finally, never quote something simply because you find it difficult to express in your own words. You will have to compose the idea in your own words when you write your paper, and it is best to think about the meaning of your research material now.

The most important points made by an author usually cannot be summed up in easily quotable form. When you want to record general arguments and conclusions, it is best to write your own paraphrase or summary of particular points. If the author has spent several pages relating the decline in trade between Spain and Mexico to the Wars of Mexican Independence, you may want to summarize the findings by noting that the author feels that the diminishing economic tie between colony and mother country was one of the major factors leading to Mexican independence. If you wish to note the evidence itself, you may want to paraphrase the author's description of the decline in trade with several sentences of your own that include the main factors of this decline.

Whether you are quoting an author's exact words or summarizing a point, the rules of note taking are the same. As you read, it is best to have a pile of index cards beside you (4″ × 6″ or 5″ × 8″).[5] When you come to something you want to note, write the author's name, the book title, and the page number or numbers at the top of the card.[6] The exact page numbers are essential because you will have to use them when you write your footnotes. If your quote or paraphrase covers more than one page from your source, be sure to make that fact clear on your note card. Also, it is essential to place each paraphrase or quotation on a separate card so that you can arrange them by period or subject or topic when you prepare your paper. Placing a brief topic heading in the corner of each card will make such arrangement easier. (See Figure 4.3.)

If you are quoting, be sure to use quotation marks and to copy the quotation word for word. If you are quoting something that the author has quoted, you must be sure to point this out when you use the material and to identify the original source. Be sure to include in your note an introduction to the quoted material in your own words, stating who said it (if other than the author) and in what context. This will ensure that you use it properly in your paper. If a quotation is very long and if there are parts that relate to matters other than the one you are referring to, then you may omit portions of the original quote by inserting **ellipses** — three periods (. . .) — in the quoted material.[7] For example, if the quotation reads "Feudalism, despite later idealizations of it, was maintained by an oppressive social order," you may want to leave out "despite later idealizations of it," and quote the sentence as "Feudalism . . . was maintained by an oppressive social order." However, never omit anything if doing so would change the meaning of the material. If the sentence had read "Feudalism in its later stages in Moravia was maintained by an oppressive social order," the entire sentence would have to be quoted, or its meaning would be seriously altered.

To give a clearer sense of what note taking involves, there are two sample note cards in Figure 4.3. The first contains a quotation from a book and the second a paraphrasing of several paragraphs from an article.

---

[5]Some students have begun to take notes on their computers. In this case, you still need to take down all of the same information that you would have put on index cards. Also, be sure to learn about the *searching* ability of your word processing program so that you can code your notes in a way that enables you to organize them by category.

[6]If you are taking notes on a journal or newspaper article, you will need to record such information as date, volume number, section, and page number.

[7]If the portion omitted is the end of a sentence, this is indicated by inserting four periods — three to indicate omission and the fourth to indicate the end of the original sentence. In this case, the closing quotation mark appears after the fourth period.

First note card on each source must include a full citation for use in footnotes/endnotes and bibliography

GT 2869.M56   *Sugar comes to*
                     the New World

Topic heading

    Sidney W. Mintz
    Sweetness and Power: The Place
    of Sugar in Modern History
    N.Y.: Penguin Books, 1985, p. 32

Library call number in case you need to locate the book again.

Sugar cane brought by Columbus in 1493.
First grown in Spanish Santo Domingo. First
shipment to Europe around 1519. " . . . it was
Spain that pioneered sugar cane, sugar making, African slave labor, and the plantation
form in the Americas."

Student's summary comments set context for quoted material

                                        1

Number keeps several notes from same source in order

E171.J87   Not widely
    Michael A. Bellesiles   used before
    "The Origins of Gun Culture in the United   1865
    States, 1760–1865"
    The Journal of American History 83
    (1996): 425–55
Author argues that guns were not as important before the Civil War as they became later.
"Judging from the popular literature of the
day, the public seemed completely uninter-
ested in firearms." (439)
"Even western magazines showed a decided
coolness toward hunting and militarism. . . ."
(440)

Quotations from different pages must be identified separately

                                        1

FIGURE 4.3   Sample Note Cards

Avoiding Plagiarism

The only thing worse than misquoting from your sources is plagiarizing from them. Plagiarism is easy to fall into. Because of your inexperience with your subject, it will be tempting to use the more sophisticated language of the historians you are reading. In most cases, their expertise will enable them to make their point clearly, and it is easy to get into the habit of using their words instead of your own. Don't fall into this trap. First of all, your instructor is also a historian and can tell the difference between the language of someone who has spent years researching a topic and that of the average history student. Second, and more important, is that thinking is learning. If you substitute the simple task of copying for the more difficult but rewarding one of thinking about something and then putting it into your own words, then you are doing yourself a disservice. Finally, plagiarism is dishonest and is considered a very serious violation of college rules. The penalty can be severe, sometimes leading to suspension.

When taking notes, *never* copy the author's words unless you intend to quote them in your paper. In that case, be sure to put very clear quotation marks on your note card at the beginning and end of each word-for-word passage. In all other instances, summarize the author's ideas and information *in your own words*. Of course, proper names, dates, statistics, and other very specific facts need to be recorded just as they appear in the material you are using. Even here, you must be careful. If the source says: "George Washington, a great patriot, a great general and our greatest president, was born in 1732," you can put the date of his birth in your paper without quotation, but you cannot say he was "a great patriot, a great general and our greatest president" *or anything very close to this* without plagiarizing.

There will always be some resemblance between the points that you make in your paper and those that were in your research sources. This is even necessary if you are to correctly interpret your sources. *However, all the words in your paper (except for quoted material) must be your own.*

The Art of Paraphrasing

To help you avoid plagiarism, here is a passage from J. Joseph Hutchmaker and Warren I. Sussman, eds., *Wilson's Diplomacy: An International Symposium* (Cambridge, Mass.: Schenckman, 1973), p. 13, followed by two paraphrasings. Paraphrase *a* constitutes plagiarism, but *b* does not. The subject is the diplomacy of Woodrow Wilson. Here is the original text:

> Wilson took personal responsibility for the conduct of the important diplomacy of the United States chiefly because he believed that it was wise, right, and necessary for him to do so. Believing as he did that the people had tem-

porarily vested their sovereignty in foreign affairs in him, he could not delegate responsibility in this field to any individual. His scholarly training and self-disciplined habits of work made him so much more efficient than his advisors that he must have thought that the most economical way of doing important diplomatic business was for him to do it himself. Experience in dealing with subordinates who sometimes tried to defeat his purposes also led him to conclude that it was the safest method, for he, and not his subordinates, bore the responsibility to the American people and to history for the consequences of his policies.

PARAPHRASE A: Wilson took personal responsibility for conducting diplomacy because he believed it was right for him to do so. Believing that the people had vested their sovereignty in foreign affairs in him, he couldn't delegate this responsibility. His scholarly training and self-discipline made him more efficient than his advisers. He thought that the most economical way of doing important business was to do it himself. Experience in dealing with subordinates who sometimes tried to defeat his purposes led him to conclude that it was the safest method because he bore responsibility to the American people for the consequences.

PARAPHRASE B: Wilson felt personally responsible for major diplomacy because he believed that the voters had entrusted him with such matters. He was more capable than his advisers in this area. He, and not his advisors, was responsible to the people.

Paraphrase A is too close to the original. Rather than recording the main points of the passage, it repeats many phrases word for word. Not only is it time consuming to take such lengthy notes, but the identical and almost identical phrases, if used as your own, would constitute plagiarism. Paraphrase B records only the principal point of the passage — that Wilson decided major foreign policy issues on his own because he felt personally responsible to the people in such matters. It does not copy the phraseology of the original. In this way, you save time, protect yourself from the danger of plagiarism, and still are able to use the central idea of the passage. Paraphrasing that reduces your readings to their essential points and uses your own words is not easy at first. But mastering this technique will prevent plagiarism and produce a finished paper that is truly yours.

Organizing Your Research

During the process of research you are aided by your research outline (see pp. 62–64) which helps you to determine what sources to seek first and when to read them. When your reading is finished (or almost finished), it is time to arrange all those notes and note cards so that you can create a paper out of them. It is time to prepare a **writing** (as opposed to a *research*) **outline.** Take a good look at your note cards and especially at the headings that you placed in the corners of the cards. It is from among these headings that you should find the major parts of your theme.

Preparing a Writing Outline

If your topic is the conflict between Israel and its Arab neighbors, and you have narrowed it to the theme, "Origins of the 1947 Partition of Palestine," several major points should have appeared in your reading and should be reflected in your notes and in the headings to your note cards. The claims of three parties (Arab, Jewish, British) were no doubt mentioned in many of your readings. As a result, you should have notes concerning Arab nationalism, Zionism, and British colonial policy. These three perspectives are natural sections of your paper, each with a place in the writing outline. The shifting state of opinion within the United Nations (the body that would vote on the partition of Palestine) and the role of the United States (the most important power outside the region) should have appeared in your research and in your notes as well. This suggests two more possible sections for your paper. If your notes reflect what your research uncovered about your theme, you should have more notes, say, on the British decision to withdraw from Palestine than you do, say, on the Balfour Declaration of 1917. That declaration should be *mentioned* in your paper, but the British decision to withdraw is much closer to your topic and thus deserves a section rather than a mention. That is why, as noted above, British colonial policy should be an important part of your writing outline. Be guided by your notes. If your research has been broad and thorough and your notes contain material closely related to your theme, you will end up with more notes on some points than others.

Once you have a general plan for the *parts* of your paper, the next question is: In what *order* should you include them in your paper? If your theme is "The Impact of the Great Depression on African Americans," you may decide to deal with the theme chronologically and separate your paper into sections dealing with the period before 1929, the Hoover years, the early New Deal, and the late New Deal. Or perhaps you want to cover the subject topically, setting up separate sections on African American reactions to economic discrimination, the National Association for the Advancement of Colored People, the U.S. Communist Party, organized labor, and New Deal legislation. Or perhaps you will want to consider the ideas of important African American leaders and writers of the day, setting up sections dealing with E. Franklin Frazier, Richard Wright, Ralph Bunche, W.E.B. Du Bois, A. Philip Randolph, Langston Hughes, Zora Neale Hurston, and Claude McKay.

A *chronological* approach begins with events that predate those that are the main focus of the paper. It then moves, step by step, through stages that group together spans of time. These spans may be in years, decades, or — for a very broad topic — centuries. Each time span is later than the one preceding it, and they generally do not overlap.

Time spans do not have to be the same length. It is best to use larger time units when discussing events that occurred long before the main events covered in the paper and to use smaller units when covering the period closest to the main events. A different rule applies to the length of each *section* of the paper: those portions dealing with periods removed from central events should be briefer than those portions close in time to such events.

A common problem with chronological organization is determining how far back in time to begin. Do you start ten or a hundred years before the time of the main events of the paper? A similar problem is determining where to stop. Do you stop with the main events themselves, or do you add short sections covering later periods as well? There is no hard and fast rule, but it is wise not to cover too much ground. That is, don't start too long before or end too long after the principal events of your topic. A paper covering a long period of time can be very unwieldy, and is best handled by another form of organization.

A *topical* form of organization is suited for more general themes — those that deal with ideas, social systems, or other complex phenomena that involve a mixture of political, social, economic, cultural, and intellectual backgrounds. In this form of organization, the task is not so much to build a historical sequence leading up to a particular event, but to weave a fabric composed of the many separate lines of historical development that form the background to the main topic. In some cases, the same topic can be organized by either method.

To give you an idea of how the same topic might be organized by each of the two methods, here are sample outlines of each kind. The student's research dealt with the topic of the United States and Vietnam and was narrowed to the theme "How Did the United States Become Involved in the War in Vietnam?"

CHRONOLOGICAL ORGANIZATION

Japanese invasion of Indochina turns U.S. attention to the area. (1940–41)

U.S. policy toward Southeast Asia in W. W. II (1942–45)
  Strategy against Japan
  Aid for anti-Japanese guerrillas in Vietnam
  The U.S. military and the Viet Minh

U.S. attitude toward the return of French control (1945–49)
  Defeat of Japan
  Creation of a government by the Viet Minh under Ho Chi Minh
  Tensions between U.S. and French goals in Vietnam

Impact of the Cold War (1949–54)
  The "fall" of China and its impact on U.S. policy
  Need for French involvement in NATO
  War in Korea and the "Containment" of Communism

Geneva Conference and the Creation of the Republic of South Vietnam
(1954–1960)
- France defeated by the Viet Minh
- The Geneva Conference
  - The roles in the conference of: France, China, the Soviet Union, and
    the United States
- The United States and the Government of Ngo Dinh Diem
  - The failure of reform efforts in the South
- The rise of insurgency in the South
  - Aid from the North

United States defends the South from "aggression" from the North
(1960–1963)
- The role of U.S. advisors
- Instability in the government of South Vietnam
- The overthrow of Diem's government

Growing U.S. military involvement to prevent the defeat of the Saigon government (1963–68)
- U.S. ground troops sent to Vietnam
- The escalation of the air war

Conclusion (1968–)
- Military stalemate in Vietnam
- Growing domestic opposition to the war
- The decision to withdraw from Vietnam
- The lessons to be learned

Note that the sections are in almost perfect chronological order. Don't
expect to write your paper in fixed time compartments, however.
There are bound to be sections that run into each other. In fact, to tie
your paper together, some overlap between sections is necessary. (See
the section on organizing your paper in Chapter 5.)

TOPICAL ORGANIZATION

Anti-communism in America
- The Red Scare after World War I
- The New Deal and the debate over American "socialism"
- The cultural bases of anticommunism

The Cold War and resurgence of anticommunism in the United States
- The Soviet Union as a threat to the American "way of life"
- The "loss" of China — the domestic political debate
- Stalemate in Korea — the domestic political debate

U.S. interests in Southeast Asia
- Strategic positions and economic investments
- The "domino theory"

Debate over U.S. involvement in Vietnam
- The debate within the U.S. government
- The debate in Congress
- The debate in the universities

Conclusion
>The forces that drew the United States into Vietnam
>Contemporary judgments about U.S. involvement in Vietnam

This paper covers some of the same ground as the chronologically organized one. Nevertheless, this particular organization leads to a different paper from the first one. In the final analysis, the outline that you create will reflect the nature of your interest in your theme, the kind of research materials you have uncovered, and the way they have influenced your thinking. (For another example of organizing a paper see the outline to the sample student paper in Chapter 5.)

Organizing Your Notes

The piles of note cards and the kinds of information they contain have helped you to create a writing outline (at least a tentative one) for your paper. Now that the outline is done, go back to your notes and decide which section of the paper they are most relevant to. For example, the notes concerning the impact of the Korean war on U.S. involvement in Vietnam, which you took from a book about the Cold War in Asia, should become the basis for the section in the chronologically organized paper named "War in Korea and the 'Containment' of Communism," or the section in the topically organized paper named "Stalemate in Korea — the domestic political debate." Mark each group of notes (usually in the upper right-hand corner) with the name of the section of the outline to which they are most directly related. Some groups of notes will not neatly fit in just one section; in that case, mark two or more section headings in the corner. If you cannot find any place in your outline where certain notes go, then something is wrong. Either don't use this set of notes, because they are not dealt with in the outline, or change the outline to accommodate them.

Make sure that you have enough information on each section of your outline to do it justice. If, looking at your notes, you see a mismatch between a section of the outline and the notes needed to support it, you must alter or eliminate that section or, more likely, reread the relevant sources and take notes more directly connected with the point you want to cover in your outline. Notes and outlines are rarely in perfect harmony at the outset. Be sure you have the notes you need. Don't wait until the paper is half written to discover that an important part lacks the kind of documentation it should have. (See the section on why your paper needs a theme in Chapter 5.)

Budgeting Your Research Time

If you are writing, say, a fifteen- to thirty-page paper, expect to read about a dozen sources. This is not a firm figure, however, and your teacher and the subject you choose are the best guides to the proper amount of research. If you read too few sources, your work will be shallow and perhaps unsatisfactory. If you read too many, you will not complete your work in the allotted time. It is best to make a tentative bibliography early in your research and discuss its adequacy in terms of topicality, authoritativeness, and length with your instructor. In addition, discuss with your teacher the outline for your paper.

If you have never written a long research paper before, you may be unsure as to how much time to allow for each aspect of your research and writing. Only experience will tell you the best budget of time for your particular work habits, but here are some general rules.

For a paper of fifteen to thirty pages due at the end of a fifteen-week semester, you should allow approximately 10 percent of your time (one to two weeks) for choosing a topic and theme, preparing a tentative bibliography, and familiarizing yourself with the general contours of your topic; about 60 percent (seven to eight weeks) for reading the available research materials and taking notes from them; about 10 percent (another week) for thinking and talking about what you have read and organizing your notes; and about 20 percent (two to four weeks) for writing and typing the preliminary and final drafts.

If your term is much shorter than fifteen weeks, or if your assignment must be finished before the end of the semester, you will need to shorten your budget accordingly. (For a discussion of the preparation of papers of five to fifteen pages, see Chapter 3.) Remember that by the end of the term, exams will dominate your attention, and a paper due the final week of classes is best finished at least a week before that time so as not to conflict with studying for finals.

Historical Materials
Outside the Library

If you are fortunate, your topic will be one on which special historical materials are available at a nearby special collections library, a museum, a historical society, the archives of an institution or corporation, or film and audiotape libraries of television and radio studios. (See the section on research in primary sources earlier in this chapter.)

Older members of your community or your own family also can be sources of historical information. People who have been leaders in local and national affairs have personal knowledge of important historical events. Perhaps you could prepare a series of questions concerning past events in which they were participants. You can write to these individuals, or perhaps speak with them. They may also have personal papers they would permit you to see. This kind of historical research is exciting and satisfying, and it may enable you to use primary historical material that no other historian has uncovered.

Elderly people are very good sources of historical material. They can tell of their years in another country or describe the America in which they grew up. They may not have been important historical figures, but they reflect the experiences of countless others and are thus the stuff of which history is made. Their recollections of how they felt and of what they and others did and said when, for example, the *Titanic* sank, when women won the right to vote, or when Lindbergh flew across the Atlantic, are priceless pieces of the historical puzzle. (See also Appendix B, pp. 177–78.)

How to Research Your Family History

One of the most pleasurable kinds of historical research is the composition of your own family's history. Moreover, to research it is to re-create a portion of the historical experience of our nation. Because most of our ancestors came from other nations, a family history also will connect us with the historical experience of other lands. By studying the history of your family, you become aware of your own place within these broader historical experiences. Perhaps most important, knowledge of your family's history and its meaning can give you a strong sense of your cultural roots that will strengthen you throughout your lifetime.

The best sources — and in many cases the only sources — of information on the history of your family are the recollections, understandings, and long-term possessions of your relatives. Researching a family history involves investigating these sources as thoroughly and creatively as possible. This kind of research involves: (1) familiarizing yourself with the general history of the nations and regions, and of the specific times and places, in which your ancestors lived; (2) studying all available family records, such as diaries, photographs, heirlooms; and finally, and most important, (3) interviewing all available family members.

The interview is the core of a family history because, in most instances, it is the only way of uncovering the nature of your family's life. Without the recollections of your relations, you would not be able to discover more than a handful of names, dates, and places — only the barest outline of your family's history.

In preparing for this crucial aspect of family research, you must familiarize yourself with the basic history of your family so that you can place in proper context the information you obtain from the people you interview. You will need to prepare your questions beforehand, focusing on important aspects of family life and of the larger social and political life surrounding the family. Be sure that your questions establish the basics: the names, relationships, and principal home and workplace activities of each member of the family in each generation, going as far down the trunk and out on the limbs of the family tree as possible given the scope of your project and the memories of your relatives. Keep away from trivia (your great-uncle's favorite dessert), and look for information that will enable you to make comparisons between generations of your family and between it and other families. Investigate such topics as the type of dwelling and neighborhood, parent-child and husband-wife relationships, authority and status patterns, income and social mobility. When you come across major family events — immigration, military service, job and residence changes, involvement in political movements — probe the reasons for them, as they will illuminate the ties between your family and the nation's history.

In actually conducting the interview, use your prepared questions, taking care to make them as broad as possible; for example, "What was the neighborhood like when you lived there?" not simply "What was your address in 1936?" When you get an answer that seems to lead in the direction of important material, ignore your prepared questions temporarily and probe further. However, never interrupt an answer, even when the response seems unimportant. Your informants are the experts on their lives, and their self-perceptions — even if illogical or factually incorrect — are essential ingredients of family history. Finally, because the intricate web of your relatives' feelings is as important as the milestones of their lives, it is best to tape-record the interview if possible rather than rely on written notes. Record it all and then collect from your tapes the information which, on the one hand, best reflects your informants' testimony about their lives and, on the other, enables you to say something of importance about those lives and the times in which they were lived.

How to Write
a Research Paper

Preparing to Write

Why Your Paper Needs a Theme

Before you begin to write, you need to have narrowed your topic to a theme, to have fully researched that theme, and to have organized your research according to your *writing* outline. (See the section on organizing your research in Chapter 4.)

As you prepare to write, keep the limitations of your theme and of your research in mind. Be sure to confine your writing to these limits. Avoid the temptation to go beyond your theme, or you may end up back at the broad *topic* with which you started. Let your theme guide your paper. Don't attempt to record in your paper *everything* on which you took notes. Just because you have read something doesn't mean that it belongs in your paper. Look carefully at your outline. It should have excluded peripheral material that turned up in your notes. As you write, ask yourself, "Does what I am writing belong in my paper? Is it part of my outline?" If the material isn't in your outline, then don't write about it. (Or, if necessary, change your outline to include it.) Then ask yourself, "Does what I am saying belong in *this* part of my paper, or should it be in some other part?" Be sure that your notes are organized according to your outline or you will be putting material in the wrong place, and your paper will not be logically developed.

Your Writing Outline

By the time you begin to write, your writing outline may look different than it did when you first put it together. There is nothing wrong with that. The effort to match research to your outline usually leads either to further research (if you don't have documentation for part of the outline) or to expansion of the outline (if you find important documentation for a relevant point that was not originally included). If you discover that your sources make an important point that you had not intended to cover, you must make room for it in your outline so that it appears in your paper. Another reason for changing an outline is finding material that differs strongly with one of the points you had intended to make. Always make room in your paper for *counterevidence,* that is, for points made by authors that disagree with part (or all) of your interpretation of the theme. Having done so, be sure to explain why you believe the evidence in support of your interpretation is stronger. You should not claim that your ideas are the *only* correct ones. You should show, however, that there are compelling reasons for your interpretation.

If you have not already done so, review your notes now and arrange them according to the section of your outline (and the section of your paper) that they most directly refer to. Now, finally, you are prepared to write. The goal of your writing should be to: (1) introduce your theme clearly and briefly, (2) describe it in a series of well documented parts, and (3) draw clear and brief conclusions concerning what you have said about your theme.

Writing the Text

The Rough Draft

Your first draft will change, perhaps many times, so don't worry too much about the exact wording when you write it. Your introductory paragraph (or two) will certainly have to be rewritten after the rough draft is done, but it is still a good place to start. By setting out in your introduction the points that you wish to make in the paper, you will make it easier to confine your writing to statements that develop your theme. For example, a paper on the independence of Texas that concerns the theme "The Role of Sam Houston in Texan Independence" needs to focus tightly on Houston's role. By saying in your introduction that this is your goal (and why it is worth writing about), you will keep yourself on track. Of course, other people will appear in your paper (the Mexican general Santa Anna, for example) but a clear focus on Houston in your draft introduction will keep you from writing a long section of your paper on Santa Anna or having too much to say about the defense of the Alamo. While these subjects should be mentioned in your paper, only the parts that directly bear upon the issue of Houston's leadership should be included. Always use the test of relevance to the theme as you write your paper.

How long should each section of your paper be? There is no correct length, of course, but each section should be long enough to make the point you want to cover in it. As you write the rough draft of each section, keep in mind the information you want to include. Develop each section from the notes that support it, but don't feel obliged to use all of these notes. When you have made the point you intended to make — stop. In addition, you need to write a connecting sentence — either at the end of one section or at the beginning of the next — that introduces the next point you intend to make. Now you are prepared to repeat the process in the next section of your paper, and in the next, until you reach your conclusion.

Keep the overall length of the paper in mind as well. If your paper is limited to twenty-five pages and your outline has seven points to it, don't start out with a section six pages long. Of course, sections may be of unequal length; some points are more important than others or take more space to document. Here is a very general guide: for a paper of twenty-five to thirty pages, it is best to have no more than six to eight sections. You will need at least two, and perhaps as many as four pages, to make the points you wish to cover in each section. You also need to leave a few pages at the end for your conclusion, endnotes (unless you use footnotes, which also lengthen your text), and bibliography. Keep your overall limit in mind, or you can end up with too many (or too few) pages.

The last section of your paper is, of course, the conclusion. It is usually wise *not* to include it in your rough draft. If you change your paper in subsequent drafts, your conclusion would then need a complete rewriting. Still, it is worth pointing out here that the goal of your conclusion is to summarize briefly the points you have made concerning your theme. In the paper about Sam Houston's leadership, for example, you would briefly refer to the evidence, both positive and negative, that you presented about him.

The conclusion is also the place for any opinions you may have formed as a result of your research and writing. Unless you are asked to write an opinion piece, don't load your paper with personal comments. Instructors will likely consider this a weakness. Still, unless told not to, you may include some personal remarks in your conclusion. After all, if your topic is worth writing about it *should* leave you with plenty to think about. Should you decide to say something of your own, however, make your remarks clear. Take the trouble to set down your own thoughts as carefully as you did those of the authors whose works you read.

Clear Writing: A Matter of Continuity

As you write the rough draft of each section keep in mind the information you wish to include and the points you wish to make. If your theme is "German Aid to the Forces of General Franco in the Spanish Civil War," then the section that deals with the reasons behind the German support might begin by briefly describing the circumstances surrounding Franco's appeal to Hitler in 1936. The main body of the section would explain in some detail Hitler's reasons for giving aid (for example, strategic and economic considerations, ideological and diplomatic factors) and would conclude by relating these reasons to the subject of later sections, such as the actual aid given and its effect on the course of the war. Your principal concerns as you construct each section of your paper should be: Does this section follow logically from the one preceding it; does it adequately support and develop the central theme; and does it establish the necessary background for the section that follows?

As each section mirrors the overall structure of the paper by containing an introduction, a main body, and a transition to the next section, so each paragraph of which the section is composed contains a similar structure. A well-constructed paragraph begins with a sentence that introduces the information to be developed and concludes with a sentence that leads to the next paragraph. If each paragraph is developed in this way, and if sentences explaining the relationship between paragraphs are included where necessary, then the paper as a whole becomes a tightly knit series of related statements rather than a random group of facts that do not seem to move in any clear direction. The key to tight construction is for each sentence to have two components: it must be related to the one preceding it, and it must continue the development of the theme to which it is related.

Here are two groups of sentences. The first is tightly constructed; the second is not.

> In 1919, most Germans felt that the terms of the Versailles Treaty were harsh. In particular, they believed that the reparations and war-guilt clauses of the Treaty were unjust. When Hitler rose to power fourteen years later, he appealed to this sense of injustice in order to gain support for his program of denouncing the Treaty.

> In 1919, most Germans felt that the terms of the Versailles Treaty were harsh. The French hoped to weaken German war-making capacity by forcing her to pay heavy war reparations. Hitler appealed to the German people to support his program to denounce the Treaty.

Although each sentence in the second version is true, the paragraph does not hang together because the sentences are not clearly related. The first sentence refers to German feelings about the treaty, and then the second jumps to a discussion of French attitudes and drops the reference to the Versailles Treaty, which is the common theme that ties together the sentences of the first version. The third sentence further confuses the situation by jumping back to Germany and forward in time without any proper transition. On the other hand, the first version is tightly constructed because the second sentence, rather than breaking the line of development by bringing in a new element, expands and accentuates the point made in the first. The third sentence explains the forward jump in time and relates the events of the later period (Hitler's denunciation of the Treaty) to the German people's sense of injustice established in the first two sentences.

The best way to ensure that there are no logical gaps between your sentences is to construct each paragraph from the viewpoint of the average person who might read your paper. Very often, a disconnected set of sentences may seem clear to you because as you write them you unconsciously fill in the gaps with your own knowledge. Your reader most likely does not have this knowledge and has to depend entirely on the words you write. If these are not enough to make your point clearly, you must be more explicit.[1]

Documenting Your Paper:
Citing Your Sources

Documentation means telling your reader where the material in your paper comes from; documentation says to the reader, in effect, "here is the source for the information." Documentation usually takes the form of footnotes or endnotes (to be explained below), but it can also include illustrations, diagrams, photographs, or any special material that you place in your paper to support your theme.

Footnotes and Endnotes:
When and How to Use Them

Footnotes are forms of documentation that appear at the foot of the page while endnotes appear at the end of the paper. They both include the same information. If your instructor has no preference, you can choose to put your documentation in either place, but you must be consistent throughout the paper. You must number your notes consecutively. (When proofreading be sure that the number in the text matches the number in the note.) As both footnotes and endnotes have the same

---

[1]The other basic component of clarity is a well-constructed sentence. No matter how well sentences are linked to one another, if the sentences themselves have faulty grammatical construction, the result will be unsatisfactory. If your sentence-writing ability is weak, you should study one of the grammar and style manuals listed in Appendix B.

form, the following discussion that describes how to write them will, for convenience, use the word "footnotes" to refer to both types.

If you quote from or closely summarize your research sources, you must tell your reader where the original information can be found. In this way, the reader can check the accuracy of your quotes and statements, judge the bias and credibility of your sources, or carry out research of his or her own. On occasion, you may also want to use footnotes to make comments that qualify or supplement statements in your paper.

The question that troubles students the most is: Which of the statements that I make in my paper need footnotes? There are only a few hard and fast rules to guide you. However, three types of statements *must* be footnoted: (1) direct quotations, (2) controversial facts or opinions, and (3) statements that directly support the main points made in your paper. Another group of statements — those which summarize important points from your sources — should be footnoted and *must* be if they are used to sustain an important part of your argument. Finally, statistics are almost always footnoted.

Some clarification concerning rules 2 (controversial points) and 3 (support for main points) may be helpful here. Controversial facts or opinions are those on which your sources disagree or which will surprise your reader. Suppose, in your theme "Treatment of Slaves on Mississippi Plantations," you write that some slaveowners were kind to their slaves. This statement may surprise the reader and thus must be footnoted. Researching "European Discoverers of America" you find that all sources agree that Vikings visited the New World long before Columbus. However, if most people believe that Columbus was the first European to see the New World, then it is necessary to show the reader the source of your information with a footnote. Finally, statements of fact or opinion that directly support main points should be footnoted. If your theme concerns the Protestant Reformation, and you treat nationalism as a major factor in the break with Catholicism, then your references in the text to nationalist forces should be footnoted. On the other hand, if you treat the wealth of the Catholic Church as a very minor factor, then your references to that need not be footnoted.

The number of footnotes to use is another thorny problem. Some papers have more factual or controversial material than others and thus need more footnotes. As a rule of thumb, if your paper has quite a few pages without any footnotes, then you are probably not documenting as much as you should. On the other hand, if you are writing five or more footnotes per page, you may be overdoing it. There is no such thing as the *right* number of footnotes, but a twenty-five-page paper might contain anywhere from fifteen to seventy-five footnotes, depending on the subject.

One final point about what to footnote. Using a footnote does not give you permission to plagiarize. (See Chapter 4, the section on

"Avoiding Plagiarism.") You should not use sentences or even phrases from your research sources. Your ideas may come from your sources, but the words must be your own.

How to Write Footnotes

When you decide that a footnote is necessary, place a number at the end of the sentence that contains the information to be documented. Occasionally, you may want to footnote two different things in the same sentence. In this case, place each number right after the word or phrase you want to footnote. Some writers place the number at the end of a paragraph rather than at the end of a sentence. This is proper only if the footnote refers to the material in the paragraph as a whole. If you are footnoting specific facts or quotations, the number should appear right after the facts or quoted material. If you are footnoting a general idea or opinion, place the number at the end of the paragraph or paragraphs that discuss it. All footnote numbers in the text should be in superscript — that is, a half-line above the line of type. The number should not be put in parentheses and should be inserted after any punctuation (except a dash).

Footnote Form.   Here are examples of footnotes showing the different forms required for citing different kinds of sources. Unless your instructor tells you to use a different form, follow the examples below. (An extended list of examples covering a larger variety of sources can be found in Appendix B.)

FOOTNOTE FOR A BOOK (FIRST REFERENCE)

The *first time* you refer to a book, list all of the information as in the example:

    1. Edward Countryman, Americans (New York: Hill and
    Wang, 1996), 58.

A first reference to a book should include:

1. Author's full name, followed by a comma.
2. Book title in full, underlined (or italicized[2]).
3. Publication information (enclosed in parentheses and followed by a comma): place of publication, followed by a colon; name of publisher followed by a comma; date of publication.
4. Page number(s) cited, followed by a period.

---

[2]If you are writing with a word processing program that has italics, the book title may be italicized rather than underlined.

BOOK (SECOND REFERENCE)

The second and any later reference *to the same* book is in shortened form, as in the example:

```
2. Countryman, 98.
```

A second or later reference need only use the author's last name and the page number. If, however, you cite more than one book (or article, etc.) by the *same author,* any second or later reference must include a shortened form of the title. If, for example, you cite two books by Countryman (*Americans* and *People in Revolution*), your second and later references to both books must make clear to the reader *which* of the two you are citing. To cite the first book a second time, the form is:

```
3. Countryman, Americans, 144.
```

To cite the second book a second time, the form is:

```
4. Countryman, People, 56.
```

Some book footnotes are more complex. If a book has *several authors,* if it has a *translator* or *editor,* or was published in *several volumes,* or *editions,* then the footnote has to include such information as in the example:

```
5. T. W. Wallbank and A. M. Taylor, Civilization Past
and Present, rev. ed. (Chicago: Scott Foresman, 1954),
2:104-17.
```

Notice that when there are two authors, both are listed. If there are more than three authors, the footnote includes the name of the one listed first on the title page followed by "et al." ("and others"). If there is more than one volume to the work, the number of the specific volume used is placed before the page numbers and is separated from them by a colon. If you are using a *later edition* of a work, that too is placed after the title. If there is an editor or translator, that person's name, followed by "ed." or "trans.," appears in the place reserved for the author's name:

```
6. Thomas Dublin, ed., Immigrant Voices: New Lives in
America 1773-1986, (Urbana: University of Illinois Press,
1993), 182.
```

FOOTNOTE FOR JOURNAL ARTICLE (FIRST REFERENCE)

The first time you cite an article, include all of the information as in the example:

```
7. I. C. Campbell, "Culture Contact and Polynesian
Identity in the European Age," The Journal of World
History 8 (1997): 46.
```

A first reference to an article should include:

1. Author's full name followed by comma.
2. Title of article followed by comma, all in quotation marks.
3. Title of the journal (or magazine), underlined or in italics.
4. Volume number of the journal and, in parentheses, the year of the volume, followed by a colon.
5. Page number(s) cited, followed by a period.

JOURNAL ARTICLE (SECOND REFERENCE)

The second and any later reference to the *same article* is in shortened form as in the example:

        8. Campbell, 47.

If you cite more than one article (or book, etc.) *by the same author* a second or later reference must include a short title. For example, if you cite two (or more) articles by Campbell, the second and later references must make clear to the reader *which* article by Campbell you are referring to as in the example:

        9. Campbell, "Culture Contact," 48.

Some journal article footnotes are more complex. (See Appendix B.)

MAGAZINE ARTICLE

Reference to a popular magazine requires author, title of article, title of magazine, date, but no volume number or page number:

        10. Stacy Sullivan, "A Case of Alarming Anarchy,"
        Newsweek, 24 March 1997.

NEWSPAPER ARTICLE

Reference to a newspaper article requires year, month, *and* day (and edition if more than one) as well as author, title, name of paper, and section if appropriate.

        11. Michael R. Gordon, "Russia-China Theme: Contain the
        West," New York Times, 24 April 1997, sec. A, p. 3.

If the newspaper article has no author, the citation begins with the name of the article.

(For information about citing such sources as anonymous works, works with *both* an author and editor, translated works, essays, articles or documents published in books, book reviews, public documents, unpublished theses, films and videos, sound recordings, reference works, and sources found on the computer, see Appendix B. A list of abbreviations found in footnotes is also in Appendix B.)

Quotations: When and How to Use Them

Good general rules are: don't quote too often, don't quote too much, and rely on your own words unless there is a good reason for quoting those of your source. Unless it is necessary to use the *very same* words found in a source to make a point that is crucial to your argument, don't use a quotation. However, if your source has said something highly controversial, you may want to make it clear to the reader that you have not misinterpreted it. In this case a direct quotation may be useful. If you do quote, be sure to include enough of the original statement to make its meaning clear. On the other hand, don't make a quote any longer than is necessary. Finally, set off quoted words with quotation marks at the beginning and end. (A common error is forgetting one set of quotation marks.)

Quotation Form. In most cases a paraphrase or summary of your source, properly footnoted, is sufficient. If you need to quote, however, here is how you should do it.

If a quotation is brief, taking up no more than two or three lines of your paper, then it should be written as a part of the text and surrounded by quotation marks. You should introduce the quotation by clearly identifying the speaker. The reader will always want to know who is speaking and in what context. Don't say: *The strikers were "a dangerous mob."* Say: *According to D. H. Dyson, the plant manager, the strikers were "a dangerous mob."* If you do not wish to quote a whole statement, it is necessary to indicate those parts that you are leaving out by inserting **ellipses** (three periods ". . .") wherever words are missing. (See the example that follows.)

If your quotation is very long, it must be separated from the sentences that precede and follow it. It should be indented ten or more spaces and appear in single-spaced type. Do not surround it with quotation marks.

SHORT QUOTATION EXAMPLE: The early settlers were not hostile to the Native Americans. As pointed out by the Claxton *Banner* in 1836: "Our Sioux neighbors, despite their fierce reputation, are a friendly and peaceable people."[1]

SHORT QUOTATION EXAMPLE WITH OMISSION: As pointed out by the Claxton *Banner* in 1836: "Our Sioux neighbors . . . are a friendly and peaceable people."[1]

LONG QUOTATION EXAMPLE: The early settlers were not hostile to the Native Americans. As pointed out by the Claxton *Banner* in 1836:

> Our Sioux neighbors, despite their fierce reputation, are a friendly and peaceable people. No livestock have been disturbed, and the outermost cabins are unmolested. We trust in God that our two peoples may live in harmony in this territory.[1]

Remember that all quotations must be footnoted.

Organizing a Bibliography

A bibliography is an alphabetical listing of the sources you have used in writing your paper. It must include *all* of the sources that appear in your footnotes or endnotes. However, do not include all of the sources you looked at in the course of your research. If your bibliography is long (say, more than twenty items) you should separate it into several categories: (1) primary sources and documents, (2) books, (3) articles, (4) nonprinted sources (tables, pictures, Internet pages, etc.). The list is alphabetized according to the last name of the author. If a work has no author (or editor or translator), alphabetize it according to the first word (except for "A," "An", "The") of the title. Begin each entry at the left margin and indent any additional lines five spaces. Each item in a bibliography is single-spaced with double-spacing between items.

LISTING A BOOK

The form is:

```
Countryman, Edward. Americans. New York: Hill and Wang,
    1996.
```

An entry in a bibliography for a book should include:

1. Author, last name first, followed by a period.
2. Title of work underlined or in italics, followed by a period.
3. Place of publication, followed by a colon.
4. Publisher, followed by a comma.
5. Date of publication, followed by a period.

If you include more than one source *by the same author,* use three hyphens instead of repeating the name.

```
---. People in Revolution. New York: W. W. Norton, 1989.
```

LISTING A JOURNAL ARTICLE

The form is:

```
Campbell, I. C. "Culture Contact and Polynesian Identity
    in the European Age." The Journal of World History 8
    (1997): 46-53.
```

An entry in a bibliography for a journal article should include:

1. Author, last name first, followed by a period.
2. Title of article followed by period, all in quotation marks.
3. Title of the journal (or magazine), underlined or in italics.
4. Volume number of the journal and, in parentheses, the year of the volume, followed by a colon.
5. Pages on which the article begins and ends, followed by a period.

If a work has more than one author, alphabetize according to the last name of the first author mentioned on the title page of the book or article. That name should be followed by *all* of the others, though these with first names first. As with footnotes, if there is an author or translator, or more than one volume, or if the source is unusual, say, pictorial, microprinted or electronic, a special form must be followed. (See Appendix B, pp. 188–93.)

Revising and Rewriting

Leave time in your writing schedule for revising your paper. Before writing your final draft, put the paper aside for a day or two (another reason to leave time) and then reread it. This way, you will gain a fresh perspective and may detect weaknesses that you hadn't noticed before.

A rough draft always needs smoothing out. As you reread your paper, ask these questions: (1) Does the paper have thematic unity, and do its parts clearly follow one another? (2) Is there adequate support for the major claims and interpretations? (3) Are the points made clearly and convincingly?

While you examine the overall structure of the paper for defects, you also need to look closely at the language itself. If you have repeated yourself, eliminate the repetition; if you have included material that is unrelated to your theme, discard it. Check the connections between paragraphs to see if the reader can follow your argument. Make sure that you accomplish what you set out to do in your introduction and that your conclusion makes it clear that you have done so. Go over the footnotes or endnotes and the bibliography to check style and accuracy.

Finally, examine your writing for errors in spelling and grammar. Proofread carefully and slowly. At normal reading speed your eyes can go right by major errors. You are so familiar with your paper that you may not see what is on the page. Reading your paper aloud will help you catch unclear phrases. Showing it to a friend will let you know where your readers might have problems. (Some of the mechanics of correcting errors in writing will be discussed in the section "Word Processing.")

Word Processing: Advantages and Dangers

If you have access to a computer, the rough-draft stage (and then the rewriting stage) is the best time to use it. You can also use a computer to take your research notes but only if you can bring your source to the computer or (as with a laptop) bring the computer to the source. (See the section on how to take notes from your sources in Chapter 4.)

Word processing programs are similar, but each has some differences. You need to become familiar with the program that you intend to use. The advantages of word processing are apparent only if you are not constantly at war with the program. Take the time to learn the basic commands: how to move around the screen, to delete, to move blocks, to save, to print, etc. There is no need to be afraid of a computer, but big chunks of what you have written can disappear if you don't know how to save what you write or if you forget to do so regularly. It can be costly to learn a program *after* you have begun to use it.

Know the basics of your keyboard and of your printer also. Don't tackle a twenty-five page paper on a machine that is new to you. Warm up with smaller projects first. If you are faced with a new machine or program just before beginning a big project, take some time to learn your way around.

One thing that word processing programs cannot do for you is type. If you are a weak typist, *take your time.* You may hit the wrong letters so often that constant deleting and rewriting slows you to the pace of the old typewriter. Worse yet, your stumbling fingers may hit a control or function key and do real damage to your draft. Don't be intimidated, but be sure to type at a speed that you can handle.

The great advantage of word processing is that you can see what you have written as you write it. This will only happen, however, if you look at the screen. If you cannot type without looking at the keyboard, don't type more than a sentence without reading it on the screen!

Changing what you have written either because it is wrong or because you think of a better way of saying it is the greatest advantage of composing with a computer. Read each sentence as it appears on the screen. Does it make sense? Does it say what you want it to say? Will your reader understand it? Does it take your theme another step along the way? If not, revise it; don't wait until you have written more. If you wait, you will only entangle your weak sentence with others. When you go back to change the weak one, you will probably have to change surrounding sentences also so that they are connected to one another in a clear way.

The same advice for sentences holds true for paragraphs. Don't write too many paragraphs without rereading to see if they make sense together. Remember, you can only see one screen at a time. This can give you a tunnel-like vision of your paper. The paragraph on the screen may read well, but the one that just scrolled off the top of the screen may not be logically connected. Every few paragraphs, scroll back to earlier paragraphs (or even earlier pages) to ensure that whole sections of your paper hold together. If you lose a sense of the structure of any part of your paper, print it out and read it on the printed page. Don't let big pieces of your writing go by without rereading them — *and saving them.*

When you have finished a draft, print it out and read it as a whole. Mark any changes in red and save them on disk right away. If you don't do this, you may lose track of which changes you have and have not made. On the other hand, since rewriting is so easy on a computer, what is on your disk can quickly jump ahead of what you have printed. Be vigilant or your "final" hard copy may not reflect all the changes that are on the disk.

Guidelines for Formatting Your Paper
1. Always set at least one inch margins when you type.
2. Print out your text double-spaced. (Long quotes and footnotes/endnotes can be single-spaced.)
3. Make sure that all pages are numbered consecutively.
4. Prepare a separate title page that includes at least: your name, the name of the course and instructor, the date, and your title.
5. Don't use spelling or style checkers as substitutes for proofreading.

Example of a Research Paper

As a final aid in preparing your research paper, this chapter ends with a full-scale example. The examination of the research paper begins with a discussion of how the topic and theme were chosen and then moves on to the writing outline that the student developed. Finally, there is the paper itself, including endnotes and a bibliography, all of which follow the rules and suggestions made earlier in this chapter.

Several aspects of the sample research paper are designed to aid students. Annotations in the margin help you to see what the text is trying to accomplish. Also in the margin are a series of subtitles to the paper. Note how each one represents a stage in the unfolding story and is related to part of the writing outline. Finally, a comment in the margin of each endnote tells you what point in the paper is being supported. As you read the paper, ask yourself about the point the author is making and how she is accomplishing the goal. Pay special attention to the way in which the parts are put together and how each section adds strength to the effort to describe and support the theme. Read through the endnotes also to determine why a citation is full or shortened and to see the form used for writing them. Note also the form of the bibliography. If anything is unclear, refer back to the section of the *Guide* that talks about writing research papers.

There are two important ways in which this sample research paper can help you. First, you can read the paper as a whole *before* you write your own. This will give you a clearer sense of what your paper should look like, how it should be developed, and the kind of documentation it should have. Second, you can refer to the paper *while* you are writing your own in order to answer specific questions you may have about such issues as the introduction, continuity between paragraphs, the form of quotations and endnotes (or footnotes), the bibliography, and conclusion.

How the Theme Was Chosen

The theme chosen for this paper would fit a variety of courses: Pre–Civil War U.S. History, American Labor History, Women's History, and the History of Industrialization, among others. Within the framework of one of these courses, the student became curious about the lives of workers in the earliest factories. This led to a *topic* about industrialization in New England where the student had grown up. Preliminary research indicated that textiles were the first goods to be made in factories, so the topic was narrowed to workers in that industry. When the student discovered that many of the earliest workers were young women who were the same age as she was, she decided to look at their lives in particular. The largest number of these women worked in mills in Lowell, Massachusetts, so that town was chosen. (The student's research also made it clear that there were numerous sources that discussed Lowell mill workers.) The time period to be covered was the one during which women workers were the principal work force in Lowell. Finally, the student discovered from preliminary research that in the early nineteenth century there was great concern about the impact of industrial work on American society and especially on women. All of this narrowing led to the theme "Wage Slavery or True Independence: Women Workers in the Lowell, Massachusetts, Textile Mills, 1820–1850." (See the section on coming up with a theme for your paper in Chapter 4.)

The Writing Outline for the Theme

The writing outline was created from the student's research outline and subsequent research notes. See the section on creating a research outline in Chapter 4. The research phase had made clear that several important aspects of the theme had to be examined in the paper. Several sources gave detailed accounts of the experiences of the women workers, showing both positive and negative aspects of their working lives. It became clear that this subject should have an important place in the paper. Sections 4, 5, and 6 of the outline focus on this subject. Section 4 talks about work life, section 5 social life, and section 6 the women's response to changes in the mills. Having decided on the importance of the work experience, it became necessary to give the reader an understanding of how these women came to be mill workers in the first place. Section 3 examines this subject. Showing how the women came to be mill workers required an explanation to the reader of where the mills themselves came from. This is necessary because the mills represent the first stage of industrialization in America, one of the points of the theme. Sections 1 and 2 deal with industrialization. Section 7 covers the end of the period during which women workers predominated in textile work. The other two sections, of course, are the introduction and conclusion.

The subheadings within each section are divisions of the larger subject and determine the order in which a section will be developed. For example, section 4, "Life in a mill town," examines, in order, adjusting to life in a mill town, a typical work day, the work itself, the pay received, and the mill-owned boarding houses where the girls lived. Look at each part of the outline to see the function it serves and how the whole of the outline fully covers the important parts of the theme. Try to be sure that your own outline sets the stage for writing the paper the way this one does.

Wage Slavery or True Independence:
Women Workers in the Lowell, Massachusetts,
Textile Mills, 1820–1850

Introduction
1. Attitudes toward industrialization in the United States
   a. Prejudice against industry by Americans
   b. Early industrialization in England
2. The origins of the textile industry in eastern Massachusetts
   a. The pre-industrial economy in America
   b. Slater-type mills
   c. Plans for a textile mill in Lowell, Massachusetts
3. Recruiting women workers
   a. The choice of a female work force
   b. Overcoming the prejudice against women working outside the home
   c. Building a "moral" community
   d. Why young women chose to work in the mills
4. Life in a mill town
   a. Adjusting to life in the mills
   b. Typical work day
   c. Nature of work
   d. Rate of pay
   e. The boarding house
5. Social life
   a. Leisure hours
   b. Female companionship
   c. The *Lowell Offering*

    6. Women workers' resistance to factory discipline
      a. "Turnouts"
      b. Slavery or independence?
    7. Declining conditions of work in the Lowell mills
      a. End of paternalism
      b. The coming of the Irish workers
Conclusion
      a. Young women's experience of early industrialization

Wage Slavery or True Independence:
Women Workers in the Lowell, Massachusetts,
Textile Mills, 1820-1850

Unless your instructor has a special format, your title page should look something like this one. Whatever layout you choose (don't get carried away with exotic ones) be sure to include: paper title, course name and number (and section, if necessary), instructor name, your name, and the date.

American History 200,
Section 4   Jane Q. Student
Professor Jones   December 8, 1997

1

Introduction.   This paper will examine the development of
the textile industry in Lowell, Massachusetts,
and the young women who served as its principal
work force between 1820 and 1850. It will attempt to show how these women came to accept
what was for them an unusual form of labor and
Thesis   how they shaped it to serve their own purposes.
statement.   Such a story helps to explain much about early
industrialization in America and particularly
about the role of women in the early factory
system. The paper also addresses the issue of
whether these women workers were mere laborers
exploited by the mill owners or were actively
engaged in expanding the constricted opportunities for women.

Attitudes toward   Until the early nineteenth century, the
industrialization
in the United   vast majority of Americans grew up in farm fami-
States.   lies. As the industrial revolution spread across
England, rural Americans felt certain that the
dark and dreary factory towns that were beginning to dot the English countryside would not
arise in America. News coming from England contained reports that a permanent class of exploited workers was being created there. America, with its commitment to opportunity, would
not, people were sure, experience such a fate.
New England had been in the forefront of the
struggle against British rule. Rural people in
that region were especially proud of their independence and suspicious of anything that seemed
Superscript num-   to copy the ways of the English.[1]
bers refer to end-
notes.

2

New Englanders watched the rise of industrialization in England with concern. Changes in production there were most noticeable in the making of cloth. As late as the 1760s, English textile merchants were still making cloth by the age-old "putting out" system. They bought raw wool and hired women to spin it at home. When the wool had been spun into yarn, the merchant then sent it to weavers who also worked in their homes. In that decade, however, new machinery (the carding cylinder, spinning jenny, and most important, the water frame) was developed that made possible the shift of spinning and weaving from homes to what were called "factories." By 1800, many such factories had been established in England, usually employing children to do most of the work. Many of these children were orphans or "paupers" from families so poor that they could not even afford to feed them. Conditions in these factories were very bad, and stories of these dark and dangerous mills (some accurate, some exaggerated) filtered back to America reinforcing the prejudice against England and industry.[2]

The economy of New England early in the nineteenth century was tied to commerce and agriculture, not industry. The wealth of New England merchants had been made in foreign trade, and few of them saw the need to turn to other pursuits. Some worried that the development of American manufactures would cut down on the need to import foreign goods. Until the War of 1812, which cut the United States off from

3

trade in English goods, most wealthy merchants
in the Northeast were content to stay in the
business that had made their riches.[3] Moreover,
where would American factory workers come from?
England had a large class of peasants who served
as a pool of potential factory labor. In America, however, when land wore out or harvests
were poor, Yankee farmers could move west to the
vast territories being taken from Native Americans.

*The origins of the
textile industry in
eastern Massachu-
setts.*

While great changes in the production of
textiles were taking place in England, most New
Englanders still spun yarn at home and some also
wove their own cloth. In most cases they were
simply making clothes for their families. Much
of this work was done by women. A spinning wheel
was a possession of almost every household.[4] Despite their anti-industrial prejudice, however,
New England farmers witnessed, in the first two
decades of the nineteenth century, a slow shift
in the way cloth was made in America. Home production gradually gave way to "putting out" and
that system was eventually replaced by factory
production. Why did this change occur?

Unlike most merchants in America, a few,
like Samuel Slater and Francis Cabot Lowell,
were impressed by the mechanization of English
textile production and began to think about an
American textile industry. Men like these noted
the massive increase in productivity in the English textile industry. At first, Slater, and
others who followed his lead, built small mills

4

in rural villages and employed not children as in England but whole families. The building of Slater-type mills did not directly challenge the New England way of living. Most villages already contained small mills run by water power (streams pushing paddle wheels) that ground corn or wheat. Since the textile mills hired whole families who already lived in the villages, family and village life was not greatly altered.[5]

One new development in textile production, however, did raise troublesome questions about the impact of industrialization on America's rural way of life. This change came from a new type of mill. The first of its type was built in Waltham, Massachusetts, in 1813 by Francis Lowell and a small group of wealthy Boston merchants.[6] Three years earlier, Lowell had returned from a long trip to England. The British government would not allow the plans for the new power looms to be taken out of the country, but Lowell had paid close attention to their construction on his many tours of English mills and returned to America with enough knowledge in his head to eventually reproduce a machine comparable to the English power loom.[7]

Transition sentence introduces discussion of new type of mill.

In Waltham, Francis Lowell built a large mill that carried out both the spinning and weaving processes. In fact, every step of the production process was done in a series of connected steps. Waltham was not a village with a textile mill in it, it was a "mill town" in which the factory dominated the economic life of a rapidly growing city. Most significantly, Lowell's system of production brought important changes in the lives of his workers. He hired them as individuals, not as families, and many came from great distances to live and work in the new mill town. When Lowell died in 1817, the small group of Boston businessmen who had invested in his mill at Waltham spread the new factory system to other places. Their biggest investment was in the small village of East Chelmsford about twenty-seven miles from Boston and lying along the swift-flowing Concord and Merrimack Rivers. There they built what was soon the biggest mill town in the nation with more than a dozen large integrated mills based upon mechanical looms. In honor of their friend, they called the new town Lowell.[8]

The growth of Lowell between 1821 and 1840 was unprecedented.[9] A rapidly developing textile industry like the one at Lowell needed larger and larger numbers of people to work the mechanical looms and other machines in their factories. Given the prejudice against factory work in New England, how could large numbers of natives be drawn to work in the mills? It was a question that had been carefully pondered by the wealthy men who built the big textile mills at Lowell, Massachusetts.

Recruiting women workers.

The mill owners, aware of the negative view of English mill towns, decided to confront the problem by creating a planned community where workers would live in solid, clean housing rather than slums. Their source of workers would

6

also be different. The rapidly running rivers
that ran their mills were not near the major
coastal cities. No large pool of potential laborers lived near their new town. The mill owners
had to find a large group of people whose labor
was not absolutely necessary to the farm economy. The solution to their labor problem came in
the form of hundreds (later thousands) of young
women who lived on the farms of the region.[10]

Several developments in the social and economic history of New England tended to make this
group of workers available. Population growth
was making it more and more difficult for farmers to find land close by for their sons (and
their sons' families). Generations of the same
family had hoped to live near one another. By
the 1820s, however, many farms in New England,
especially those on the less productive land of
Maine and New Hampshire, had run out of good
land and had to find sources of income outside
of agriculture. While some farmers went west to
find more fertile land and a less harsh climate,
others sent their sons to work on neighboring
farms, or as apprentices to craftsmen (shoemak-
ers, blacksmiths, or leather workers). Extra
cash was something that most farm families were
in great need of.[11]

Another factor helped set the stage for the
successful industrialization of textile production. This one was within the structure of the
family itself and worked in favor of producing a
new group of workers for the mills. The position
of women (wives and, especially, daughters) in

the family was an inferior one. While adult,
property-holding males were citizens with full
civil rights, the same was not true for women of
any age. The father of the family had the legal
right to control most aspects of the life of his
wife and daughters. His wife could own no prop-
erty. Her signature on a document meant nothing
as only her husband could transact business.
Daughters had even less independence. They were
bound by social conventions to obey their fathers and rarely were able to earn money of
their own. In fact, even travel away from home
was unusual. The idea that a woman's place was
in the home was not merely a powerful concept,
it was, with rare exceptions, a rule binding a
woman's behavior. While the work of daughters
and wives was important to the family economy
(it literally could not have functioned without
their labor at field work, food preparation,
cleaning, washing, etc.) they gained no independent income or freedom as a result. Indeed, so
strong was the belief that daughters' lives would
be bound by decisions made by their fathers,
older brothers, and, eventually, their husbands
that many could not imagine for themselves a
life of active, public involvement of the kind
expected of men. For some women, however, their
inferior position in family and society gave
them an incentive to take hold of any opportunity to weaken their bonds of inferiority.[12]

Women's motives were economic as well as
social. Very few opportunities for employment
outside the home existed; teaching in a local

school was one of the most common, but that was very poorly paid and lasted for only a few months a year. The new mill work was steady work, and it paid more than any alternative available to women.[13] The young girls could thus contribute to their family's welfare by sending home a portion of their pay. This economic motive added to their desire to move outside the traditional sphere of the family. For many of them, the chance to live away from home and with other young women like themselves offered an independence that was otherwise impossible.[14]

Hiring young women, of course, ran up against strong Yankee resistance. As noted above, fathers rarely allowed their daughters to leave home when they were young. According to the prejudices of the period, young women were unprepared for a life among adult, male strangers. Their "innocence" and "purity" had to be protected by their family. The goal held out for these girls (almost the only respectable one) was eventual marriage. To prepare for that, they had to learn wifely duties and practical household skills. God-fearing New England fathers were very reluctant to let their daughters leave the farm to live and work among strangers in a faraway town.[15]

To confront this prejudice, the mill owners created boarding houses around the mills where groups of girls would live and take their meals under the care of a boarding housekeeper who was usually an older woman, perhaps a widow. Strict boarding house rules were laid down by the com-

pany; rules that served the company's purposes
but also reassured parents that their daughters'
behavior would still be monitored even though
they were away from home. For example, the young
women could not have visitors in the late
evening. (See the reproduction of boarding house
regulations on page 10.) Moreover, the girls
would never grow into a permanent working
class--something that no one wished to see--as
it was expected that they would return to their
homes for visits and after a year or two would
go back to their villages. While they stayed in
Lowell, their reputations (and thus their opportunity for marriage) would be protected by the
town fathers.[16]

The mill owners did not advertise for help.
They sent recruiters into the countryside to explain the special nature of Lowell and to soothe
parents' fears. Because of the farmers' need for
extra income, and the women's desire for independence, this effort was often successful.[17]
Over the years, thousands of young women took
the long trip by stagecoach or wagon from their
rural homes to mill towns like Lowell.

Life in a mill town.

Upon first arriving in Lowell, the young
girls were naturally nervous. They had not lived
away from home or ever worked in a factory. They
were not used to the atmosphere of a city. The
boarding house was new also. Living with a
strange woman (and probably her family) who
might or might not be a caring mother-substi-
tute, also required adjustment. The girls shared

10

REGULATIONS

FOR THE

BOARDING HOUSES

OF THE

MIDDLESEX COMPANY.

THE tenants of the Boarding Houses are not to board, or permit any part of their houses to be occupied by any person except those in the employ of the Company.

They will be considered answerable for any improper conduct in their houses, and are not to permit their boarders to have company at unseasonable hours.

The doors must be closed at ten o'clock in the evening, and no one admitted after that time without some reasonable excuse.

The keepers of the Boarding Houses must give an account of the number, names, and employment of their boarders, when required; and report the names of such as are guilty of any improper conduct, or are not in the regular habit of attending public worship.

The buildings and yards about them must be kept clean and in good order, and if they are injured otherwise than from ordinary use, all necessary repairs will be made, and charged to the occupant.

It is indispensable that all persons in the employ of the Middlesex Company should be vaccinated who have not been, as also the families with whom they board; which will be done at the expense of the Company.

SAMUEL LAWRENCE, Agent.

JOEL TAYLOR, PRINTER, Daily Courier Office.

11

the home with a dozen or more other girls and
usually roomed with three or four of them. Most
were homesick for a time. While all this was
happening, of course, the girls had to make the
difficult adjustment to the rigorous rules and
long hours at the mill.[18]

Mill work was not only an opportunity, like
so much of early factory labor, it was hard
work. The typical work day began at five a.m.
and did not end until seven in the evening, or
later. Thus the women worked an average of
twelve hours a day. They were given only thirty
minutes for lunch and forty-five for dinner.
Since they took their meals at the boarding
house, the thirty minutes for lunch had to include a quick walk (perhaps a run) to and from
the house, leaving only fifteen or twenty minutes for the meal.[19] The mills operated six days
a week so that the only day off was Sunday, part
of which was usually spent at church. Thus free
time was confined to two or three hours in the
evening (boarding house rules required them to
go to bed at ten) and to Sunday afternoon.[20] For
many, however, this was still more leisure (and
more freedom) than they would have had at home.

Despite a work day which, including meals,
took up fourteen hours, most of the young women
did not find the work very strenuous or particularly dangerous. As the mill owners had claimed,
Lowell did not resemble the grimy, packed mill
towns of England.[21] Still, the work was tedious
and confining--doing the same operation over and

12

over again and under the watchful eye of the
overseer. In the ideal plan for Lowell, the
overseer was to take the place of the absent father (just as the boarding-house widow was to be
the substitute mother), someone responsible for
seeing to the safety and welfare of the girls on
the job. Of course, the overseer was also hired
by the company to assure that the mill ran
smoothly and efficiently. He saw to it that the
women worked steadily and recorded their hours
of labor; any possibility of time off required
his approval.[22]

The young women earned an average of three
to four dollars a week from which their board of
$1.25 a week was deducted.[23] At that time there
were no other jobs open to women that paid as
well. As noted above, rural school teachers
earned less than one dollar a week and taught
for only three months of the year.[24] Three or
four dollars a week was enough to pay their
board, send badly needed money home and still
have enough left over for new clothes once in a
while. Many women workers even established savings accounts, and some eventually left work
with several hundred dollars, something that
they could never have done at home.[25]

In Lowell the women became part of a grow-   *Social life.*
ing city that had shops, social events, and ca-
maraderie that were absent in their rural villages and farms. While most felt responsible to
send part of their earnings home, enough was
left over to give them consumer choices unavail-

13

able to their rural sisters, cousins, and
friends. Also, unlike farm and family chores,
mill work offered free time on Sundays and in
the evenings.[26]

Even though their free time was very limited, the women engaged in a wide variety of activities. In the evening they wrote letters
home, entertained visitors (though there was
little privacy), repaired their clothing, and
talked among themselves. They could go out to
the shops, especially clothing shops. The mill
girls at Lowell prided themselves on a wardrobe
that, at least on Sunday, was not inferior to
that of the wives of prosperous citizens.[27]
One of the most surprising uses of their free
time was the number of meetings attended by mill
girls. There were evening courses that enabled
the young women to extend their education beyond
the few years of schooling they had received in
the countryside. They could also attend lectures
by prominent speakers. It was not unusual for
the audience for serious presentations to be
composed mostly of mill girls. In their spare
time, they also read novels and essays. So
strong was the girls' interest in reading that
many mills put up signs "No reading in the
mills."[28] Perhaps the most unusual pursuit of at
least some mill girls was writing. Determined to
challenge the idea that mill girls were mindless
drones of the factory and that they had not the
refinement necessary to make them good wives,
about seventy-five mill girls and women
contributed in the 1840s to a series of publica-

14

tions that featured stories and essays by the workers themselves. Indeed, much of the editorial work was done by these women as well.[29]

The most well-known of these publications was the Lowell Offering. The Offering stayed away from sensitive issues concerning working conditions, and the mill owners certainly benefited from the reputation for seriousness that it earned their workers. Still, the women controlled the content of the publication and wrote on subjects (family, courtship, fashion, morality, nature, etc.) that interested them.[30] A few of the Offering writers even went on to literary careers, not the kind of future that most people expected of factory workers. Charles Dickens toured the mills in 1842 and later said of the girls' writing that: "Of the merits of the Lowell Offering, as a literary production, I will only observe . . . that it will compare advantageously with a great many English annuals."[31]

Though the Offering was a sign that something unusual was happening in this factory town, the women still worked in an industry that caused them hardship. In the early years, the owners had tried to keep up the image of the factory as a pleasant place. Buildings had many windows and much sunlight. The town had large green spaces and the atmosphere of a country village.[32] As time went on, however, the mill companies became more interested in profits and less concerned about their role as protectors of their young workers.

Example of a quotation with ellipsis. Short quotations are integrated into the text.

15

By the 1830s, tensions in the mills had
begun to rise. Factory owners, observing a decline in the price of their cloth and the growth
of unsold inventories, decided to lower their
workers' wages.[33] When the reduction was announced in February 1834, the women workers cir-

*Women workers'
resistance to fac-
tory discipline.*

culated petitions among themselves pledging to
stop work ("turn out") if wages were lowered.[34]
When the leader of the petition drive at one
mill was fired, many of the women protested.
They left work and marched to the other mills to
call out their workers. It is estimated that
one-sixth of all women mill workers walked out
as a result. The strikers wrote another petition
stating that "we will not go back into the mills
to work until our wages are continued . . . as
they have been."[35] While the "turn out" was
brief and did not achieve its purpose, it did
demonstrate the attitude of many of the women
workers. They did not accept the owners' view
that they were minors under their benevolent
care. The petitions prepared by the strikers indicate that they thought of themselves as the
equal of their employers. The sense of independence gained by factory work and cash wages led
them to reject the idea that they were mere factory hands. Petitions referred to their "unques-
tionable rights," and to "the spirit of our pa-
triotic ancestors, who preferred privation to
bondage. . . ." One petition ended "we are free,
we would remain in possession of what kind prov-

*Example of a
quotation with
emphasis added.*

idence has bestowed upon us, and remain <u>daugh-
ters of free men still</u>."[36] This language indi-

16

cates that the women did not think of themselves
as laborers complaining about low wages. They
were free citizens of a republic and deserved
respect as such. Since many of the young women
had older relatives who had fought in the Revolutionary War, they felt that they were protect-
ing not only their jobs but also their indepe-
dence. While it is true that the strike failed
and that these women did not really have the
"independence" they were so proud of, this issue
was so important to them that many left the
mills and went home when it became clear that
mill work required a lessening of their status.
They had accepted mill work because life away
from home and good wages gave them greater freedom. When mill work came to seem more like
"slavery" (a comparison that also appeared in
the petitions) than independence, many changed
their minds. In 1836, a similar effort to lower
wages led to an even larger "turn out."[37] The
willingness of these young women to challenge
the authority of the mill owners is a sign that
their new lives had given them a feeling of mutual strength.[38]

Economic recession in the late 1830s and
early 1840s led to the layoff of hundreds of
the women workers. Many of the mills were forced
to part-time schedules. In the 1840s and 1850s,
the mill owners tried to maintain profits despite increased competition and lessened demand.
They did so by intensifying the work process.
The speed of the machinery was increased as was

*Declining condi-
tions of work in
the Lowell mills.*

17

the number of machines tended by each worker.
Paternalism was discarded. To save money the
companies stopped building boarding houses.[39]
The look of Lowell changed as well. Mill buildings took up more of the green space that had
been part of the original plan.

By 1850, Lowell did indeed look something
like an English mill town. By then, however, the
need to pacify the fears of potential workers
and their families was gone. Terrible famine in
Ireland in 1845 and 1846 had caused a large number of Irish to immigrate to the United
States.[40] As conditions in the mills declined,
more and more young Yankee women left the mills
for home or other work. Their places were
rapidly taken up by the very poor Irish for whom
work of any kind in America was an opportunity,
and who did not have the option of returning to
their homes. Slowly, Lowell had become just another industrial city. It was dirty and over-
crowded, and its mills were beginning to look
run-down.

Conclusion.   By 1850, an era had passed. By then most of
the mill workers were recruited from newly
arrived immigrants with backgrounds very different from those of the young New England women.
During the period from the 1820s to the 1840s,
however, young women from rural New England made
up the majority of the textile workers in the
area. At that time, an unusual era in the development of industrialization took place. Large
textile mills with complex production systems

18

were operated largely by young women who did not
think of themselves as workers but as free citizens of a republic earning an independent existence for a few years before returning to their
homes. These women gave the mill owners the work-
force that was needed to make the U.S. textile
industry large and profitable. Many fortunes
were made for investors living in Boston and
other major cities.[41] But the farmers' daughters
profited as well. Not only did they earn more
money than earlier generations of women had been
able to, they did so outside the home.

A great debate had raged during the 1830s
and 1840s about the impact of industrialization
on American life. Because of the general belief
that women were weak, it was presumed that they
would be taken advantage of as workers, especially as they were away from the protection of
the male members of their families. Further, it
was feared that mill work would "defeminize"
them and that young men would not marry them because they had not been brought up in an environment of modesty, deference to their fathers
and brothers, and daily practice in domestic
tasks such as cleaning, sewing, and cooking.[42]
Seen from a longer perspective, however, the
women showed these fears to be unfounded. Even
more importantly, as effective workers they un-
dermined the stereotype of women as frail and as
thriving only in a domestic environment. While
these young women helped make possible the industrialization of New England, at the same time
they expanded their opportunities. Many women

*Restatement of
thesis.*

reformers and radicals in later years, as they
raised the banner for equal rights for women in
more and more areas of life, referred back to
the example of the independent mill girls of the
1830s and 1840s who resisted pressures from
their employers, gained both freedom and matu-
rity by living and working on their own, and
showed an intense desire for independence and
learning.[43] Great fortunes were made from the
textile mills of that era, but within those
mills a generation of young women gained something even more precious--a sense of self-
respect.

20

Endnotes

Endnotes begin on a new page.

1. Caroline F. Ware, The Early New England Cotton Manufacture (Boston: Houghton-Mifflin Co., 1931), 4-8; Barbara M. Tucker, Samuel Slater and the Origins of the American Textile Industry: 1790-1860 (Ithaca: Cornell University Press, 1984), 38-41; Robert F. Dalzell, Enterprising Elite: The Boston Associates and the World They Made (Cambridge: Harvard University Press, 1987), 12-13; Jonathan Prude, The Coming of Industrial Order: Town and Factory Life in Rural Massachusetts, 1810-1860 (Cambridge: Cambridge University Press, 1983), 6-12; Allan Kulikoff, "The Transition to Capitalism in Rural America," William and Mary Quarterly 46 (1989): 129-30, 141-42.

1. American attitudes toward industrialization in England and mill work in general.

2. Tucker, Slater, 33-40.

2. The rise of industrialization in England.

3. Dalzell, 41-42; Ware, 3-8, 62.

3. The origins of industrialization in America.

4. Thomas Dublin, Women at Work: The Transformation of Work and Community in Lowell, Massachusetts, 1826-1860 (New York: Columbia University Press, 1979), 14; Adrienne D. Hood, "The Gender Division of Labor in the Production of Textiles in Eighteenth Century Rural Pennsylvania," Journal of Social History 27, spring 1994, <http://www.searchbank.com/infotrac/session/4/0/82904/3?xrn_7> (9 September 1996).

4. Home spinning in America.

Example of citation from the Internet.

5. Tucker, Slater, 79, 85, 99-100, 111; Barbara M. Tucker, "The Family and Industrial Discipline in Ante-Bellum New England," Labor History 21 (winter 1979-80): 56-60.

5. Slater-type mills and family production.

6. Dalzell, 26-30; Tucker, Slater, 111-16.

6. The creation of Waltham mills.

21

7. H.C. Lowell and power loom.

7. Dalzell, 5-6.

8. The founding of Lowell.

8. Tucker, 116-17.

9. The growth of Lowell.

9. Dublin, 19-21, 133-35.

10. The owners' choice of a female work force.

10. Dublin, 26, 76; Benita Eisler, ed., The Lowell Offering: Writings by New England Mill Women (1840-1845) (Philadelphia: J.B. Lippincott Co., 1977), 15-16.

11. Problems of the farm economy.

11. Christopher Clark, "The Household Economy: Market Exchange and the Rise of Capitalism in the Connecticut Valley, 1800-1860," Journal of Social History 13 (winter 1979): 175-76; Gail Fowler Mohanty, "Handloom Outwork and Outwork Weaving in Rural Rhode Island, 1810-1821," American Studies 30 (fall 1989): 42-43, 48-49.

12. The inferior position of women.

12. Eisler, 16, 19, 62; Barbara Welter, "The Cult of True Womanhood," American Quarterly 18 (1966): 155, 162-65.

13. Limited opportunities for women in New England.

13. Eisler, 16, 193; Clark, 178-79; Dalzell, 33.

14. Women's desire for independence.

14. Dublin, 40; Tucker, Slater, 255-56; Harriet H. Robinson, Loom and Spindle (1898; reprinted in Women of Lowell, New York: Arno Press, 1974), 194; Eisler, 61-63, 81-82.

15. Early nineteenth-century rural attitudes toward women.

15. On the influence of patriarchy see Tucker, Slater, 25-26; Robinson, 61; Welter, 152, 170-71. Also see Sins of Our Mothers, 58 min., WGBH/WNET/KLET/PBS, 1988, videocassette.

Example of a film citation.

16. Early Lowell paternalism.

16. Dublin, 77-79; Eisler, 19-24.

17. The method of recruiting women workers.

17. Eisler, 18-19. On the decline of New England agriculture see Clark, 176; Ware, 14.

18. Getting used to town life and the boarding house.

18. Dublin, 80; Eisler, 73-74.

19. The nature of mill work and the work day.

19. Dublin, 80; Robinson, 31; Lucy Larcom, "Among Lowell Mill Girls: A Reminiscence" (1881;

22

reprinted in <u>Women of Lowell</u>), 602; Eisler, 75-77.

20. See table of mill hours printed in Eisler, 30. Boarding house curfew is listed in "Regulations for the Boarding Houses," contained in illustration on page 10. For a very negative view of work hours and conditions, see A Citizen of Lowell, <u>Corporations and Operatives: Being an Exposition of the Condition [of the] Factory Operatives</u> . . . (1843; reprinted in <u>Women of Lowell</u>), 15-19.21.

21. Larcom, 599-602; Eisler, 56-66.

22. "Factory Rules from the Handbook to Lowell, 1848," n.d., <http://www.kentlaw.edu/ilhs/lowell.htm> (9 August 1996).

23. Dublin, 66, 183, 185; Ware, 239.

24. Ware, 240-42. For teachers' pay see Eisler, 193.

25. Elisha Bartlett, <u>A Vindication of the Character and Condition of the Females Employed in the Lowell Mills</u>, . . . (Lowell, Massachusetts: Leonard Huntress, Printer, 1841), 21; Dublin, 188.

26. Larcom, 599-600.

27. Eisler, 49-50.

28. Robinson, 91-93; Eisler, 113-32. For mill rules concerning reading, see Eisler, 31.

29. Robinson, 97-102.

30. Eisler, 33-40; Dublin, 123-24, 129-30; Robinson, 114-120; Bertha Monica Stearns, "Early Factory Magazines in New England: The <u>Lowell Offering</u> and Its Contemporaries," <u>Journal of Eco-</u>

20. Work hours and free time.

21. Favorable comments on mill work by the Lowell mill girls.

22. The role of the overseer.

23. The rate of women's pay.

24. Low alternative pay for women.

25. Savings accounts.

26. Free time.

27. Leisure time and wardrobe.

28. Reading and education.

29. Women's writing.

30. The Lowell Offering

23

nomic and Business History (August 1930):
690-91, 698.

31. Dickens is quoted in Robinson, 11. Also see Larcom, 609; Eisler, 41.

32. Larcom, 598, 609; Eisler, 63-65.

33. Dublin, 87-90.

34. Robinson, 84; Dublin, 89-91.

35. Dublin, 91.

36. Dublin, 93.

37. Dublin, 98-99.

38. Dublin, 44, 82-83, 103.

39. Dublin, 108, 134; Robinson, 204, 208-09; Eisler, 215.

40. Dublin, 140, 156, 197. On the decline of Lowell, see Dalzell, 69.

41. Dalzell, 60-61, 70-73.

42. Dublin 32; Welter, 151-74. For the contemporary debate about the impact of factory work on women, see the pamphlets: Bartlett, <u>A Vindication of the Character and Condition</u> . . . and A Citizen, <u>Corporations and Operatives</u>. . .

43. Dublin, 127-29; Ware, 292.

31. Dickens commenting on the Lowell Offering.

32. The early Lowell setting.

33. The tensions of the 1830s; lowered wages.

34. The 1834 "Turnout."

35. Strikers' petitions.

36. More quotes from petitions.

37. The 1836 "Turnout."

38. Mutual support.

39. Declining working conditions.

40. The work force after 1845; Irish immigration.

41. Profits for owners.

42. The status of women.

43. Lowell women activists and later movements.

24

Bibliography

Books

Bartlett, Elisha. <u>A Vindication of the Character
and Condition of the Females Employed in the
Lowell Mills</u>, . . . Lowell, Massachusetts:
Leonard Huntress, Printer, 1841. Reprinted
in <u>Women of Lowell</u>. New York: Arno Press,
1974.

Citizen of Lowell, A. <u>Corporations and Operatives: Being an Exposition of the Condition
[of the] Factory Operatives</u>. . . . 1843.
Reprinted in <u>Women of Lowell</u>. New York: Arno
Press, 1974.

Dalzell, Robert F. <u>Enterprising Elite: The Boston
Associates and the World They Made</u>. Cambridge: Harvard University Press, 1987.

Dublin, Thomas. <u>Women at Work: The Transformation
of Work and Community in Lowell, Massachusetts, 1826-1860</u>. New York: Columbia University Press, 1979.

Eisler, Benita, ed. <u>The Lowell Offering: Writings
by New England Mill Women (1840-1845)</u>.
Philadelphia: J.B. Lippincott Co., 1977.

Prude, Jonathan. <u>The Coming of Industrial Order:
Town and Factory Life in Rural Massachusetts, 1810-1860</u>. Cambridge: Cambridge University Press, 1983.

Robinson, Harriet H. <u>Loom and Spindle; Or, Life
Among the Early Mill Girls.</u> 1898. Reprinted
in <u>Women of Lowell</u>. New York: Arno Press,
1974.

*Bibliography be-
gins on a new
page.*

*Citations are
listed alphabeti-
cally under each
heading.*

*Second and fol-
lowing lines of
each citation are
indented.*

25

Tucker, Barbara M. <u>Samuel Slater and the Origins</u>
<u>of the American Textile Industry: 1790-1860.</u>
Ithaca: Cornell University Press, 1984.

Ware, Caroline F. <u>The Early New England Cotton</u>
<u>Manufacture</u>. Boston: Houghton Mifflin Com-
pany, 1931.

Articles

Clark, Christopher. "The Household Economy, Market Exchange, and the Rise of Capitalism in
the Connecticut Valley, 1800-1860." <u>Journal</u>
<u>of Social History</u> 13 (winter 1979): 169-89.

Hood, Adrienne D. "The Gender Division of Labor
in the Production of Textiles in the Eighteenth Century." <u>Journal of Social History</u>
27. Spring 1994. <http://www.searchbank.com/
infotrac/session/4/0/82904/3?xrn_7> (9 September 1996).

Kulikoff, Allen. "The Transition to Capitalism in
Rural America." <u>William and Mary Quarterly</u>
46 (1989): 120-144.

Larcom, Lucy. "Among Lowell Mill Girls: A Reminiscence." 1881. Reprinted in <u>Women of Low-</u>
<u>ell</u>. New York: Arno Press, 1974.

Mohanty, Gail Fowler. "Handloom Outwork and Outwork Weaving in Rural Rhode Island,
1810-1821." <u>American Studies</u> 30 (fall 1989):
41-68.

Stearns, Bertha Monica. "Early Factory Magazines
in New England: The Lowell Offering and Its
Contemporaries." <u>Journal of Economic and</u>
<u>Business History</u> (Aug. 1930): 685-705.

26

Tucker, Barbara M. "The Family and Industrial
  Discipline in Ante-Bellum New England."
  <u>Labor History</u> 21 (winter 1979-80): 55-74.
Welter, Barbara. "The Cult of True Womanhood."
  <u>American Quarterly</u> 18 (1966): 151-74.

      Films
<u>Sins of Our Mothers</u> 58 min. WGBH/WNET/KCET/PBS,
  1988. Videocassette.

     Documents
"Factory Rules from the Handbook to Lowell,
  1848." N.d. <http://www.kentlaw.edu/ilhs.
  lowell.htm> (9 August 1996).

A P P E N D I X A

Basic Reference Sources
for History Study
and Research

Chapter 4, "How to Research a History Topic," describes the ways of searching for information on a history topic in your library. This appendix makes that job easier by separating different kinds of reference sources by type so that you know what *kind* of printed or online finding aid will get you where you want to go.

This list of reference sources is especially designed for undergraduate historical research. It contains several kinds of sources: (1) *reference works* (dictionaries, **encyclopedias, atlases, yearbooks**); (2) *guides* to biographies, newspaper articles, journal articles, book reviews, and government documents; and (3) several hundred *subject bibliographies* arranged according to topic. While reference works contain brief descriptions of aspects of your historical topic, guides and subject bibliographies lead you to specific studies of the topic itself. If, for example, your topic is nineteenth-century Asian immigration to the United States and you are seeking information on the theme "Chinese Immigrant Labor on the Transcontinental Railroad," the section of the subject bibliographies entitled "Asian Immigrant and Ethnic History" is a good place to begin. Here you will find a work entitled *Asian American Studies: An Annotated Bibliography and Research Guide.*

Also included in this appendix is a section called "Electronic Reference Sources" (see p. 173). This section includes the rapidly growing world of information sources on computer. A tour of your library's computer terminals will let you know which of these sources is available to you. Some computer terminals will give you access to the holdings of your own library, others may have access to CD-ROM discs owned by your library and yet others will have access to the World Wide Web by way of the Internet. In the future, more and more historical research is likely to be done online, so it is important that you know your way around the universe of electronic information. For the present, however, more information on your topic/theme will probably be available in your library's *printed* reference works.

Many of the works cited in this appendix should be available in the reference section of your own library. If your library is small, however, you may not find some of them. On the other hand, if your school's library is large, you will have even more sources available to you. Within each group of sources, those that should be found in most reference collections or that are particularly useful for undergraduate research are designated by an asterisk. Other sources listed are prepared for advanced students or professionals. If your library includes them, however, you will probably find them valuable for your own research.

Nonelectronic entries in the appendix are listed by title first so that you can more easily spot the work that seems closest to your topic. Following the title is publication information and then the name of the editor or compiler (if available). When looking for one of these works in a catalog, however, first conduct an "author" search under the name of the editor or compiler. If the book does not turn up this way, then search for the work by title. When you have access to more than one edition of a work, it is usually best to use the most recent one. As always, the reference librarian is your best guide to your school's information resources.

Dictionaries, Encyclopedias, Atlases, and Yearbooks

These sources are general reference works. They can help you to define and correctly spell important terms, gather general information on your topic/theme, locate geographical areas, obtain statistical data, and much more. These sources are a good point at which to begin any historical investigation. You can also consult them for specific facts. However, these sources do not contain extensive examinations or interpretations of historical subjects, and therefore you should not depend upon them for the substance of your work.

General Dictionaries

Webster's New International Dictionary
Funk and Wagnall's New Standard Dictionary
The Random House Dictionary of the American Language
Oxford English Dictionary, 2d ed. Oxford: Clarendon Press, 1989. This is the most complete English-language dictionary. If you are studying the historical development of the meaning of a word, it is an essential reference. If, however, you wish to determine the contemporary spelling or definition of a term, the unabridged language dictionaries are better sources. If the term is colloquial or is a recent derivation, be sure to use the most recent edition available.

Historical Dictionaries

Historical dictionaries define only historical terms. Unlike language dictionaries, they briefly describe the origin and general historical context of the term. Some historical dictionaries give extensive explanations of terms and thus are similar to encyclopedias.

Concise Dictionary of American History. New York: Charles Scribner's Sons, 1983. David William Voorhees, ed. This is an abridgement of the eight-volume *Dictionary of American History.*

Macmillan Concise Dictionary of World History. New York: Macmillan, 1983. Bruce Wetterau, comp. and ed.

A Dictionary of Twentieth Century History, 1914–1990. Oxford: Oxford University Press, 1992. Peter Teed, ed.

A Dictionary of Modern History, 1789–1945. Baltimore: Penguin Books, 1975. Alan W. Palmer, ed.

Dictionary of American History. Rev. ed. New York: Scribner's, 1976. James T. Adams and Roy V. Coleman, eds. *Supplement,* 1996.

The Harper Dictionary of Modern Thought. New York: Harper & Row, 1988. Alan Bullock and Stephen Trombley, eds.

A Dictionary of Ancient History. Oxford: Blackwell, 1994.

Oxford Dictionary of Byzantium. 3 vols. Oxford University Press, 1991. Alex P. Kazhdan, ed.

A Dictionary of American History. Oxford: Blackwell, 1995. Thomas L. Purvis, ed.

Dictionary of Afro-American Slavery. New York: Greenwood, 1988. Randall M. Miller, ed.

A Dictionary of Contemporary American History, 1945 to the Present. New York: Meridian, 1996. Stanley Hochman and Eleanor Hockman, eds.

Specialized Dictionaries

A Dictionary of the Social Sciences. New York: The Free Press, 1964. J. Gould and W. Kolb, eds.

The New Grove Dictionary of Music and Musicians. 20 vols. New York: Macmillan, 1980. Stanley Sadie, ed.

Baker's Biographical Dictionary of Musicians. 8th ed. New York: Schirmer, 1992. Theodore Baker, comp.

The Oxford Dictionary of Philosophy. Oxford: Oxford University Press, 1994. Simon Blackburn, comp.

General Encyclopedias

If your subject is a recent one, or if important new facts and interpretations have arisen in recent years, be sure to obtain the latest edition of whatever encyclopedia you use. If a recent edition is not available, check the annual supplements published by most good encyclopedias. Online versions of encyclopedias may be available to you.

Encyclopaedia Britannica. Chicago: Encyclopaedia Britannica Educational Corporation.
This is one of the best encyclopedias.

Encyclopedia Americana. Danbury, Conn.: Grolier Educational Corporation.

Collier's Encyclopedia. New York: Crowell Collier and Macmillan.

The Columbia Encyclopedia. New York: Columbia University Press.

Historical Encyclopedias

An Encyclopedia of World History, Ancient, Medieval and Modern, Chronologically Arranged. Boston: Houghton Mifflin, 1972. William L. Langer, ed.

Harper Encyclopedia of the Modern World [1760 to present]. New York: Harper & Row, 1970. Richard B. Morris and Graham W. Irwin, eds.

Encyclopedia of American History. New York: Harper & Row, 1982. Richard B. Morris et al., eds.

Encyclopedia of American Political History: Studies of the Principal Movements and Ideas. 3 vols. New York: Scribner's, 1984. Jack P. Green, ed.

Women's Studies Encyclopedia: History, Philosophy, and Religion. Vol. 3. Westport, Conn.: Greenwood Press, 1991. Helen Tierney, ed.

Specialized Encyclopedias

International Encyclopedia of the Social Sciences. New York: Macmillan, 1968–1991. David L. Sills, ed. If your research takes you into such fields as political science, economics, anthropology, law, sociology, and psychology, this is an important sourcebook for you. (A biographical supplement, published in 1979, includes biographies of famous social scientists.) An earlier work, *Encyclopedia of the Social Sciences* (New York: Macmillan, 1930–1934), edited by Edwin R. A. Seligman and Alvin Johnson, is also valuable for such subjects, although it is now out of date.

Encyclopedia of Philosophy. New York: Free Press, 1973. Paul Edwards, ed.

Encyclopedia Judaica. 16 vols. Jerusalem: Keter Publishing House, 1972. Geoffrey Wigoder, ed.

New Catholic Encyclopedia. Palantine, Ill.: J. Heraty, 1981.

Encyclopedia of Religion. 16 vols. New York: Macmillan, 1987. Mircea Eliade, ed.

Encyclopedia of World Art. New York: McGraw Hill, 1959–1968. Supplements, 1987.

Benets' Readers Encyclopedia of American Literature. New York: Harper Collins, 1991. George Perkins, ed.

The Concise Encyclopedia of Islam. New York: Harper & Row, 1989. Cyril Glasse, ed.

McGraw-Hill Encyclopedia of Science and Technology. 8th ed. New York: McGraw-Hill, 1997.

Encyclopedia of the American Military. New York: Scribner's, 1994. John E. Jessup, ed.

Encyclopedia of the United States in the Twentieth Century. 4 vols. New York: Scribner's, 1996. Stanley Kutler, ed.

The New Grove Dictionary of Music and Musicians. 20 vols. New York: Macmillan, 1980. Stanley Sadie, ed.

General Atlases

Webster's New Geographical Dictionary. Springfield Mass.: G. and C. Merriam, 1984. Although this source is not useful for map reference, it is a convenient source for determining the spelling, location, and description of geographical terms.

The Times Atlas of the World. London: Times Publishing Company, 1955–1959. John Bartholomew, ed. Vol. 1 — World, Australia, East Asia; vol. 2 — India, Middle East, Russia; vol. 3 — Northern Europe; vol. 4 — Mediterranean and Africa; vol. 5 — Americas. A one-volume edition was published in 1985. The newest edition was published by Hammond, 1991.

National Geographic Atlas of the World. Washington, D.C.: National Geographic Society, 1981.

Historical Atlases

**Rand McNally Historical Atlas of the World.* Chicago: Rand McNally, 1981. R. I. Moore, gen. ed.

**Muir's Historical Atlas: Ancient, Medieval & Modern.* London: George Philips, 1976.

**Times Atlas of World History.* 4th ed. New York: Hammond, 1993.

**Atlas of American History.* New York: Scribner's, 1984. Kenneth T. Jackson, ed.

The Atlas of Medieval Man. New York: Crescent Books, 1985. Colin Platt, ed.

Shepherd's Historical Atlas. New York: Harper & Row, 1980. William R. Shepherd, ed.

Harper Atlas of World History. New York: Harper Collins, 1992.

Times Atlas of European History. New York: Times/Harper Collins, 1994. Thomas Cussans, ed.

Historical Atlas of the United States. Washington D.C.: National Geographic Society, 1988. Wilbur E. Garrett, ed.

Historical Atlas of Britain. New York: Continuum, 1981. Malcolm Falkus, ed.

Muir's Atlas of Ancient and Classical History. London: George Philips, 1982.

Atlas of World History. Rev. ed. Chicago: Rand McNally, 1995. Robert R. Palmer et al., eds.

Atlas of the Greek World. New York: Facts on File, 1982. Peter Levi, comp.

Atlas of the Roman World. New York: Facts on File, 1982. Tim Cornell and John Matthews, comps.

Yearbooks

**Statesman's Yearbook.* New York: St. Martin's Press, 1864–present. This and the following yearbooks provide up-to-date political information, especially of a governmental nature.

Political Handbook of the World. New York: McGraw-Hill, 1927–present. Arthur S. Banks and William Overstreet, eds.

United Nations Statistical Yearbook. New York: United Nations Statistical Office, 1949–present. There is also a *United Nations Demographic Yearbook,* which provides world and national population statistics.

Facts on File. New York: Facts on File, 1940–.

Biography Collections

Biography collections consist of short biographies of well-known persons. They contain a general outline of the milestones and accomplishments of individuals who have made notable contributions to the times in which they lived and/or to posterity. These works are useful as a first step in biographical research on persons central to your topic or as a way of identifying characters peripheral to it. Each collection has different criteria for determining which individuals it includes. Take care to select the biography collection that is most likely to include the type of individual on whom you are seeking information. Some are also available on CD-ROM.

Guides to Biography Collections

*Biography Index: A Cumulative Guide to Biographical Material in Books and Magazines. New York: H. W. Wilson, 1949–present.

*Biography and Genealogy Master Index. 8 vols. Detroit: Gale, 1980. Miranda C. Herbert and Barbara McNeil, eds. Supplements issued annually. Also available on CD-ROM.

Biographical Dictionaries Master Index. Detroit: Gale, 1975–. Dennis La Beau and Gary C. Tarbert, eds.

British and Canadian Biography Collections

*Dictionary of National Biography. Oxford: Oxford University Press, 1908–present. Leslie Stephen and Sidney Lee, eds. A summary of this large multivolume collection can be found in A Concise Dictionary of National Biography, vol. 1, to 1900; vol. 2, 1901–1970.

Who's Who. London: Allen & Unwin, 1849–present. Annual. This volume covers living individuals. For historical research, you must choose a year during which your subject was most active, or preferably use the Who Was Who collection that follows.

Who Was Who. Vol. 1, 1897–1915; vol. 2, 1916–1928; vol. 3, 1929–1940; vol. 4, 1941–1950; vol. 5, 1951–1960; vol. 6, 1961–1970; vol. 7, 1971–1980. A cumulative index for 1897–1980 was published in 1981. (See annotation to Who Was Who in America for further information.)

Canadian Who's Who. 19 vols. Toronto: University of Toronto Press, 1984.

Dictionary of Canadian Biography. Toronto: University of Toronto Press, 1966–present. An index to this multivolume work is listed below.

Dictionary of Canadian Biography: Index. Volumes I to XII, 1000 to 1900. Toronto: University of Toronto Press, 1991.

American Biography Collections

*Dictionary of American Biography. New York: Scribner's, 1928–1958, including supplements. This is the best source for biographies of historical personages of the United States. It includes both American citizens and people who lived much of their lives in this country even if they were not citizens. It lists only individuals who are no longer living. As with most biography collections, the date of original publication is the best key to determining who is included. Most of the original volumes were written between 1928 and 1936. If your subject died after 1928, check the numerous supplements. A one-volume work containing shortened versions of these biographies is published under the title *Concise Dictionary of American Biography*, 3d ed., 1980. An index was published in 1990.

*_Who Was Who in America: Historical Volume, 1607–1896._ Chicago: Marquis Who's Who, 1967. If you are uncertain about your subject's death date, check *Who Was Who Index, 1607–1993.*

*_Who Was Who in America._ Vol. 1, 1897–1942; vol. 2, 1943–1950; vol. 3, 1951–1960; vol. 4, 1961–1968; vol. 5, 1969–1973; vol. 6, 1974–1976; vol. 7, 1977–1981; vol. 8, 1982–1985. Chicago: Marquis Who's Who. The years covered in each volume indicate the dates of death for those included in it. For example, if your subject died in 1945, he or she should be included in volume 2. For individuals who died before 1897, see the preceding citation.

Who's Who in America. Chicago: Marquis Who's Who, 1897–present. This volume covers living individuals. For purposes of historical research, you must obtain the older volumes or, preferably, use the *Who Was Who* collections that follow.

*_Notable American Women 1607–1950: A Bibliographical Dictionary._ 3 vols. Cambridge, Mass.: Harvard University Press, 1971. Edward T. James, ed. Supplemented by: *Notable American Women: The Modern Period.* 1980. This volume includes women who died between 1951 and 1975.

National Cyclopedia of American Biography. Ann Arbor, Mich.: University Microfilms, 1967. Unlike the *Dictionary of American Biography*, this is not an alphabetical listing, but it does have an alphabetical index at the end of each volume. This collection is published in two series: a "Current" series and a "Permanent" series. The Permanent series includes only individuals no longer living at date of publication for the volume in which they were to be included. Although this work was reprinted in 1967, the original volumes of the Permanent series were written in the 1890s. If your subject was living in the twentieth century, consult the Current series, which includes only persons living at date of publication. A cumulative index to both the Permanent and Current series has been published by J. T. White and Co., 1984.

Research Guide to American Historical Biography. New York: Beacham, 1988. Robert Muccigrosso, ed.

Biographical Directory of the American Congress, 1774–1989. Washington, D.C.: Government Printing Office, 1989.

Biographical Directory of the United States Executive Branch, 1774–1989. Westport, Conn.: Greenwood Press, 1990.

Who's Who of American Women. Chicago: Marquis Who's Who, 1958–.

Dictionary of American Negro Biography. New York: W. W. Norton, 1982. Rayford W. Logan and Michael Winston, eds.

Biographical Directory of American Labor. Westport, Conn.: Greenwood Press, 1984. Gary M. Fink, ed.

A Bibliography of American Autobiographies. Madison: University of Wisconsin Press, 1961. Louis Kaplan et al., comps.

American Autobiography, 1945–1980: A Bibliography. Madison: University of Wisconsin Press, 1982.

American Men and Women of Science. New York: Bowker, 1906–present.

Directory of American Scholars. New York: Bowker. American Council of Learned Societies. New York: R. R. Bowker, 1982.

American Diaries: An Annotated Bibliography of Published American Diaries and Journals. Detroit: Gale, 1983–1987.

The Encyclopedia of American Biography. New York: Harper Collins, 1996. John Garraty and Jerome Sternstein, eds.

International Biography Collections

International biography collections list persons of all national origins.

*Current Biography. New York: H. W. Wilson, 1940–present. This covers living persons. Older volumes, however, may list individuals who are now of historical significance. Only useful for historical research for the period since the 1930s. To locate the volume you need, check *Current Biography: Cumulated Index, 1940–1970.*

International Who's Who. London: Europa, 1935–present.

New York Times Obituary Index, 1858–1968, 1969–1980. New York: New York Times, 1970, 1980.

Who's Who in the World. Chicago: Marquis, 1971–present.

The International Dictionary of Women's Biography. New York: Continuum, 1982. Jennifer S. Uglow, ed.

Makers of Nineteenth-Century Culture, 1800–1914. London: Routledge & Kegan Paul, 1982. Justin Wintle, ed.

Makers of Modern Culture. New York: Facts on File, 1981. Justin Wintle, ed.

Biographical Directory of Modern Peace Leaders. Westport, Conn.: Greenwood Press, 1985. Harold Josephson, ed.-in-chief.

National Biography Collections

Most national biography collections deal with contemporary personages. However, such collections may be useful for research into recent history or for obtaining information on the early careers of contemporary figures. Here is a brief selection.

Dictionary of Canadian Biography. Toronto: University of Toronto Press, 1966–present.

Who's Who in Latin America. Chicago: A. N. Marquis, 1946–1951. Percy A. Martin, ed.

Dictionary of African Historical Biography. Berkeley, CA: University of California Press, 1986. Mark R. Lipschultz and R. Kent Rasmusson, eds.

Dictionary of African Biography. New York: Reference Publications, 1977–present. Volumes expected on each African country.

Japan Biographical Encyclopedia and Who's Who. Tokyo: Rengo Press, 1958–present.

Australian Dictionary of Biography. 12 v. Carlton, Victoria: Melbourne University Press, 1966–1991. Douglas Pike et al.

Specialized Biography Collections

A Biographical Dictionary of World War II. New York: St. Martin's Press, 1972. Christopher Tunney, ed.

Biographical Dictionary of World War I. Westport, Conn.: Greenwood Press, 1982. Holger H. Herwig and Heil M. Heyman, eds.

Biographical Encyclopedia of Science and Technology. Garden City, N.Y.: Doubleday, 1982. Isaac Asimov, ed.

Dictionary of Scientific Biography. 16 vols. New York: Scribner's, 1970–1980. Charles C. Gillispie, ed. Includes index.

Newspaper Directories and Indexes

In most cases, the beginning student will have access only to the few newspapers held in the school or local public library. If you determine, however, that a particular newspaper is especially important to you, the best way to locate back issues is to check a newspaper directory. These directories can tell you in which libraries that newspaper can be found and how complete the collection is. Remember, the newspaper directory is useful only if you know the name of the paper for which you are looking. Moreover, unless you have easy access to a large university or public library, most of the newspapers in a directory will be located far from your school. You might be able to obtain the newspapers you need if they are on microfilm or microfiche, but this can take several weeks. In most cases, it is best to limit yourself to the newspaper collections in your nearby libraries. Some newspaper directories and indexes are available on CD-ROM.

Newspaper Directories

American Newspapers, 1821–1936: A Union List of Files Available in the United States and Canada. New York: H. W. Wilson, 1937. Winifred Gerould, ed. Also available on microfilm. Ann Arbor: University Microfilms, 1966.

Newspapers on Microfilm: A Union Check List. Washington, D.C.: Library of Congress, 1963. George Schwegman Jr., ed. This volume is supplemented by *Newspapers in Microform: United States, 1948–1984.*

African Newspapers in Selected American Libraries. Washington, D.C.: Library of Congress, 1965.

Latin American Newspapers in United States Libraries. Austin: University of Texas Press, 1969. Steven M. Charno, ed.

Newspaper Indexes

Once you have access to a particular newspaper, you must determine which issues contain articles on your theme. If your theme is a specific event, then merely check the issues of the newspaper published at the time of or shortly after the event. However, if you are seeking articles about an event that was not confined to a particular day or week (for example, the stock market crash of 1929), then you will have to check newspaper issues covering many weeks or even months. An indispensable aid in such a task is the newspaper index.

If you know the year in which the event occurred, then a newspaper index can tell you the days in that year when a particular paper contained related articles or editorials. The only problem with newspaper indexes is that so few of them exist. If there is no index to the paper you wish to read, check the index of another newspaper. This will tell you the dates on which that newspaper carried articles on your subject. You can then go back to the newspaper in which you were initially interested and read it for those dates. In most cases, you will find what you need.

New York Times Index. New York: New York Times, 1913–present. This is usually the best source for beginning students. Most libraries have files of the *New York Times,* and the index has been extended back to 1851.

New York Daily Tribune Index. New York: Tribune Association, 1841–1907.

Palmer's Index to The Times [of London] *Newspaper,* 1790–1941. London: 1868–1943.

Official Index to The Times [of London]. London: 1907–present.

Christian Science Monitor Index. Corvallis, Oregon: 1960–present. Because this index goes back only to 1960, it is of limited use for historical research.

Periodical Guides and Indexes

Periodical guides describe the location and general content of periodicals. Like newspaper guides, they are most useful if you already know which periodical you need and want to find out where collections of it are located. If the periodical guide lists no library convenient to you, it is best to check into other periodicals.

Periodical Guides

Union List of Serials in Libraries of the United States and Canada. New York: H. W. Wilson, 1943.

Historical Periodicals: An Annotated World List of Historical and Related Serial Publications. Santa Barbara, Cal.: ABC-Clio, 1961. Eric H. Boehm and Lalit Adolphus, eds. This volume is brought up to date by the directory that follows.

Historical Periodicals Directory. Vol. 1, United States and Canada, 1981; vol. 2, Europe (West), 1982; vol. 3, Europe (East), 1982; vol. 4, Africa, Asia, and Latin America, 1983. Santa Barbara, Cal.: ABC-Clio. Eric H. Boehm, Barbara H. Pope, and Marie Ensign, eds.

Ulrich's International Periodicals Directory. New York: Bowker, 1985.

Magazines for Libraries. 8th ed. New York: Bowker, 1995. This guide describes each publication and helps to determine which are best for historical research.

General Periodical Indexes

General periodical indexes list articles that have appeared in periodical publications. Usually organized by subject, they contain all of the articles on a given topic that appeared in the periodicals that are indexed. The periodicals covered by a particular index are usually listed. When you choose an index, be sure that it covers the kind of periodical likely to contain articles on your theme and that these articles are written for a serious or scholarly audience. There are also many electronic databases that index periodicals.

*Historical Abstracts. Santa Barbara, Cal.: ABC-Clio, 1955–present. Part A: Modern History (1450–1914); Part B: The Twentieth Century (1914–present). Eric H. Boehm, ed. This is the best source for articles in history journals. It covers a wide range of subjects. A brief description of each article is included. After 1964, it does not include articles on United States or Canadian history. Also available in database form.

*America: History and Life: A Guide to Periodical Literature. Santa Barbara, Cal.: ABC-Clio, 1965–present. Supplement, 1980. A brief description of each article is included. It covers the United States and Canada. Also available in database form.

*Reader's Guide to Periodical Literature. New York: H. W. Wilson, 1900–present. These volumes cover the twentieth century. Be selective when using them because many of the periodicals included are written for a popular rather than a scholarly audience. However, the magazines listed are valuable as records of popular opinions and interests.

*Nineteenth Century Reader's Guide to Periodical Literature. New York: H. W. Wilson, 1944.

*Public Affairs Information Service Bulletin. New York: P.A.I.S., 1915–present. This work emphasizes periodicals and other publications in the social sciences and includes many government publications.

* The Combined Retrospective Index Set to Journals in History, 1838–1974. Washington, D.C.: Carrollton, 1977. Annadel N. Wile, exec. ed.

*Social Science and Humanities Index. New York: H. W. Wilson, 1907–1973. This is often the best single guide for historical researchers.

Poole's Index to Periodical Literature, 1802–1881. Boston: Houghton Mifflin, 1891. There is a supplement covering 1882–1906.

Social Sciences Index. New York: H. W. Wilson, 1974–present. For the period prior to 1974, see *Social Science and Humanities Index.*

Humanities Index. New York: H. W. Wilson, 1974–present. For the period prior to 1974, see *Social Science and Humanities Index.*

Specialized Periodical Indexes

There are many periodical indexes on specialized topics. If your research takes you into a specialized field, the indexes listed here may be worth looking into.

Agricultural Index; Applied Science and Technology Index; Art Index; Business Periodi-

cals Index; Education Index; Index to Legal Periodicals; Index Medicus; Music Index. These and other indexes are also available in database format.

Some specialized periodical indexes of value in historical research are:

American Historical Review: General Index for Volumes XLI–LXX, 1935–1965. New York: Macmillan, 1965.

Guide to the American Historical Review, 1895–1945. Washington, D.C.: Government Printing Office, 1945. Franklin D. Scott and Elaine Tegler, comps. (This work is found in American Historical Association, *Annual Report for the Year 1944,* Vol. I, pt. 2, pp. 65–292.)

Women's Magazines, 1693–1968. London: Michael Joseph, 1970. Cynthia White, comp.

Hispanic American Periodicals Index. Los Angeles: U.C.L.A. Latin American Center Publications, 1974–. Barbara H. Valk, ed.

Foreign Affairs 50-Year Index: Vols. 1–50, 1922–1972. New York: Council on Foreign Relations, 1973. Robert J. Palmer, comp.

The Pacific Historical Review: A Cumulative Index to Volumes I–XLIII, 1932–1974. Berkeley: University of California Press, 1976. Anne M. Hager and Everett Gordon, comps.

Fifty Year Index: Mississippi Valley Historical Review, 1914–1964. Bloomington, Ind.: Organization of American Historians, 1973. Francis J. Krauskopf, comp.

Index to Economic Journals. American Economic Association, 1886–present. Homewood, Ill.: R. D. Irwin.

Guide to the Hispanic American Historical Review: 1918–1945, 1945–1955. Durham, N.C.: Duke University Press, 1956–1975. Durham N.C.: Duke University Press, 1980. Stanley R. Ross, Wilbur Chaffee, eds.

Index to the Canadian Historical Review. Toronto: University of Toronto Press, 1920–.

Historical Periodicals

Following is a list of some of the best-known historical periodicals published in the United States, Britain, and Canada and written for professional and student researchers. Some of these journals have their own cumulative indexes (like that to the *American Historical Review* listed previously) and thus can be useful places to begin the search for historical material. There are also many highly specialized periodicals in history. For example, most state historical societies publish journals. Be sure to examine periodical indexes that include the journals most closely related to your subject.

United States, British, and Canadian Historical Journals

Agricultural History
American Historical Review

American Jewish History
The American Journal of Legal History
American Quarterly
The Americas
Bulletin of the Institute of Historical Research
Business History Review
Cambridge Historical Journal
Canadian Historical Review
Canadian Journal of History
Central European History
China Quarterly
Comparative Studies in Society and History
Current History
Daedalus
Diplomatic History
Early Medieval History
Economic History Review
Economic Journal
Eighteenth Century Studies
English Historical Review
Ethnohistory
Feminist Studies
Film and History
French Historical Studies
Gender and History
Hispanic American Historical Review
The Historian
Historical Journal
Historical Methods
Historical Research
History
History and Theory
History of Education Quarterly
History of Political Economy
History of Religions
The History Teacher
International Journal of African Historical Studies
International Review of Social History
Irish Historical Studies
Isis
Journal of African History
Journal of American History
Journal of American Studies
Journal of Asian Studies
Journal of Black Studies
Journal of British Studies
Journal of Canadian Studies
Journal of Contemporary History
Journal of the Early Republic
Journal of Ecclesiastical History

Journal of Economic History
Journal of the History of Biology
Journal of the History of Ideas
Journal of Imperial and Commonwealth History
Journal of Interdisciplinary History
Journal of Japanese Studies
Journal of Latin American History
Journal of Modern History
Journal of Near Eastern Studies
Journal of Negro History
Journal of Popular Culture
The Journal of Psychohistory
Journal of Religious History
Journal of Social History
Journal of Southern History
Journal of Sports History
Journal of Women's History
Journal of Urban History
Journal of World History
Labor History
Latin American Research Review
Mid-America
Middle East Review
Oral History Review
Pacific Affairs
Pacific Historical Review
Past and Present
Political Studies
The Public Historian
Renaissance Quarterly
Russian History
Scottish History Review
Slavic Review
Slavic Studies
Social History
Social Science History
Speculum
Transactions of the Royal Historical Society
Western Historical Quarterly
William and Mary Quarterly

Book Review Indexes

In addition to articles, historical periodicals usually contain reviews of recently published books on historical subjects. If you wish to know the content of a particular book or to find out what other historians thought of it, you can look up the reviews of it. The indexes in the following list organize book reviews by author, title, and sometimes by subject. They indicate which periodicals reviewed the book and in what issue. If the index is annual, you will need to know the year of publication of the book in which you are interested. Most books are reviewed within one to two years after publication. Book reviews are also available in electronic format.

Index to Book Reviews in Historical Periodicals. Metuchen, N.J.: Scarecrow, 1974–.

Combined Retrospective Index to Book Reviews in Scholarly Journals, 1886–1974. 15 vols. Arlington, Va.: Carrollton Press, 1982.

Book Review Digest. New York: Wilson, 1905–present. Monthly.

Index to Book Reviews in the Humanities. Detroit: Gale, 1960–present. Annual.

Book Review Digest: Author/Title Index, 1905–1974. 4 vols. New York: Wilson, 1976. Leslie Dunmore-Lieber, ed.

New York Times Book Review Index, 1896–1970. 5 vols. New York: New York Times, 1973.

National Library Service Cumulative Book Review Index, 1905–1974. 6 vols. Princeton: National Library Service Co., 1975.

Book Review Index. Detroit: Gale, 1965–present. Bimonthly.

Book Review Index: A Master Accumulation, 1969–1979. 7 vols. Detroit: Gale, 1980. Gary C. Tarbert, ed.

Government Publications and Public Documents

The works included here are guides to books, pamphlets, speeches, treaties, hearings, reports, and so on, published by public agencies. This list, like most in this appendix, is confined to works in English and is by no means complete. If your research topic is related to governmental affairs at any level, these works can lead you to documents and publications by or about the agencies you are studying. The major publications of the U.S. government are available at many libraries. Some U.S. government documents are also available online.

International Agencies

Guide to League of Nations Publications: A Bibliographical Survey of the Work of the League, 1920–1947. New York: Columbia University Press, 1951. Hans Aufricht, comp.

United Nations Documents Index. New York: United Nations Library, 1950–1977. These volumes are supplemented by *UNDOC: Current Index.*

Foreign Government Publications

Manual of Government Publications, United States and Foreign. New York: Appleton-Century-Crofts, 1950. Everett S. Brown, comp.

Great Britain, Parliament: Parliamentary Debates. London: 1803–present.

United States Government Publications

Introduction to United States Government Information Sources. 5th ed. Englewood: Libraries Unlimited, 1996. Joe Morehead and Mary Fetzer, eds.

New Guide to Popular Government Publications. Littleton, Colo.: Libraries Unlimited, 1978. Walter L. Newsome, ed.

Subject Guide to Major United States Government Publications. Chicago: American Library Association, 1987. William J. Wiley, comp.

Guide to United States Government Publications. McLean, Va.: Documents Index, 1985, John L. Andriot, ed. Cumulative bimonthly supplements.

Monthly Catalogue of United States Government Publications. Washington, D.C.: Government Printing Office, 1895–present.

United States Congressional Committee Hearings Index, 1833–1969. Washington, D.C.: CIS, 1981–.

United States Congressional Committee Prints Index from Earliest Publications through 1969. 5 vols. Washington, D.C.: CIS, 1980.

United States Serial Set Indexes: American State Papers . . . 1789–1969. Washington, D.C.: CIS, 1975.

Subject Guide to United States Reference Sources. Littleton, Colo.: Libraries Unlimited, 1985. Judith Schick Robinson, ed.

Annotated Bibliography of Bibliographies on Selected Government Publications and Supplementary Guides to the Superintendent of Documents Classification System. Kalamazoo, Mich.: Western Michigan University, 1967–1990. Alexander C. Body, ed.

Cumulative Subject Guide to United States Government Bibliographies, 1924–1973. Arlington, Va.: Carrollton Press, 1976. Edna A. Kanely, comp.

United States State and Local Government Publications

State Government Reference Publications: An Annotated Bibliography. Littleton, Colo.: Libraries Unlimited, 1981. David W. Parish, ed.

Bibliography of County Histories in Fifty States in 1961. Baltimore: Genealogical Publishing Company, 1963. Clarence Peterson, ed.

Subject Bibliographies

A subject bibliography lists printed works on a particular topic. The ones listed here are those that the beginning student is most likely to obtain. Emphasis has been placed on bibliographies that (1) are written especially for students, (2) are of recent publication or republication and therefore likely to be in new library collections, (3) contain predominantly or solely works in the English language, and (4) are general rather than specialized. Bibliographies that are especially useful to beginning students are designated by an asterisk (*).[1] (In some instances, helpful sources that are not bibliographies have been included.)

Disciplines Other than History

The following bibliographies list works in fields other than history. If an important aspect of your research topic falls under other major branches of knowledge, then you might find valuable materials in nonhistorical publications.

A Select Bibliography: Asia, Africa, Eastern Europe, Latin America. New York: American University, 1960, plus supplements. These are studies in the social sciences covering the developing countries of the world. For more recent works, see *Cumulative Supplement, 1961–1971* and *1972–1982.*

*Reference Sources in History: An Introductory Guide. Santa Barbara: ABC-Clio, 1990.

Sources of Information in the Social Sciences. Chicago: American Library Association, 1986. William H. Webb, ed.

Sources of Information in the Humanities. 3 vols. Chicago: American Library Association, 1982. John F. Wilson, ed.

The Humanities: A Selective Guide to Information Sources. Englewood, Colo.: Libraries Unlimited, 1994. Ron Blazek and Elizabeth Aversa, eds.

Specialized Branches of History

Encyclopedia of Medical History. New York: McGraw-Hill, 1985. Roderick E. McGrew, ed.

Dictionary of the History of Ideas. New York: Scribner's, 1968–1974. Philip P. Wiener, ed.

History of Psychology: A Guide to Information Sources. Detroit: Gale, 1979. Wayne Viney, Michael Wertheimer, and Marilyn Lou Wertheimer, eds.

ISIS Cumulative Bibliography: A Bibliography of the History of Science from Isis Critical Bibliographies 1–90 (1913–1965). 3 vols. London: History of Science Society, 1971–1975. Magda Whitrow, ed.

Bibliography of the History of Medicine. Bethesda, Md.: National Library of Medicine, 1965–.

New Oxford History of Music. 10 vols. Oxford: Oxford University Press, 1954–1985.

Bibliography of Military History: A Revised, Expanded, and Selected Annotated Listing of Reference Sources. West Point, N.Y.: U.S. Military Academy, 1982.

The Encyclopedia of Military History: From 3500 B.C. to the Present. New York: Harper & Row, 1985. Ernest R. Dupuy and Trevor N. Dupuy, eds.

The Holocaust: An Annotated Bibliography. Haverford, Pa.: Catholic Libraries Association, 1985. Harry James Cargas, ed.

---

[1]If the title of a bibliography indicates that it is annotated, this means that it not only *lists* books on a particular topic but also provides a brief description of their contents.

The New Standard Jewish Encyclopedia. Garden City, N.Y.: Doubleday, 1977. Geoffrey Wigoder, ed.

Psychohistorical Inquiry: A Comprehensive Research Bibliography. New York: Garland, 1984. William J. Gilmore, ed.

History of the Family and Kinship: A Select International Bibliography. Millwood, N.Y.: Kraus International Publications, 1980. Gerald L. Soliday, ed.

Companion Encyclopedia of the History of Medicine. New York: Routledge, 1993.

Encyclopedia of the Holocaust. New York: Macmillan, 1990.

The Cold War, 1945–1991. 3 vols. Detroit: Gale, 1992. Benjamin Frankel, ed.

Dictionary of Concepts in History. New York: Greenwood, 1988. Harry Ritter.

Church History: An Introduction to Research, Reference Works, and Methods. Grand Rapids, Mich.: Wm. B. Erdmans, 1996. James E. Bradley and Richard A. Muller, eds.

General World History

The remainder of this appendix contains the basic source material for historical research — history bibliographies. Once you have chosen your research topic, these bibliographies and the reference collection of your library should be your initial step in finding sources. For the convenience of the beginning student, the list of subject bibliographies is separated according to the chronological period or geographical area that the works cover. The bibliographies themselves break down the topics even further.

Don't expect to find an entire bibliography dedicated to your particular topic. Choose the ones that cover the period or area into which your topic falls. Remember, your library will probably not have all of these books. If the most promising bibliography is not there, try a different work. As with other reference sources, some of these works are available in electronic form.

*American Historical Associations: A Guide to Historical Literature. Oxford: Oxford University Press, 1995. Mary Beth Norton, ed. This work has chapters on all periods and areas, and on many specialized topics.

*Historical Abstracts. Santa Barbara, Cal.: ABC-Clio, 1955–present. Part A: Modern History (1450–1914); Part B: The Twentieth Century (1914–present). Eric H. Boehm, ed. This is the best source for articles in history journals. Also available on CD-ROM.

Books for College Libraries. Chicago: American Library Association, 1988. Melvin Voigt and Joseph Treyz, comps. See volume 3: History. It contains chapters on each geographical area.

*World Historical Fiction Guide. Metuchen, N.J.: Scarecrow Press, 1973. Daniel McGarry and Sarah White, eds. If you are studying historical novels, this is an important source.

Serial Bibliographies and Abstracts in History: An Annotated Guide. Westport, Conn.: Greenwood Press, 1986. David Henige, ed.

Bibliographies in History. Santa Barbara, Cal.: ABC-Clio, 1988.

*Reference Sources in History: An Introductory Guide. Santa Barbara, Cal.: ABC-Clio, 1990. Ronald H. Fritze et al., eds.

World History from Earliest Times to 1800. Oxford: Oxford University Press, 1988. H. Judge, ed.

Encyclopedia of Nationalism. New York: Paragon House, 1990. Louis L. Snyder, ed.

Ancient History

The Encyclopedia of Ancient Civilizations. New York: Mayflower Books, 1980. Arthur Cotterell, ed.

The Cambridge Ancient History. Cambridge: Cambridge University Press, 1923–1939, 1951–1954, 1970–present. This is a multivolume historical work with extensive bibliographies.

Who Was Who in the Greek World, 776 B.C.–30 B.C. Ithaca, N.Y.: Cornell University Press, 1982. Diana Bowder, ed.

Who Was Who in the Roman World, 753 B.C.–A.D. 476. Ithaca, N.Y.: Cornell University Press, 1980. Diana Bowder, ed.

The Oxford History of the Classical World. Oxford: Oxford University Press, 1986. John Boardman et al., eds. An excellent bibliography is included.

The Encyclopedia of Ancient Egypt. New York: Facts on File, 1991. Margaret Bunson, ed.

Civilizations of the Ancient Near East. New York: Scribner's, 1995. Jack S. Sasson, ed.

Civilizations of the Ancient Mediterranean Greece and Rome. New York: Scribner's, 1988. Michael Grant and Paul A. Cimbala, eds.

Medieval History

*A Guide to the Study of Medieval History. New York: F. S. Crofts & Sons, 1931. Louis J. Paetow. This guide is updated in a supplement by Gray C. Boyce, Medieval Academy of America, 1980, and by:

*Literature of Medieval History, 1930–1975. 5 vols. Millwood, N.Y.: Kraus International Publisher, 1981. Gray C. Boyce, ed.

Cambridge Medieval History. Cambridge: Cambridge University Press, 1911–1936.

Who's Who in the Middle Ages. New York: Stein and Day, 1980. John Fines, ed.

Dictionary of the Middle Ages. New York: Scribner's, 1982–1989. Joseph R. Strayer, ed.

The Middle Ages: A Concise Encyclopedia. New York: Thames and Hudson/Norton, 1989. H. R. Loyn, ed.

Atlas of Medieval Europe. New York: Facts on File, 1983. Donald Matthew, comp.

Dictionary of Medieval Civilization. New York: Macmillan, 1984. Joseph Dahmus, ed.

The New Cambridge Medieval History. New York: Cambridge, 1995. Rosamond McKitterick, ed.

Early Modern and Modern European History

*Modern European History, 1494–1789: A Select Bibliography. London: Historical Association of London, 1966. Alun Davies, comp.

*Modern European History, 1789–1945: A Select Bibliography. London: Historical Association of London, 1960. William N. Medlicott, comp.

Cambridge Modern History. Cambridge: Cambridge University Press, 1902–1911; reissued, 1970. These history volumes have large bibliographies. *The New Cambridge Modern History,* however, has no bibliography.

Renaissance Humanism, 1300–1550: A Bibliography of Materials in English. New York: Garland, 1985. Benjamin Kohl, ed.

A Bibliography of Modern History. Cambridge: Cambridge University Press, 1968. John Roach, ed. This bibliography was created to accompany *The New Cambridge Modern History.*

Modern European Imperialism: A Bibliography of Books and Articles, 1815–1972. Boston: G. K. Hall, 1974. John P. Halstead, comp.

Women in Western European History: A Select Chronological, Geographical and Topical Bibliography from Antiquity to the French Revolution. Westport, Conn.: Greenwood Press, 1982. Linda Frey, Marsha Frey, and Joanne Schneider, eds.

Women in Western European History: A Select Chronological, Geographical, and Topical Bibliography: The Nineteenth and Twentieth Centuries. Westport, Conn.: Greenwood Press, 1984. Linda Frey and Marsha Frey, eds.

The Columbia Dictionary of European Political History Since 1914. Berkeley, Cal.: University of California Press, 1992. John Stevenson, gen. ed.

The Oxford Encyclopedia of the Reformation. New York: Oxford, 1996. Hans J. Hillerbrand, ed.

Modern Europe: France, Italy, Spain, Germany, Scandinavia

Historical Dictionary of the French Fourth and Fifth Republics, 1946–1991. Westport, Conn.: Greenwood Press, 1992. Wayne Northcutt, ed.

Dictionary of Modern Italian History. Westport, Conn.: Greenwood Press, 1985. Frank J. Coppa, ed.-in-chief.

Modern Italian History: An Annotated Bibliography. Westport, Conn.: Greenwood Press, 1990. Frank J. Cappa and William Roberts, comps. A companion to *Dictionary of Modern Italian History.*

Historical Dictionary of Modern Spain, 1700–1988. Westport, Conn.: Greenwood Press, 1990. Robert W. Kern, ed.-in-chief.

Nazism, Resistance, and the Holocaust in World War II: A Bibliography. Metuchen, N.J.: Scarecrow Press, 1985. Vera Laska, ed.

Dictionary of Scandinavian History. Westport, Conn.: Greenwood Press, 1986. Byron J. Nordstrom, ed.

Historical Dictionary of Germany. Metuchen, N.J.: Scarecrow, 1994. Wayne C. Thompson, Susan L. Thompson, and Juliet S. Thompson, eds.

France. ABC-Clio, 1990. Frances Chambers, ed.

Scandinavian History: 1520–1970. London: Historical Association, 1984.

British History

British History to 1789

A Bibliography of English History to 1485. Oxford: Clarendon Press, 1975. Edgar B. Graves, ed.

Tudor England, 1485–1603: A Bibliographical Handbook. Cambridge: Cambridge University Press, 1968. Mortimer Levine, comp.

A Bibliography of British History, Stuart Period, 1603–1714. Oxford: Clarendon Press, 1970. Mary Keeler, ed.

Early Modern British History, 1485–1760. London: Historical Association of London, 1970. Helen Miller and Aubrey Newman, comps.

A Bibliography of British History, The Eighteenth Century, 1714–1789. Oxford: Clarendon Press, 1951. Stanley Pargellis and D. J. Medley, eds.

British History Since 1789

British History Since 1760: A Select Bibliography. London: Historical Association of London, 1970. Ian R. Christie, comp.

A Bibliography of British History, 1789–1851. Oxford: Clarendon Press, 1977. Lucy Brown and Ian R. Christie, eds.

A Bibliography of British History, 1914–1989. Oxford: Clarendon Press, 1996. Keith Robbins, ed.

Modern England, 1901–1970: A Bibliographical Handbook. Cambridge: Cambridge University Press, 1976. Alfred F. Havighurst, comp.

British Economic and Social History: A Bibliographical Guide. 3d ed. Manchester: Manchester University Press, 1995. W. H. Chaloner and R. C. Richardson, eds.

A Dictionary of British History. New York: Stein and Day, 1983. J. P. Kenyon, ed.

The Oxford History of England: Consolidated Index. Oxford: Clarendon/Oxford University Press, 1991. Richard Raper, comp.

Victorian Britain: An Encyclopedia. New York: Garland, 1988. Sally Mitchell, ed.

The Cambridge Historical Encyclopedia of Great Britain and Ireland. Cambridge: Cambridge University Press, 1985. Christopher Haigh, ed.

Irish, Scottish, and British Empire History

A Dictionary of Irish History Since 1800. Totawa, N.J.: Barnes & Noble, 1980. D. J. Hickey and J. E. Doherty, eds.

A Bibliography of Works Relating to Scotland, 1916–1950. Edinburgh: Edinburgh University Press, 1959–1960. P. D. Hancock, ed.

Cambridge History of the British Empire. Cambridge: Cambridge University Press, 1929–1959. John Rose, Arthur Newton, and Ernest Benians, comps.

A Chronicle of Irish History Since 1500. Savage, Md.: Rowman and Littlefield, 1990. J. E. Doherty and D. J. Hickey, eds.

East European History

*The Soviet Union and Eastern Europe. New York: Facts on File, 1985. George Schoepflin. This is a general handbook but includes bibliographies.

The American Bibliography of Slavic and East European Studies. Columbus, Ohio: American Association for the Advancement of Slavic Studies, 1957–present.

Junior Slavica: A Selected, Annotated Bibliography of Books in English on Russian and

Eastern Europe. Littleton, Colo.: Libraries Unlimited, 1968. Stephan M. Horak, ed.

Poland's Past and Present: A Select Bibliography of Works in English. Newtonville, Mass.: Oriental Research Partners, 1977. Norman Davies, ed.

Yugoslavia: A Comprehensive English-Language Bibliography. Wilmington, Del.: Scholarly Resources, 1993. Francine Friedman, ed.

Russian History (and USSR)

*A Bibliography of Works in English on Early Russian History to 1800. New York: Barnes & Noble, 1969. Peter A. Crowther, comp.

*Books in English on the Soviet Union, 1917–1973: A Bibliography. New York: Garland, 1975. David L. Jones, comp.

*The Rise and Fall of the Soviet Union: A Selected Bibliography of Sources in English. Westport, Conn.: Greenwood Press, 1992. Abraham J. Edelheit and Hershel Edelheit, eds.

The American Bibliography of Slavic and East European Studies. Columbus, Ohio: American Association for the Advancement of Slavic Studies, 1957–present.

Russia and the Former Soviet Union: A Bibliographic Guide to English Publications, 1986–1991. Englewood: Libraries Unlimited, 1994. Helen F. Sullivan and Robert H. Burger, eds.

An Atlas of Russian History. New Haven, Conn.: Yale University Press, 1970. Allen F. Chew, ed.

The Modern Encyclopedia of Russian and Soviet History. Gulf Breeze, Fla.: Academic International Press, 1976–. Plus supplements.

The Soviet Union: A Biographical Dictionary. New York: Macmillan, 1991. Archie Brown, ed.

Soviet Foreign Policy, 1918–1945: A Guide to Research and Research Materials. Wilmington, Del.: Scholarly Resources, 1991. Robert H. Johnston, ed.

Dictionary of the Russian Revolution. Westport, Conn.: Greenwood Press, 1989. George Jackson, ed.

The Russian Revolution, 1905–1921: A Bibliographic Guide to the Works in English. Westport, Conn.: Greenwood, 1985. Murray Frame, ed.

Ukraine: A Bibliographic Guide to English Language Publications. Englewood, Colo.: Ukranian Academic Press, 1990. Bohdan Wynar, ed.

African History[2]

*An Atlas of African History. New York: Africana Publisher, 1978. J. D. Fage, ed.

Cambridge History of Africa. 8 vols. Cambridge University Press, 1975–1986.

---

[2]For the northern African states that border on the Mediterranean, see Near and Middle Eastern History.

Africa South of the Sahara: A Bibliography for Undergraduate Libraries. Williamsport, Pa.: Bro-Dart, 1971. Peter Duignan, ed.

Africa and the World: An Introduction to the History of Sub-Saharan Africa from Antiquity to 1840. San Francisco: Chandler, 1972. Peter Duignan and Lewis H. Gann, eds.

Historical Dictionary of——. Metuchen, N.J.: Scarecrow Press, 1972–. This is a series of historical dictionaries including separate volumes for most African nations.

Makers of Modern Africa. London: Africa Journal Ltd., 1981.

South African History: A Bibliographic Guide with Special Reference to Territorial Expansion and Colonization. New York: Garland Publishing, 1984. Naomi Musiker, ed.

Dictionary of African Historical Biography. Berkeley: University of California Press, 1986. Mark R. Lipschultz and R. Kent Rasmusson, eds.

African Bibliography. Manchester, Eng.: Manchester University Press, 1984–.

Near and Middle Eastern History

*The Islamic Near East and North Africa: An Annotated Guide to Books in English for Non-Specialists. Littleton, Colo.: Libraries Unlimited, 1977. David W. Littlefield, ed.

*Concise Encyclopedia of Arabic Civilizations. New York: Praeger, 1960–1966. Stephan and Nandy Ronart, eds.

*Books on Asia from the Near East to the Far East: A Guide for General Readers. Toronto: University of Toronto Press, 1981. Eleazir Birnbaum, ed.

Concise Encyclopedia of the Middle East. Washington, D.C.: Public Affairs Press, 1973. Mehdi Heravi, ed.

Middle East and Islam: A Bibliographical Introduction. Geneva: Inter Documentation, 1979. Derek Hopwood and Diana Grimwood-Jones, eds.

Encyclopedia of Islam. Leiden, Netherlands: E. J. Brill, 1960–present. C. E. Botsworth et al., eds.

The Cambridge Encyclopedia of the Middle East and North Africa. Cambridge: Cambridge University Press, 1988. Trevor Mostyn, exec. ed.

The Oxford Dictionary of Byzantium. Oxford: Oxford University Press, 1991. Alexander P. Kazhdan, ed.

Oxford Encyclopedia of the Modern Islamic World. New York: Oxford, 1995. This covers the eighteenth century to the present.

General Asian History

*Encyclopedia of Asian History. New York: Scribner's, 1988. Ainslis T. Embree, ed.

*Books on Asia from the Near East to the Far East: A Guide for General Readers. Toronto: University of Toronto Press, 1971. Eleazir Birnbaum, ed.

Cumulative Bibliography of Asian Studies, 1941–1965, 1966–1970. Boston: G. K. Hall, 1972.

Bibliography of Asian Studies. Ann Arbor, Mich.: Association for Asian Studies, 1941–present.

Historical and Cultural Dictionary of ———. Metuchen, N.J.: Scarecrow Press, 1972–present. This is a series of dictionaries including separate volumes for most Asian nations.

Indian, Pakistani, and Sri Lankan History

*India: A Critical Bibliography. Tucson: University of Arizona Press, 1980. J. Michael Mahar, ed.

*Cambridge History of India. New York: Macmillan, 1922–1953. See bibliography at end of volumes.

*An Historical Atlas of South Asia. Chicago: University of Chicago Press, 1978. Joseph E. Schwartzberg, ed.

A Dictionary of Indian History. New York: Braziller, 1967. Sachchidananda Bhattacharya.

South Asian Civilizations: A Bibliographical Synthesis. Chicago: University of Chicago Press, 1981. Maureen Patterson, ed.

Cambridge Encyclopedia of India, Pakistan, Sri Lanka, Nepal, Bhutan and the Maldives. Cambridge: Cambridge University Press, 1989. Francis Robinson, ed.

Southeast Asian History

*Southeast Asia: A Critical Bibliography. Tucson: University of Arizona Press, 1969. Kennedy G. Tregonning, ed.

Southeast Asia: An Annotated Bibliography. Westport, Conn.: Greenwood Press, 1968. Cecil C. Hobbs, ed.

Vietnam: A Guide to Reference Sources. Boston: G. K. Hall, 1977. Michael Cotter, ed.

The Wars in Vietnam, Cambodia, and Laos, 1945–1982: A Bibliographic Guide. Santa Barbara, Cal.: ABC-Clio, 1984. Richard Dean Burns and Milton Leitenberg, eds.

Vietnam Studies: An Annotated Bibliography. Lanham, Md.: Scarecrow Press, 1997. Carl Singleton, ed.

Chinese History

*China: A Critical Bibliography. Tucson: University of Arizona Press, 1962. Charles O. Hucker, ed.

*Dictionary of Chinese History. London: Frank Cass, 1979. Michael Dillon, ed.

Historical Atlas of China. Chicago: Aldine, 1966. Albert Herrmann, ed.

China and America: A Bibliography of Interactions, Foreign and Domestic. Honolulu: University of Hawaii Press, 1972. James M. McCutcheon, comp.

Chinese History: A Bibliography. New York: Gordon Press, 1978. Leona Rasmussen Phillips, ed.

China Bibliography: A Research Guide to Reference Works about China Past and Present. Kinderhook: E. J. Brill, 1995. Harriet T. Zurndorfer, ed.

Japanese and Korean History

Japan and Korea: A Critical Bibliography. Westport, Conn.: Greenwood Press, 1982. Bernard Silberman, ed.

A Guide to Reference and Research Materials on Korean History: An Annotated Bibliography. Honolulu: East-West Center, 1968. William E. Hentworth, ed.

The Cambridge Dictionary of Japan, Volume 4: Early Modern Japan. Cambridge: Cambridge University Press, 1991. John Whitney Hall, ed.

Japanese History and Culture from Ancient to Modern Times: Seven Basic Bibliographies. New York: Markus Wiener, 1993. John Dower and Timothy George, eds.

Japanese Studies from Pre-History to 1990: A Bibliographical Guide. Manchester, Eng.: Manchester University Press, 1992. Richard Perren, ed.

Japan. Santa Barbara, Cal.: ABC-Clio, 1990. Frank L. Shulman, ed.

Studies on Korea: A Scholar's Guide. Honolulu: University of Hawaii Press, 1980. Han-kyo Kim, ed.

Latin American and Caribbean History

Latin America: A Guide to the Historical Literature. Austin: University of Texas Press, 1971. Charles C. Griffin, ed.

Encyclopedia of Latin American History and Culture. New York: Scribner's, 1995. Barbara Tenenbaum, ed.

A Guide to the History of Brazil, 1500–1822: The Literature in English. Santa Barbara, Cal.: ABC-Clio, 1980. Francis A. Dutra, ed.

Handbook of Latin American Studies. Cambridge, Mass.: Harvard University Press, 1936–1947; and Gainesville: University of Florida Press, 1948–present. Annual volume.

Latin America and the Caribbean: A Bibliographic Guide to Works in English. Coral Gables: University of Miami Press, 1967. Stojan A. Bayitch, ed.

The Complete Caribbeana, 1900–1975: A Bibliographical Guide to the Scholarly Literature. Millwood, New York: KTO Press, 1978. Comitas Lambros, ed.

The Cambridge Encyclopedia of Latin America and the Caribbean. Cambridge: Cambridge University Press, 1992. Simon Collier et al., eds.

Latin America and the Caribbean: A Critical Guide to Research Sources. New York: Greenwood, 1992. Paula H. Covington et al., eds.

Index to Latin American Periodical Literature, 1929–1960. New York: G. K. Hall, 1962. Pan American Union. Updated through 1970 by G. K. Hall, 1980.

Latin America: A Guide to Economic History, 1830–1930. Berkeley: University of California Press, 1977. Stanley Stein and R. Cortés Conde, eds.

Historical Dictionary of ——. Metuchen, N.J.: Scarecrow Press. This is a series of historical dictionaries including separate volumes for most Latin American nations.·

Latin American Politics: A Historical Bibliography. Santa Barbara, Cal.: ABC-Clio, 1986.

Canadian History

Encyclopedia Canadiana. Toronto: Grolier, 1977.

Bibliographia Canadiana. Don Mills, Ont.: Longman Canada Limited, 1973. Claude Thibault, comp.

The Oxford Companion to Canadian History and Literature. Toronto: Oxford University Press, 1967, *Supplement,* 1973. Norah Story, comp.

Canadian Reference Sources: A Select Guide. 2nd ed. Ottawa: Canadian Library Association, 1973, *Supplement,* 1981. Dorothy E. Ryder, ed.

*Canada Since 1867: A Bibliographical Guide. Toronto: Samuel Stevens, 1977. J. L. Granatstein and Paul Stevens, eds.

Western Canada Since 1870: A Select Bibliography and Guide. Vancouver: University of British Columbia Press, 1978. Alan F. J. Artibise, ed.

Bibliography of Ontario History, 1867–1976: Cultural, Economic, Political and Social. 2 vols. Buffalo: University of Toronto Press, 1980. Olga B. Bishop, ed.

Economic History of Canada: A Guide for Information Sources. Detroit: Gale, 1978. Trevor J. O. Dick, ed.

Canadian Urban History: A Select Bibliography. Sudbury: Laurentian University Press, 1972. Gilbert A. Stelter, ed.

Historical Atlas of Canada. Toronto: University of Toronto Press, 1987. R. Cole Harris and Donald Kerr, eds.

The Canadian Encyclopedia. Edmonton: Hurtig, 1985. James H. March, ed.-in-chief.

United States History

In the case of U.S. history, the bibliographies have been arranged by certain topics of special interest to students.

Many of this first group of bibliographies have separate chapters on specialized topics.

*Harvard Guide to American History. Rev. ed. Cambridge, Mass.: Harvard University Press, 1979. Oscar Handlin et al., eds. Chapters six through thirty contain detailed reading lists for many periods and topics in U.S. history.

*The Reader's Companion to American History. Boston, Mass.: Houghton Mifflin, 1991. Eric Foner and John A. Garraty, eds.

*The American Historical Association's Guide to Historical Literature. Ithaca: Cornell University Press, 1995. Mary Beth Norton, ed. Third Edition, 2 vols. This guide contains a large section on U.S. history.

*Writings on American History. Washington, D.C.: American Historical Association, 1956; and Millwood, N.Y.: KTO Press, 1976–present. The original series of volumes covers (with two brief lapses) books and articles written between 1902 and 1961. The new series is now annual and covers only articles written since 1962. Coverage of books is continued in:

*Writings on American History, 1962–1973: A Subject Bibliography of Books and Monographs. 10 vols. White Plains, N.Y.: Kraus International Publications, 1985. James R. Masterson, comp.

*Writings on American History, 1962–1973: A Subject Bibliography of Articles. 4 vols. Millwood, N.Y.: KTO Press, 1976. James J. Dougherty, ed. This work is continued in:

*Writings on American History: A Subject Bibliography of Articles. 1974–1990.

*America: History and Life. Santa Barbara, Cal.: ABC-Clio, 1954–present. After 1965, titled *America: History and Life: A Guide to Periodical Literature.* Each volume now has four parts: (1) abstracts of journal articles, (2) an index to

book reviews, (3) a bibliography of articles and dissertations and (4) an annual index. The best source for articles on U.S. history. Also on CD-ROM.

Encyclopedia of American History. New York: Harper & Row, 1982. Richard B. Morris, ed.

Concise Dictionary of American History. New York: Scribner's, 1983. David W. Voorhees, ed. This is an abridgement of the eight-volume *Dictionary of American History.*

The Encyclopedia of Colonial and Revolutionary America. New York: Facts on File, 1989. John Faragher, ed.

Handbook for Research in American History: A Guide to Bibliographies and Other Reference Works. 1994. 2d ed. Lincoln: University of Nebraska Press, Francis Paul Prucha, ed.

A Bibliography of American Autobiographies. Madison: University of Wisconsin Press, 1961. Louis Kaplan et al., comps. An important source if you are researching the life of a historical figure.

American Autobiography, 1945–1980: A Bibliography. Madison: University of Wisconsin, 1982. Mary Louise Briscoe, ed. Companion to Kaplan's *Bibliography.*

Dictionary of American History. New York: Scribner's, 1942–1961. James T. Adams and Roy V. Coleman, eds. Revised, 1976. Supplement, 1996.

Encyclopedia of American Political History: Studies of the Principal Movements and Ideas. 3 vols. New York: Scribner's, 1984. Jack P. Greene, ed.

Recently Published Articles. Washington, D.C.: American Historical Association, 1976–1990.

A Guide to the Study of the United States of America. Washington, D.C.: Library of Congress, 1960. Supplement, 1976. This work covers all fields of knowledge. It has several chapters on aspects of U.S. history.

For sources on the United States government, see "United States Government Publications" on page 151.

Regional, State, County, and Local United States History

The sources listed here can be supplemented by the appropriate sections of the *Harvard Guide to American History, Writings on American History,* and *America: History and Life.*

Directory of Historical Organizations in the United States and Canada, 1990. Nashville: American Association for State and Local History, 1990. Mary Bray Wheeler, comp. This volume includes the addresses of state and local historical societies.

Directory of State and Local History Periodicals. Chicago: American Library Association, 1977. Milton Crouch and Hans Raum, comps.

A Bibliography of American County Histories. Baltimore: Genealogical Publishing Co., 1985. P. William Filby.

State Censuses: An Annotated Bibliography to Censuses of Population Taken after 1790 by States and Territories of the United States. New York: Burt Franklin, 1969. Henry J. Dubester, ed.

The Encyclopedia of Southern History. Baton Rouge: Louisiana State University, 1979. David C. Roller, ed.

The Frontier and the American West. Northbrook, Ill.: AHM Publishing, 1976. Rodman W. Paul and Richard W. Etulain, comps.

The Old South. Northbrook, Ill.: AHM Publishing, 1980. Fletcher M. Greene and J. Isaac Copeland, comps.

Encyclopedia of Southern Culture. Chapel Hill, N.C.: University of North Carolina Press, 1989. Charles Reagan Wilson and William Ferris, eds.

Localized History Series. New York: Teachers College Press, 1965–1971. Clifford L. Lord, ed. A multivolume series; each volume contains a bibliography of works on a separate state, region, city, or ethnic group.

United States Local Histories in the Library of Congress: A Bibliography. Baltimore: Magna Carta, 1975. Marion J. Kaminkow, ed.

Consolidated Bibliography of County Histories in Fifty States in 1961. Baltimore: Genealogical Publishing Co., 1963. Clarence Peterson, ed.

Genealogical and Local History Books in Print. Washington, D.C.: Genealogical Books in Print, 1985.

Encyclopedia of the American West. New York: Simon and Schuster/Macmillan, 1996.

Encyclopedia of the Confederacy. New York: Scribner's, 1993. Richard N. Current, ed.

Specific Periods

Though now somewhat out of date, the best bibliographies for the study of specific periods of United States history are the Goldentree Series published by Harlan Davidson, Inc., Arlington Heights, Illinois. The relevant items in this series, in chronological order, are listed below.

The American Colonies in the Seventeenth Century (1971). Alden T. Vaughan, comp.

The American Colonies in the Eighteenth Century, 1689–1763 (1969). Jack P. Greene, comp.

The American Revolution (1973). John Shy, comp.

Confederation, Constitution and Early National Period, 1781–1815 (1975). E. James Ferguson, comp.

The Era of Good Feeling and the Age of Jackson, 1816–1841 (1979). Edwin A. Miles and Robert Remini, comps.

Manifest Destiny and the Coming of the Civil War, 1841–1860 (1970). Don E. Fehrenbacher comp.

The Nation in Crisis, 1861–1877 (1969). David Donald, comp.

The Gilded Age, 1877–1896 (1973). Vincent P. DeSantis, comp.

The Progressive Era and the Great War, 1896–1920 (1978). Arthur S. Link and W. M. Leary, Jr., comps.

The New Era and the New Deal, 1920–1940 (1981). Robert E. Burke and Richard Lowitt, comps.

The Second World War and the Atomic Age, 1940–1973 (1975). E. David Cronon and Theodore B. Rosenof, comps.

Encyclopedia of the United States in the Twentieth Century. 4 vols. New York: Scribner's, 1996. Stanley Kutler, ed.

Encyclopedia of the North American Colonies. New York: Scribner's, 1993. Jacob E. Cooke, ed.

Diplomatic History

*Foreign Affairs Bibliography: A Selected and Annotated List of Books on International Relations [1919–present]. New York: Harper & Row, 1933, 1943, 1953; and R. R. Bowker, 1964. Vol. 1 covers 1919–1932; vol. 2, 1932–1942; vol. 3, 1942–1952; vol. 4, 1952–1962; vol. 5, 1962–1972.

*Foreign Relations of the United States. Washington, D.C.: Government Printing Office, 1861–present. United States Department of State. These volumes are issued annually and contain actual diplomatic correspondence. These are *primary* sources rather than bibliographies. They are listed because many libraries have them.

*Guide to American Foreign Relations Since 1700. Santa Barbara, Cal.: ABC-Clio, 1983. Richard Dean Burns, ed.

*Writing About Vietnam: A Bibliography of the Literature of the Vietnam Conflict. Boston, Mass.: G. K. Hall, 1989. Sandra M. Wittman, ed.

*Encyclopedia of United States Foreign Relations. Oxford: Oxford University Press, 1997. Bruce Jentleson and Thomas Patterson, eds.

*Cambridge History of American Foreign Relations. 4 vols. New York: Cambridge University Press, 1995. Bradford Perkins et al., eds. Also available on CD-ROM.

Guide to the Diplomatic History of the United States, 1775–1921. Washington, D.C.: Government Printing Office, 1935. Samuel F. Bemis and Grace G. Griffin, eds. Reprinted, 1959.

A Bibliography of United States–Latin American Relations Since 1810. Lincoln: University of Nebraska Press, 1968. David F. Trask et al., eds. *Supplement,* 1979.

American Diplomatic History Before 1900. Northbrook, Ill.: AHM Publishing, 1978. Norman A. Graebner.

American Diplomatic History Since 1890. Northbrook, Ill.: AHM Publishing, 1975. Wilton B. Fowler, comp.

Dictionary of American Diplomatic History. Westport, Conn.: Greenwood Press, 1989. John E. Findling, ed.

Encyclopedia of American Foreign Policy: Studies of the Principal Movements and Ideas. 3 vols. New York: Scribner's, 1978. Alex DeConde, ed.

Origins, Evolution and Nature of the Cold War: An Annotated Bibliography. Santa Barbara, Cal.: ABC-Clio, 1985. J. L. Black, ed.

Labor History

*Labor in America: A Historical Bibliography. Santa Barbara, Cal.: ABC-Clio, 1985.

*American Working Class History: A Representative Bibliography. New York: R. R. Bowker, 1983. Maurice Neufeld, Daniel J. Leab, and Dorothy Swanson.

Biographical Dictionary of American Labor, rev. ed. Westport, Conn.: Greenwood Press, 1984. Gary Fink, ed.

Labor Unions. Westport, Conn.: Greenwood Press, 1977. Gary M. Fink, ed. Contains a brief history and bibliography for each major union.

American Labor History and Comparative Labor Movements. Tuscon: University of Arizona Press, 1973. James C. McBrearty, comp.

Business and Economic History

American Economic History Before 1860. Northbrook, Ill.: AHM Publishing, 1969. George R. Taylor, comp.

American Economic History Since 1860. Northbrook, Ill.: AHM Publishing, 1971. Edward C. Kirkland, comp.

The Economic History of the United States Prior to 1860: An Annotated Bibliography. Santa Barbara, Cal.: ABC-Clio, 1976. Thomas Orsagh et al., eds.

Biographical Dictionary of American Business Leaders. 4 vols. Westport, Conn.: Greenwood Press, 1983. John Ingham, ed.

American Economic History: A Guide to Information Sources. Detroit: Gale, 1980. William K. Hutchinson, ed.

American Economic History: An Annotated Bibliography. Englewood Cliffs: Salem Press, 1994.

Encyclopedia of American Economic History. 3 vols. New York: Scribner's, 1980. Glen Porter, ed.

Dictionary of United States Economic History. Westport, Conn.: Greenwood Press, 1992. James S. Olson, ed.

African American History

The Negro in America: A Bibliography. Cambridge, Mass.: Harvard University Press, 1970. Elizabeth W. Miller, comp.

A Bibliographic History of Blacks in America Since 1528. New York: McKay, 1971. Edgar A. Toppin, ed.

Blacks in America: Bibliographical Essays. Garden City, N.Y.: Doubleday, 1971. James M. McPherson et al.

The Black Family in the United States: A Selected Bibliography of Annotated Books, Articles, and Dissertations on Black Families in America. Westport, Conn.: Greenwood Press, 1978. Lenwood G. Davis, ed.

Black History Viewpoints: A Selected Bibliographical Guide to Resources for Afro-American and African History. Westport, Conn.: African Bibliographic Center, 1969.

Encyclopedia of Black America. New York: McGraw-Hill, 1981. Augustus Low, ed.

Afro-American History: A Bibliography. Santa Barbara, Cal.: ABC-Clio, 1981. Dwight L. Smith, ed.

Dictionary of American Negro Biography. New York: W. W. Norton, 1982. Rayford W. Logan and Michael Winston, eds.

Dictionary of Afro-American Slavery. New York: Greenwood Press, 1988.

Black Women in America: An Historical Encyclopedia. Brooklyn: Carlson, 1993.

Encyclopedia of African-American Culture and History. New York: Simon and Schuster/Macmillan, 1996. Jack Salzman, David L. Smith and Cornel West, eds.

Mexican American History

*The Mexican American: A Selected and Annotated Bibliography. Stanford, Cal.: Stanford University Press, 1971. Luis G. Nogales, ed.

*A Bibliography for Chicano History. Westport, Conn.: Greenwood Press, 1984. Matt S. Meier and Feliciano Rivera, comps.

*Bibliography of Mexican-American History. Westport, Conn.: Greenwood Press, 1984. Matt S. Meier, comp.

Reference Materials on Mexican Americans: An Annotated Bibliography. Metuchen, N.J.: Scarecrow Press, 1976. Richard P. Woods, ed.

Dictionary of Mexican American History. Westport, Conn.: Greenwood Press, 1981. Matt Meier and Feliciano Rivera, eds.

Puerto Rican History

*Puerto Ricans on the United States Mainland. Totowa, N.J.: Rowman and Little-field, 1972. Francesco Cordasco, ed.

*The Puerto Ricans: An Annotated Bibliography. New York: Bowker, 1973. Paquita Vivó, ed.

*An Annotated, Selected Puerto Rican Bibliography. New York: Columbia University Press, 1972. Enrique R. Bravo, comp.

The Puerto Ricans 1493–1973: A Chronology and Fact Book. Dobbs Ferry, N.Y.: Oceana, 1973. Francesco Cordasco, ed.

Historical Dictionary of Puerto Rico and the United States Virgin Islands. Metuchen, N.J.: Scarecrow Press, 1973. Kenneth Farr, comp.

Women's History

*Notable American Women, 1607–1950: A Biographical Dictionary. Cambridge, Mass.: Harvard University Press, 1971. Edward T. James, ed. 3 vols. Supplemented by Notable American Women: The Modern Period. 1980. This volume includes women who died between 1951 and 1975.

The American Woman in Colonial and Revolutionary Times, 1565–1800: A Syllabus with Bibliography. Westport, Conn.: Greenwood Press, 1975. Eugenie Leonard et al.

Women's Magazines, 1693–1968. London: Michael Joseph, 1970. Cynthia White, comp.

The Female Experience in Eighteenth- and Nineteenth-Century America: A Guide to the History of American Women. New York: Garland, 1982. Jill Conway, ed.

The Female Experience in Twentieth-Century America: A Guide to the History of American Women. New York: Garland, 1986. Jill Conway, ed.

Women in American History: A Bibliography. Santa Barbara, Cal.: ABC-Clio, 1979. Cynthia E. Harrison, ed.

Women's Studies Encyclopedia: History, Philosophy, and Religion. Vol. III. Westport, Conn.: Greenwood Press, 1991. Helen Tierney, ed.

Handbook of American Women's History. New York: Garland, 1990. Angela Howard Zophy, ed.

General Immigrant and Ethnic History

General immigrant and ethnic history bibliographies are the best to use if you are researching the history of a minority group not listed separately in this appendix or if you are unsure which group you wish to study.

Minority Studies: A Select Annotated Bibliography. Boston: G. K. Hall, 1975. Priscilla Oaks, ed.

A Handbook of American Minorities. New York: New York University Press, 1976. Wayne C. Miller.

Harvard Encyclopedia of American Ethnic Groups. Cambridge: Harvard University Press, 1980. Stephen Thernstrom, ed.

A Comprehensive Bibliography for the Study of American Minorities. 2 vols. New York: New York University Press, 1976. Wayne C. Miller.

Encyclopedic Dictionary of Ethnic Newspapers and Periodicals in the United States. Littleton, Colo.: Libraries Unlimited, 1972. Lubomyr S. Wynar, ed.

Immigration and Ethnicity: A Guide to Information Sources. Detroit: Gale, 1977. John D. Buenker and Nicholas C. Burckel, eds.

Dictionary of American Immigrant History. Metuchen, N.J.: Scarecrow Press, 1990. Francesco Cordasco, ed.

European Immigrant and Ethnic History

European Immigration and Ethnicity in the United States and Canada: A Bibliography. Santa Barbara, Cal.: ABC-Clio, 1983. David L. Brye, ed.

German American History and Life: A Guide to Information Sources. Detroit: Gale, 1980. Michael Kereztesi and Gary Cocozzoli, eds.

Hungarians in the United States and Canada: A Bibliography. Minneapolis: Immigration History Research Center, 1977. Joseph Szeplaki, ed.

The British in America 1578–1970: A Chronology and Fact Book. Dobbs Ferry, N.Y.: Oceana, 1972. Howard B. Furer, ed. Volume covers the English, Scotch, Welsh, and Scotch-Irish.

The ——— in America: A Chronology and Fact Book. Dobbs Ferry, N.Y.: Oceana, 1971–present. This is a series with separate volumes on the Germans, Scandinavians, Italians, Poles, Dutch, Jews, Hungarians, and others.

Italian Americans: A Guide to Information Sources. Detroit: Gale, 1978. Francesco Cordasco, ed.

Asian Immigrant and Ethnic History

Asian American Studies: An Annotated Bibliography and Research Guide. Westport, Conn.: Greenwood Press, 1989. Hyung-Chan Kim, ed.

Asians in America: A Selected, Annotated Bibliography. Berkeley: University of California Press, 1983. Isao Fujimoto, ed.

Asian Americans: An Annotated Bibliography for Public Libraries. Chicago: American Library Association, 1977.

Dictionary of Asian American History. Westport, Conn.: Greenwood Press, 1986. Hyung-Chan Kim, ed.

Native American History

*A Bibliographical Guide to the History of Indian-White Relations in the United States. Chicago: University of Chicago Press, 1977. Francis Paul Prucha, ed. Continued in:

*Indian-White Relations in the United States: A Bibliography of Works Published 1975–1980. Lincoln: University of Nebraska Press, 1982. Francis Paul Prucha, ed.

*Indians of North America: Methods and Sources for Library Research. Hamden, Conn.: Library Professional Pubs., 1983. Marilyn L. Haas, ed.

*Indians of the United States and Canada: A Bibliography. Santa Barbara, Cal.: ABC-Clio, 1974. Dwight L. Smith, ed.

Handbook of American Indians North of Mexico. New York: Rowman and Littlefield, 1979. Frederick W. Hodge et al. This is a reprint of a 1910 work.

Encyclopedia of Native American Tribes. New York: Facts on File, 1988. Carl Waldman, ed.

Native American Periodicals and Newspapers, 1828–1982: Bibliography, Publishing Record, and Holdings. Westport, Conn.: Greenwood Press, 1984. Maureen Hardy, comp.

Ethnographic Bibliography of North America. 5 vols. New Haven, Conn.: HRAF Press, 1975. George P. Murdock and Timothy J. O'Leary, eds.

Handbook of North American Indians. Washington, D.C.: Smithsonian Institution, 1978–present. William C. Sturtevant, gen. ed. Published yearly. Twenty volumes projected.

Guide to Research on North American Indians. Chicago: American Library Association, 1983. Arlene B. Hirschfelder et al., eds.

Cambridge History of the Native Peoples of the Americas. Vol. 1. New York: Cambridge University Press, 1997. Bruce Triggas and Wilcomb Washburn, eds.

Social, Cultural, Intellectual, and Religious History

*Social Reform and Reaction in America: An Annotated Bibliography. Santa Barbara, Cal.: ABC-Clio, 1984.

Social History of the United States: A Guide to Information Sources. Detroit: Gale, 1979. D. Tingley, ed.

American Social History Before 1860. Northbrook, Ill.: AHM Publishing, 1970. Gerald N. Grob, comp.

American Social History Since 1860. Northbrook, Ill.: AHM Publishing, 1970. Robert H. Bremner, comp.

Encyclopedia of American Social History. New York: Scribner's, 1993. Mary K. Cayton, Elliott J. Gorn, Peter W. Williams, eds.

A Dictionary of American Social Change. Malabar, Fla.: Kreiger Publishing Company, 1982. Louis Filler.

Urban America: A Historical Bibliography. Santa Barbara, Cal.: ABC-Clio, 1983. Neil L. Shumsky and Timothy Crimmins, eds.

Urban History. Detroit: Gale, 1981. John D. Buenker, ed.

United States Cultural History: A Guide to Information Sources. Detroit: Gale, 1980. Philip I. Mitterling.

Religion in American Life. Northbrook, Ill.: AHM Publishing, 1971. Nelson R. Burr, comp.

Encyclopedia of the American Religious Experience. New York: Scribner's, 1988.

A Companion to American Thought. Oxford: Blackwell, 1995. Richard W. Fox and James T. Kloppenberg, eds.

Constitutional, Legal, and Military History

A Selected Bibliography of American Constitutional History. Santa Barbara, Cal.: ABC-Clio, 1975. Stephen M. Millett.

The Literature of American Legal History. New York: Oceana Pubs., 1985. William E. Nelson and John P. Reid.

Encyclopedia of the American Judicial System. New York: Scribner's, 1987. Robert J. Janosik, ed.

Encyclopedia of the American Constitution. New York: Macmillan, 1986. *Supplement,* 1992. Leonard Levy, ed.-in-chief.

Reference Guide to United States Military History, 1607–1815. New York: Facts on File, 1991. Charles R. Shrader, ed.

The Blackwell Encyclopedia of the American Revolution. Cambridge, Mass.: Basil Blackwell, 1991. Jack P. Greene and J. R. Pole, eds.

Dictionary of the Vietnam War. Westport, Conn.: Greenwood Press, 1988. James S. Olson, ed.

Guide to the Sources of United States Military History. Hamden, Conn.: Archon Books, 1975. Robin Higham. Supplements, 1981, 1993.

Bibliographic Guide to the Two World Wars. New York: Bowker, 1977. Gywn M. Bayliss, ed.

Political History

Political Parties and Elections in the United States: An Encyclopedia. 2 vols. New York: Garland, 1991. L. Sandy Maisel, gen. ed.

Guide to the Presidency. Washington, D.C.: Congressional Quarterly, 1989. Michael Nelson, ed.

Guide to United States Elections. Washington, D.C.: Congressional Quarterly, 1985. John L. Moore, ed.

The American Presidency: A Historical Bibliography. Santa Barbara, Cal.: ABC-Clio, 1984.

Herbert Hoover: A Bibliography of His Times and Presidency. Wilmington, Del.: Scholarly Resources, 1991. Richard D. Burns, comp.

Dwight D. Eisenhower: A Bibliography of His Times and Presidency. Wilmington, Del.: Scholarly Resources, 1991. R. Alton Lee, comp.

Encyclopedia of the American Left. Urbana, Ill.: University of Illinois Press, 1992. Mari Jo Buhle, ed.

Historical Dictionary of the Progressive Era, 1890–1920. Westport, Conn.: Greenwood Press, 1988. John D. Buenker, ed.

American Reform and Reformers: A Biographical Dictionary. Westport, Conn.: Greenwood Press, 1996. Randall M. Miller and Paul A. Cimbala, eds.

Encyclopedia of the American Congress. New York: Simon and Schuster, 1995.

Encyclopedia of the American Presidency. New York: Simon and Schuster, 1994.

Miscellaneous Topics in United States History

Dickinson's American Historical Fiction. Metuchen, N.J.: Scarecrow Press, 1986. Virginia B. Gerhardstein.

American Family History: A Historical Bibliography. Santa Barbara, Cal.: ABC-Clio, 1984.

Biographical Dictionary of American Sports. Westport, Conn.: Greenwood Press, 1987–1989. David L. Porter, ed.

Bibliography of North American Folklore and Folksong. New York: Dover Publications, 1961. Charles Haywood, ed.

Encyclopedia of American Agricultural History. Westport, Conn.: Greenwood Press, 1975. Edwin I. Schapsmeier and Frederick H. Schapsmeier.

A Subject Bibliography of the History of American Higher Education. Westport, Conn.: Greenwood Press, 1984. Mark Beach, comp.

Nuclear America: A Historical Bibliography. Santa Barbara, Cal.: ABC-Clio, 1984.

The History of Science and Technology in the United States: A Critical and Selective Bibliography. New York: Garland, 1982. Marc Rothenberg, ed.

The Craft of Public History: An Annotated Select Bibliography. Westport, Conn.: Greenwood Press, 1983. David F. Trask and Robert W. Pomeroy III.

Sources for Historical Statistics

World Statistical Data

Historical Tables, 58 B.C.–A.D. 1978. New York: St. Martin's Press, 1979. Sigfrid H. Steinberg.

Statistics Sources. Detroit: Gale, 1982. Paul Wasserman and Jacqueline Bernero.

The International Almanac of Electoral History. Washington, D.C.: Congressional Quarterly, 1991. Thomas Mackie and Richard Rose.

Demographic Yearbook. New York: United Nations Statistical Office, 1949–present. Annual.

Population Index. Princeton, N.J.: Office of Population Research, 1935–present.

Statistical Yearbook. New York: United Nations Statistical Office, 1949–present.

European Statistical Data

European Political Facts, 1918–1990. 3d. ed. New York: St. Martin's Press, 1992. Christopher Cook and John Paxton.

The Gallup International Public Opinion Polls. [France: 1939, 1944–1975] New York: Random House, 1976. George H. Gallup.

International Historical Statistics: Europe, 1750–1988. New York: Stockton Press, 1996. B. R. Mitchell, ed.

African, Asian, Latin American, and Middle Eastern Statistical Data

Statistical Abstract of Latin America. Los Angeles: U.C.L.A. Center of Latin American Studies, 1973–present. James W. Wilkie, ed.

The Arab World, Turkey and the Balkans, 1878–1914: A Handbook of Historical Statistics. Boston, Mass.: G. K. Hall, 1982. Justin McCarthy, ed.

International Historical Statistics: The Americas. New York: Stockton Press, 1996. B. R. Mitchell, ed.

International Historical Statistics: Africa, Asia and Oceania. 1750–1988. New York: Stockton Press, 1996. B. R. Mitchell, ed.

British Statistical Data

*Abstract of British Historical Statistics. Cambridge: Cambridge University Press, 1976. B. R. Mitchell.

National Income, Expenditures and Output of the United Kingdom, 1855–1965. Cambridge: Cambridge University Press, 1972. C. H. Feinstein.

Annual Abstract of Statistics. London: Central Statistical Office of Great Britain, 1915/1928–present.

British Labour Statistics: Historical Abstract, 1886–1968. London: Great Britain Department of Employment and Productivity, 1971.

The British Voter: An Atlas and Survey Since 1885. London: Batsford, 1981. M. Kinnear.

British Political Facts, 1900–1979. New York: St. Martin's Press, 1980. David Butler and Ann Sloman.

The Gallup International Public Opinion Polls. [Britain, 1937–1975] New York: Random House, 1976. George H. Gallup.

British Historical Statistics. Cambridge: Cambridge University Press, 1988. B. R. Mitchell, ed.

United States and Canadian Statistical Data

*Historical Statistics of the United States, Colonial Times to 1970. Washington, D.C.: Bureau of the Census, 1976. Also available on CD-ROM.

*Statistical Abstract of the United States. Washington, D.C.: Government Printing Office, 1878–present. Annual.

*Historical Statistics of Canada. Ottawa: Statistics Canada, 1983. M. C. Urquhart.

Bureau of the Census Catalog of Publications, 1790–1972. Washington, D.C.: Bureau of the Census, 1974.

American Statistics Index . . . . : A Complete Guide and Index to the Statistical Publications of the United States Government. Washington, D.C.: Congressional Information Service, 1973–present.

Federal Population Censuses 1790–1890: A Catalogue of Microfilm Copies of the Schedules. Washington, D.C.: National Archives Trust Fund Board, 1979. Catalogs of the 1900 and 1910 censuses were published in 1978 and 1982.

The Gallup Poll. New York: Random House and Scholarly Resources, 1935–present. George H. Gallup.

Guides to Photographs, Microfilms, Microforms, Movies, Recordings, and Oral History

Guide to Microforms in Print: Author, Title. Westport, Conn.: Meckler, 1985. Annual since 1961. Also see:

Guide to Microforms in Print: Subject. Westport, Conn.: Meckler, 1985. Annual since 1961. Now published by K. G. Saur Verlag, Munich.

Catalogue of National Archives Microfilm Publications. Washington, D.C.: N.A.R.S., 1974–present.

List of National Archives Microfilm Publications, 1947–1974. Washington, D.C.: National Archives and Records Service, 1974. Supplemented by:

Supplementary List of National Archives Publications, 1974–1982. Washington, D.C.: N.A.R.S., 1982.

Subject Guide to Microforms in Print. Washington, D.C.: Microcard Editions, 1962–present. Albert J. Diaz, ed.

Audiovisual Materials (1979–1982). Washington D.C.: Library of Congress, 1979–1982.

Library of Congress Catalogue: Music and Phonorecords. Washington, D.C.: Library of Congress, 1953–present. Annual.

The Oral History Collection of Columbia University. New York: Columbia University Oral History Research Office, 1979. Elizabeth Mason and Louis M. Starr.

Oral History in the United States: A Directory. New York: Oral History Association, 1971. Gary L. Shumway, comp. Locates and describes oral history collections.

Oral History Index: An International Directory of Oral History Interviews. London: Meckler, 1990.

Picture Sources. New York: Special Libraries Association, 1983. Ernest H. Robl, ed.

Microform Research Collections. Meckler, 1984, 2d ed. Suzanne Cates Dodson, ed.

Pamphlets in American History: A Bibliographical Guide to the Microfilm Collections. 4 vols. Sanford, N.C.: Microfilming Corp. of America, 1979–1983.

Newspapers on Microfilm: United States, 1948–1983. Washington, D.C.: Library of Congress, 1984.

Directory of Oral History Collections. Phoenix: Oryx, 1988. Allen Smith, ed.

Guides to Dissertations, Archives, and Manuscripts

Dissertation Abstracts International. Ann Arbor, Mich.: University Microfilms, 1938–present. Annual.

A Guide to Archives and Manuscripts in the United States. New Haven, Conn.: Yale University Press, 1965. Philip C. Hamer, ed.

Directory of Archives and Manuscript Repositories in the United States. Phoenix: Oryx, 1988. This volume updates Hamer.

Guides to Archives and Manuscript Collections in the United States: An Annotated Bibliography. Westport: Greenwood, 1994. Donald L. De Witt, ed.

The National Union Catalog of Manuscript Collections. Washington, D.C.: Library of Congress, 1962.

Electronic Reference Sources

Some of the Internet sites listed below include electronic addresses or URLs. Keep in mind that URLs often change. Those listed here may not be current when you do your research. If you cannot find the site at the URL given here, search by the name of the site using a search engine. If you are not an experienced "surfer" be sure to ask the reference librarian for assistance.

Web Sites (For Historians)

Organization of American Historians. A gateway to many history sites.
<http://www.indiana.edu/~OAH/LINKS/HTML>

The University of Kansas Virtual Library for Historians. A searchable list of over one thousand Internet sites.
<http://www.ukans.edu/history>

The Library of Congress. A complex site with access to a variety of databases organized by the largest library in the world; includes *American Memory,* a selection of primary documents.
<http//lcweb.loc.gov>

National Archives and Records Administration (NARA). Online electronic services.
<http://www.nara.gov>

History Text Archive. Primary documents.
<http://www.msstate.edu/Archives/History>

Electronic Text Center. Full-text access to historical and literary texts; some items are restricted to University of Virginia users only.
<http://www.lib.virginia.edu/etext/ETC.html>

Uncover. Online table of contents index to thousands of magazines and journals; articles written since 1987; full-text available for a fee.
<http://uncweb.carl.org/>

FirstSearch. Subscriber only, fee-based database of books and other materials.
<http://www.oclc.org>

Gateway to World History. A directory of history resources including archives and discussion groups.
<http://library.ccsu.ctstate.edu/Zhistory/world_history/>

History Reviews On-Line. An electronic journal devoted to book and web site reviews in history.
<http://www.uc.edu/www/history/reviews.htmlx>

Demography and Population Studies. Historical statistics.
<http://coombs.anu.edu.au/ResFacilities/DemographyPage.html>

Search Engines for the Web

Alta Vista:
<http://www.altavista.com>
Infoseek:
<http://guide.infoseek.com>
Lycos:
<http://www.lycos.com>
WebCrawler:
<http://www.webcrawler.com>
Excite:
<http://www.excite.com>
HotBot:
<http://www.hotbot.com>
SavvySearch (sends one search to several search engines and directories at once):
<http://guaraldi.cs.colostate.edu:2000/>

Guides and Directories

Yahoo! A vast and popular directory of web sites, constantly updated and with an easy search feature.
<http://www.yahoo.com>
The WWW Virtual Library. A large collection of guides to web resources by discipline and topic.
<http://www.w3.org/pub/Data/Sources/by Subject/Overview.html>
My Virtual Reference Desk. Thousands of links to research materials on the web, organized by category.
<http://www.refdesk.com>
Magellan. A searchable, annotated directory of rated web sites organized by category.
<http:www.mckinley.com>
The Argus Clearinghouse. A searchable, rated collection of subject guides to scholarly web resources.
<http://www.clearinghouse.net>

Electronic Discussion Lists

To be included in any of these lists, you need to "subscribe." To do this, you usually have to send an e-mail message including name of list, your name, and school. The largest site for history discussion groups can be found on "H-Net" at <http://h-net.msu.edu>

A few of the current H-Net groups are:

H-Albion (British History)
H-AmStudy (American Studies)
H-Diplo (Diplomatic History)
H-Ethnic (Ethnic and Immigration History)
H-Film (Scholarly Studies of Media)
H-Ideas (Intellectual History)
H-Labor (Labor History)
H-LatAm (Latin American History)
H-Pol (U.S. Political History)
H-Russia (Russian History)
H-SHGAPE (U.S. Guilded Age and Progressive Era)
H-South (U.S. South)
H-Urban (Urban History)
H-West (U.S. West, Frontiers)
H-Women (Women's History)
IEAHCnet (Colonial, 17th and 18th Century Americas)

Electronic Journals

Scholarly Journals Distributed via the World Wide Web. Science journal only; by subscription only.
<http://www.oclc.org/oclc/menu/ejo/htm>

Directory of Electronic Journals, Newsletters and Academic Discussion Lists. Association of Research Libraries, 1996; also in print version.
<http://arl.cni.org/scomm.edir.index.html>

History Reviews On-Line. An electronic journal devoted to book and web site reviews in history.
<http://www.uc.edu/www/history/reviews.htmlx>

Databases

These databases are updated periodically. Some of these databases are also available on the World Wide Web. Ask your librarian which of these are accessible from your library. Note that most electronic databases include only material published since about 1980. For earlier writings, you will need the printed indexes. Most databases are searchable like online catalogs. Databases have introductions and help menus, but if you run into difficulty, don't hesitate to ask for assistance.

*America: History and Life. Indexes and abstracts several thousand journals covering the history of the United States and Canada. Coverage since 1964. Also available in print.

*Historical Abstracts. Indexes and abstracts several thousand journals covering world history — excluding the United States and Canada — since 1450. Coverage since 1973. Also available in print.

*Historical Statistics of the United States: Colonial Times to 1970. Cambridge University Press, 1996.

A&H Search. A citation index to sources in the arts and humanities.

Article1st. Index of articles from thousands of journals.

Biography Database, 1680–1830. Searchable database of about one million biographical sources in English.

Biography and Genealogy Master Index. Indexes over three million biographies from biographical dictionaries. Also available in print.

BiographyInd. Guide to biographical sources.

Congressional Masterfile. Publications of the U.S. Congress since 1789.

Contents1st. Tables of contents from thousands of journals.

ERIC. Journal articles and reports in education.

FirstSearch. A collection of databases on various subjects available by subscription through the Internet.

HumanitiesIn. An index of articles in the humanities.

Index to American Periodicals of the 1700s and 1800s. Also available on microfilm and on the World Wide Web.

Infotrac-Expanded Academic Index. Indexes recent periodical articles in the humanities and sciences.

MLA-International Bibliography. Articles and other sources on literature, languages, linguistics, folklore. Also in print version.

Newspaper Abstracts. Indexes and abstracts recent articles from a group of major national newspapers.

Nineteenth-Century Short Title Catalogue, 1801–1870. A catalog of nineteenth-century publications in English.

OCLC-WorldCat. A very large catalog of books, journals, audiovisual material, etc.

PAIS Decade. Recent publications on public affairs.

PerAbs. Periodical abstracts from several thousand journals.

Periodical Abstracts. Indexes and abstracts a wide range of magazines and journals in the humanities and social sciences.

Readers' Guide Abstracts. Indexes and abstracts of the contents of 240 popular periodicals, 1983–present.

Sociofile. Indexes and abstracts leading world journals in sociology and related disciplines.

SocSciInd. Guide to the literature of the social sciences.

Statistics Masterfile. Indexes statistical information found in private, state, federal, and international publications.

WorldCat. Books and other materials in a wide range of libraries.

Useful Information for the Historian

Historical Sources in Your Own Backyard

Some of the most rewarding kinds of historical research concern people, events, and places that you can almost reach out and touch. The history of your family, of the town you grew up in, or of events that shaped your parents' lives can be uncovered not only in a library but in a nearby museum or in a local history archive filled with old photographs, land deeds, birth registers, and personal correspondence. Every state in the United States and every province in Canada has its own historical society with a library of books, photographs, and documents on the state's history. Every city and most towns, even small ones, have a historical society or a museum where they keep the documents and artifacts (for example, objects like a millstone or a carriage) that tell the story of the town's past.

Wherever your school is located, from downtown Manhattan to rural Nebraska, you are probably not more than a short drive from a local history archive. If your research concerns the town or area where your school is located, look up the address of the local historical society and visit it. One of the most enjoyable aspects of history research is to hold in your hand an actual document or artifact that makes the past come alive — a 150-year-old land deed, a photograph of the center of town in 1890, a record player from 1918, a letter from a mother to her daughter written in 1838.

If you live or go to school in a large city or if you want to research the history of a county or an area of a state, many records are available to you. Each state (each province in Canada) and each county within that state will have its own archive of historical materials. Each city will have at least one such archive. Cities and towns also have private historical societies. There are thousands of state, county, and local museums and archives. The best way to locate the major archives is to look them up in *Directory of Historical Organizations in the United States and Canada.* This work is published by the American Association for State and Local History, and the most recent volume is edited by Mary Bray Wheeler. This directory lists many hundreds of organizations. It has an index that arranges organizations alphabetically by the name of the place whose history they record. The archives are also listed alphabetically by subject if their collection of documents or artifacts is specialized in some way — say a town that was an important battlefield in the Civil War. The name, address, and telephone number of each organization is listed along with a brief description of the kind of materials it contains.

Sources for Family History

If you wish to research your family history, the following sources will be helpful.

American Families: A Research Guide and Historical Handbook. Westport Conn.: Greenwood: 1991.

American Family History: A Historical Bibliography. Santa Barbara: ABC-Clio, 1984.

Genealogical and Local History Books in Print. Wash., D.C.: Genealogical Books in Print, 1985.

A Bibliography of American County Histories. Baltimore: American Genealogical Pub. Co., 1985.

State Censuses: An Annotated Bibliography of Censuses of Population Taken After 1790 by States and Territories of the United States. New York: Burt Franklin, 1969.

Federal Population Censuses: A Catalogue of Microfilm Copies of Schedules [1790–1920]. Washington D.C., Library of Congress.

NARA. National Archives and Records Administration, *Online Electronic Services.* <http://www.nara.gov>

Biography and Genealogy Master Index. Detroit: Gale, 1980. Supplements annually. Also available on CD-ROM.

Grammar and Style Manuals

If you know that your background in grammar and composition is weak, or if you need more specific information concerning report writing, here are a few manuals that should help.

Hacker, Diana. *A Pocket Style Manual.* 2d ed. Boston: Bedford Books, 1997.

Hacker, Diana. *Rules for Writers.* 3d ed. Boston: Bedford Books, 1996.

Strunk, William Jr. and E. B. White. *Elements of Style.* 3d ed. New York: Macmillan College, 1979.

University of Chicago Press, *The Chicago Manual of Style.* 14th ed. Chicago: University of Chicago Press, 1993.

Library of Congress Subject Headings

The Library of Congress publishes a detailed list of subject headings that catalogers use when describing books. It currently fills four big red volumes which
you may find shelved near your catalog terminals. You can look up a topic in
this list and find out what the "official" name for it is. For example, catalogers
don't use "Vietnam War" as a subject heading, but if you look it up in the list,
it will tell you to use the subject heading "Vietnamese Conflict, 1961–1975."
You can then search the catalog with that heading and get better results.
Broader and narrower terms are also listed. You might check "Textile Workers" and find that while this is a subject heading, there is a narrower heading
available, "Women Textile Workers." Headings can be subdivided chronologically or geographically. Some can get quite long: "United States — History —
Civil War, 1861–1865 — Causes." An example of a listing from the *Library of
Congress Subject Headings* is shown in Figure B.1.

Call Numbers: The Library
of Congress System

The identification system of the Library of Congress divides the major subject
classifications by letter. The following are the Library of Congress subject categories and their respective letter designations.

A General works
B Philosophy, psychology, religion
C Auxiliary sciences of history
D General and Old World history
E American (Western Hemisphere) history
F American history (continued)
G Geography, anthropology, customs, sports
H Social sciences, economics, socialism
J   Political science, international law
K Law
L Education
M Music
N Fine arts
P Language, literature
Q Science
R Medicine
S Agriculture
T Technology
U Military science
V Naval science
Z Bibliography, library science

Textile waste *(May Subd Geog)*
  ₍TD899.T4₎
  BT Factory and trade waste
  NT Wool waste
    Woolen and worsted manufacture—
      Waste disposal
Textile workers *(May Subd Geog)*
  Here are entered works on modern textile workers
  in factories. Works on hand-loom weavers, including
  the medieval guild artisans, are entered under Weav-
  ers.
  UF Textile industry—Employees
  BT Employees
  NT Hosiery workers
    Lace makers
    Women textile workers
  — **Diseases** *(May Subd Geog)*
    ₍RC965.T4₎
    UF Textile workers—Diseases and
        hygiene ₍Former heading₎
    NT Byssinosis
  — Diseases and hygiene
    USE Textile workers—Diseases
        Textile workers—Health and
          hygiene
  — **Health and hygiene** *(May Subd Geog)*
    UF Textile workers—Diseases and
        hygiene ₍Former heading₎
  — **Nutrition**
  — **Trade-unions**
    USE Trade-unions—Textile workers
  — **Wages**
    USE Wages—Textile workers
  — **China**
  — **England**
  — **Great Britain**
  — **Japan**
  — **Massachusetts**
  — **Mexico**
  — **North Carolina**
  — **Soviet Union**
    NT Morozov Strike of 1885
Textile Workers' Strike, Bombay, India, 1982-
  BT Strikes and lockouts—Textile industry
      —India
Textile Workers' Strike, Catalonia, 1913
Textile Workers' Strike, Gastonia, N.C., 1929
  BT Strikes and lockouts—Textile industry
      —North Carolina

Left margin annotations:

"Used for"— "Textile workers" is used as the heading instead of this phrase.

"Broader term" — if you want to broaden your search, use this heading.

"Narrower term" — brings you to "Women textile workers," which is closer to the theme "Women Workers in the Lowell, Massachusetts, Textile Mills, 1820–1850."

Right margin annotations:

"May be subdivided geographically"— for example, "Textile workers — Japan."

Call number (not always given).

Refers to a heading that is no longer used.

Use these headings in your search rather than "Textile workers — Diseases and hygiene."

FIGURE B.1   Sample *Library of Congress Subject Headings* Listing

Each letter group is broken down further by the addition of a second letter and then by numbers. Here are some of the breakdowns of the categories D, E, and F, which deal with history.

D General history
DA Great Britain
    20–690 England
    700–745 Wales
    750–890 Scotland
    900–995 Ireland
DB Austria-Hungary
DC France
DD Germany
DE Classical antiquity
DF Greece
DG Italy
DH-DJ Netherlands
    DH   1–207 Belgium and Holland
    DH 401–811 Belgium
    DH 901–925 Luxemburg (grand duchy)
    DJ Holland
DK Russia
    1–272 Russia (general)
    401–441 Poland
    445–465 Finland
    750–891 Russia in Asia
DL Scandinavia
    1–85 Scandinavia (general)
    101–291 Denmark
    301–398 Iceland
    401–596 Norway
    601–991 Sweden
DP Spain and Portugal
    1–402 Spain
    501–900 Portugal
DQ Switzerland
DR Turkey and the Balkan States
DS Asia
DT Africa
DU Australia and Oceania
DX Gypsies
E America (General) and United States (General)
    11–143 America (general)
    31–45 North America (general)
    51–99 Indians of North America
    101–135 Discovery of America
    151–810 United States
    151–185 General history and description
        185 Afro-Americans in the United States

    186–199 Colonial period
    201–298 Revolution
    351–364 War of 1812
    401–415 War with Mexico
    441–453 Slavery
    458–655 Civil War
    482–489 Confederate States
    714–735 War with Spain
F United States (local) and America except the United States
    1–970 United States (local)
    1001–1140 British North America, Canada, Newfoundland
    1201–1392 Mexico
    1401–1419 Latin America (general)
    1421–1577 Central America
    1601–2151 West Indies
    2201–2239 South America (general)
    2251–2299 Columbia
    2301–2349 Venezuela
    2351–2471 Guiana: British, Dutch, French
    2501–2659 Brazil
    2661–2699 Paraguay
    2701–2799 Uruguay
    2801–3021 Argentine Republic
    3051–3285 Chile
    3301–3359 Bolivia
    3401–3619 Peru
    3701–3799 Ecuador

Thus a volume whose call number begins DK 408 deals with Polish history, and one which begins E 451 is about the history of slavery in the United States.

Call Numbers:
The Dewey Decimal System

The Dewey system is a decimal system. There are ten main subject headings, each containing 100 different numbers:

    000–099 General works
    100–199 Philosophy
    200–299 Religion
    300–399 Social sciences
    400–499 Language
    500–599 Pure science
    600–699 Technology
    700–799 The arts
    800–899 Literature
    900–999 History

Each of the main subject divisions is itself divided into ten sections of ten units each. The divisions of history are:

900–909 General history
910–919 Geography, travel, description
920–929 Biography
930–939 Ancient history
940–949 European history
950–959 Asian history
960–969 African history
970–979 North American history
980–989 South American history
990–999 Other regions of the world

Each of these divisions is further divided into ten parts. The divisions of 970 to 979 (North American history), for example, are as follows:

970 General North American history
971 Canadian history
972 Mexican and Caribbean history
973 General United States history
974 Northeastern states, U.S.
975 Southeastern states, U.S.
976 South-central states, U.S.
977 North-central states, U.S.
978 Western states, U.S.
979 Far-western states, U.S. and Alaska

Thus a volume whose call number begins with 934 deals with ancient history, and one that begins with 978 is concerned with the history of one or more of the western states of the United States.

Extended Footnote/Endnote Examples

Books

BASIC FORMAT FOR A BOOK

1. Edward Countryman, <u>Americans</u> (New York: Hill and Wang, 1996), 58.

TWO OR THREE AUTHORS

2. Michael Bilton and Kevin Sim, <u>Four Hours in My Lai</u> (New York: Penguin Books USA, Inc., 1992), 197.

FOUR OR MORE AUTHORS

3. James Roark et al., <u>The American Promise</u> (Boston: Bedford Books, 1998), 131.

CORPORATE AUTHOR

4. Congressional Quarterly Inc., <u>Congressional Quar-</u>
<u>terly's Guide to U.S. Elections</u> (Washington: Congres-
sional Quarterly Inc., 1985), 374.

UNKNOWN AUTHOR

5. <u>Oxford Atlas of the World</u>, 2d ed. (London: Reed International Books Limited, 1994), 39.

TRANSLATION

6. Wislawa Szymborska, <u>View With a Grain of Sand</u>,
Stanisaw Baranczak and Clare Cavanagh, trans. (New York:
Harcourt Brace, 1995), 109.

EDITORS

7. Thomas Dublin, ed., <u>Immigrant Voices: New Lives in</u>
<u>America 1773-1986</u> (Urbana: University of Illinois Press,
1993), 182.

EDITION OTHER THAN THE FIRST

8. John Hope Franklin and Alfred A. Moss, Jr., eds.,
<u>From Slavery to Freedom: A History of African Americans</u>,
7th ed. (New York: McGraw-Hill, Inc., 1994), 249.

MULTIVOLUME WORK

9. Bernard Bailyn, <u>Federalist and Antifederalist</u>
<u>Speeches, Articles, and Letters during the Struggle over</u>
<u>Ratification</u>, vol. 2 of <u>The Debate on the Constitution</u>
(New York: The Library of America, 1993), 714.

WORK IN AN ANTHOLOGY

10. Thomas Low Nichols, "Boarding Out," in <u>Witnessing</u>
<u>America</u>, comp. and ed. Noel Rae (New York: Penguin Books
USA Inc., 1996), 66.

ENCYCLOPEDIA OR DICTIONARY

With well-known reference books, facts of publication are usually omitted. However, you must cite the edition if it is not the first. When a work is arranged alphabetically, the item is preceded by *s.v.*, meaning *sub vero*, "under the word."

11. The Columbia Dictionary of Quotations, s.v. "Lincoln, Gettysburg Address."

Periodicals

ARTICLE IN A MAGAZINE

12. Stacy Sullivan, "A Case of Alarming Anarchy," Newsweek, 24 March 1997, 23.

ARTICLE IN A JOURNAL PAGINATED BY VOLUME

13. I. C. Campbell, "Culture Contact and Polynesian Identity in the European Age," The Journal of World History 8 (1997): 46-49.

ARTICLE IN A JOURNAL PAGINATED BY ISSUE

14. Susan Mann, "The History of Chinese Women Before the Age of Orientalism," Journal of Women's History, vol. 8, no. 4 (winter 1997): 164.

ARTICLE IN A NEWSPAPER

15. Michael R. Gordon, "Russia-China Theme: Contain the West," New York Times, 24 April 1997, sec. A, p. 3.

UNKNOWN AUTHOR

16. "Building Slowly for the Future," The Economist, 16 November 1996, 40.

EDITORIAL

17. Editorial, "Brutality in Vietnam," New York Times, 28 March 1997, sec A, p. 17.

LETTER TO THE EDITOR

18. Letters, Thomas Leeds, Harper's, June 1995, 5.

BOOK OR FILM REVIEW

19. David Brion Davis, "The Triumph of the Country," review of The Age of Federalism, by Stanley Elkins and Eric McKitrick, The New York Review of Books, 12 May 1994, 25.

Other Sources

MATERIAL FROM AN INFORMATION SERVICE OR DATABASE

20. Alexandra Beatty and others, "U.S. History Achievement Levels," NAEP 1994 U.S. History Report Card, ERIC ED 398 139 (1996): 157.

GOVERNMENT PUBLICATION

21. U. S. Commission on Civil Rights, Enforcement of the Indian Civil Rights Act: Hearing Held in Rapid City, South Dakota, Jul. 31-Aug. 1 and Aug. 21, 1986 (Washington: D.C.: GPO, 1988), 12.

PAMPHLET

22. Dennis Grimmestad, Britta Bloomberg, and Pat Nunnally, Preserving Minnesota: Planning for Historic Properties into a New Century (St. Paul: Minnesota Historical Society, 1991).

DISSERTATION

23. Marjorie Penn Lasky, "Off Camera: A History of the Screen Actors Guild During the Era of the Studio System" (Ph.D. diss., University of California, Davis, 1992), 322.

ABSTRACT OF A DISSERTATION

24. Catherine Elizabeth Kelly, "Between Town and Country: New England Women and the Creation of a Provincial Middle Class, 1820-1860" (Ph.D. diss., University of Rochester, 1992), abstract in Dissertation Abstracts International 53 (1992): 2076A.

COMPUTER SOFTWARE

25. The American Pageant CD-ROM, Windows 3.1 Ver., IBM, Lexington, Mass.

VIDEO

26. Incident at Oglala, dir. Michael Apted (Van Nuys: LIVE Home Video, 1991), videocassette.

SOUND RECORDING

27. Martin Luther King Jr., <u>Martin Luther King at Zion Hill</u> (Los Angeles: Dootone Records, 1962), sound cassette.

SLIDES

28. Mary Stofflet, <u>American Women Artists: The Twentieth Century</u>, (New York: Harper and Row, 1979), slides.

LECTURE OR PUBLIC ADDRESS

29. Winnie Mandela, "The Origins of Conflict and the Journey to Peace," (paper presented at Woodrow Wilson Symposium at the Johns Hopkins University, Baltimore, Maryland, 7 April 1996).

INTERVIEW

30. Carole Gallagher, "American Ground Zero: The Secret Nuclear War," interview by Vicki Kemper, <u>Common Cause Magazine</u> (summer 1993), 28.

Internet Resources

WEB SITE

31. John Kantner, "Chetro Ketl Great Kiva," n.d., <http://www.sscf.ucsb.edu/anth/projects/great.kiva/index.htmlV> (12 May 1997).

GOPHER SITE

32. "Basic Bibliography on How to Do Oral History," 1995, <gopher://gopher.ucsc.edu:/bib/> (11 May 1997).

FTP SITE

33. "Combat Casualties," 27 January 1993, n.d., ftp ftp.msstate.edu/docs/history/USA/Vietnam/ (3 May 1997).

E-MAIL MESSAGE

34. Lisa Divine, <divine@mnnf.k12.mn.us> "Re: Your Question about New Braunfels," 1 May 1997, personal e-mail (2 May 1997).

LISTSERVE MESSAGE

35. Albert Vining, <avining@tma.edu> "Lakota Diaspora after 1862," 15 April 1997, <H-ETHNIC@h-net.msu.edu> (23 April 1997).

NEWSGROUP MESSAGE

36. John Gustafson, <jgustav@aol.com> "Effects of New Technologies on Scientific Communication," 28 May 1997, <soc.history.science> (30 May 1997).

SYNCHRONOUS COMMUNICATION (MOOs, MUDs, IRCs)

37. LambdaMOO, "Discussion of Free Speech Laws," tel-netlambda.moo.mud.org/port=8888 (28 April 1997).

Subsequent References to the Same Source

A second or later reference need only use the author's last name and the page number.

2. Countryman, 98.

6. Bilton and Sim, 202.

10. Oxford Atlas, 15.

If, however, you cite more than one book (or article, etc.) by the same author, any second or later reference must include a shortened version of the title.

5. Countryman, Americans, 144

8. Countryman, People, 56.

Extended Bibliography Examples

Books

BASIC FORMAT FOR A BOOK

Countryman, Edward. Americans. New York: Hill and Wang, 1996.

TWO OR THREE AUTHORS

Bilton, Michael, and Kevin Sim. Four Hours in My Lai. New York: Penguin Books USA, Inc., 1992.

FOUR OR MORE AUTHORS

Roark, James, et al. The American Promise. Boston: Bedford Books, 1998.

CORPORATE AUTHOR

Congressional Quarterly Inc. Congressional Quarterly's Guide to U.S. Elections. Washington, D.C.: Congressional Quarterly Inc., 1985.

UNKNOWN AUTHOR

Oxford Atlas of the World. 2d ed. London: Reed International Books Limited, 1994.

TRANSLATION

Szymborska, Wislawa. View with a Grain of Sand. Stanisaw Baranczak and Clare Cavanagh, trans. New York: Harcourt Brace, 1995.

EDITORS

Dublin, Thomas, ed. Immigrant Voices: New Lives in America 1773-1986. Urbana: University of Illinois Press, 1993.

EDITION OTHER THAN THE FIRST

Franklin, John Hope, and Alfred A. Moss Jr., eds. From Slavery to Freedom: A History of African Americans. 7th ed. New York: McGraw-Hill, Inc., 1994.

MULTIVOLUME WORK

Bailyn, Bernard. Federalist and Antifederalist Speeches, Articles, and Letters during the Struggle over Ratification. Vol. 2 of The Debate on the Constitution. New York: The Library of America, 1993.

WORK IN AN ANTHOLOGY

Nichols, Thomas Low. "Boarding Out." In Witnessing America. Noel Rae, Comp. and ed. New York: Penguin Books USA Inc., 1996.

ENCYCLOPEDIA OR DICTIONARY

Well-known reference works are usually not cited in bibliographies.

Periodicals

ARTICLE IN A MAGAZINE

Remember, the pages encompassing the entire article are listed in the bibliographic entry. The specific page or pages are cited in the note.

```
Sullivan, Stacy. "A Case of Alarming Anarchy." Newsweek,
    24 March 1997, 21-24.
```

ARTICLE IN A JOURNAL PAGINATED BY VOLUME

```
Campbell, I. C. "Culture Contact and Polynesian Identity
    in the European Age." The Journal of World History 8
    (1997): 46-53.
```

ARTICLE IN A JOURNAL PAGINATED BY ISSUE

```
Mann, Susan. "The History of Chinese Women Before the Age
    of Orientalism." Journal of Women's History. Vol. 8,
    no. 4 (winter 1997): 163-76.
```

ARTICLE IN A NEWSPAPER

News items from daily papers are not listed separately in a bibliography. Instead, the name of the paper with the run of dates should be listed in a general alphabetical list or a section devoted to newspapers.

UNKNOWN AUTHOR

```
"Building Slowly for the Future." The Economist, 16 No-
    vember 1996, 40-41.
```

EDITORIAL

```
Editorial. "Brutality in Vietnam." New York Times. 28
    March 1997. Sec. A, p. 17.
```

LETTER TO THE EDITOR

```
Letters. Thomas Leeds. Harper's Magazine, June 1995, 5-7.
```

BOOK OR FILM REVIEW

```
Davis, David Brion. "The Triumph of the Country." Review
    of the The Age of Federalism, by Stanley Elkins and
    Eric Mckitrick. The New York Review of Books, 12 May
    1994, 25-28.
```

Other Sources

MATERIAL FROM AN INFORMATION SERVICE OR DATABASE

Beatty, Alexandra, et al. "U.S. History Achievement Levels." <u>NAEP 1994 U.S. History Report Card</u>. ERIC ED 398 139 (1996): 157.

GOVERNMENT PUBLICATION

U.S. Commission on Civil Rights. <u>Enforcement of the Indian Civil Rights Act: Hearing Held in Rapid City, South Dakota, Jul. 31-Aug. 1 and Aug. 21, 1986</u>. Washington D.C.: GPO, 1988, 12.

PAMPHLET

Grimmestad, Dennis, Britta Bloomberg, and Pat Nunnally. <u>Preserving Minnesota: Planning for Historic Properties into a New Century</u>. St. Paul: Minnesota Historical Society, 1991.

DISSERTATION

Lasky, Marjorie Penn. "Off Camera: A History of the Screen Actors Guild During the Era of the Studio System." Ph.D. diss., University of California, Davis, 1992.

ABSTRACT OF A DISSERTATION

Kelly, Catherine Elizabeth. "Between Town and Country: New England Women and the Creation of a Provincial Middle Class, 1820-1860." Ph.D. diss., University of Rochester, 1992. Abstract in <u>Dissertation Abstracts International</u> 53 (1992): 2076A.

COMPUTER SOFTWARE

The American Pageant CD-ROM. Windows 3.1 Ver. IBM, Lexington, Mass.

VIDEO

<u>Incident at Oglala</u>. Dir. Michael Apted. Van Nuys: LIVE Home Video, 1991. Videocassette.

SOUND RECORDING

King, Martin Luther Jr. <u>Martin Luther King at Zion Hill</u>. Los Angeles Dootone Records, 1962. Sound cassette.

SLIDES

Stufflet, Mary. <u>American Women Artists: The Twentieth Century</u>. New York: Harper and Row, 1979. Slides.

LECTURE OR PUBLIC ADDRESS

Mandela, Winnie. "The Origins of Conflict and the Journey to Peace." Paper presented at Woodrow Wilson Symposium at the Johns Hopkins University, Baltimore, Maryland, 7 April 1996.

INTERVIEW

Gallagher, Carole, "American Ground Zero: The Secret Nuclear War." Interview by Vicki Kemper. <u>Common Cause Magazine</u>, summer 1993.

Internet Resources

WEB SITE

Kantner, John. "Chetro Ketl Great Kiva." N.d. <http://www.sscf.uscb.edu/anth/projects/great.kiva/index.htmlV> (12 May 1997).

GOPHER SITE

"Basic Bibliography on How to Do Oral History." 1995. <gopher://gopher.ucsc.edu:/bib/> (11 May 1997).

FTP SITE

"Combat Casualties." 27 January 1993. ftp ftp.msstate.edu/docs/history/USA/Vietnam/ (3 May 1997).

E-MAIL MESSAGE

Divine, Lisa. <divine@mnnf.k12.mn.us> "Re: Your Question About New Braunfels." 1 May 1997. Personal e-mail (2 May 1997).

LISTSERVE MESSAGE

```
Vining, Albert. <avinging@tma.edu> "Lakota Diaspora after
    1862." 15 April 1997. <H-ETHNIC@h-net.msu.edu> (23
    April 1997).
```

NEWSGROUP MESSAGE

```
Gustafson, John. <jgustav@aol.com> "Effects of New Tech-
    nologies on Scientific Communication." 28 May 1997.
    <soc.history.science> (30 May 1997).
```

SYNCHRONOUS COMMUNICATION (MOOs, MUDs, IRCs)

```
LambdaMOO. "Discussion of Free Speech Laws." telnet-
    lambda.moo.mud.org/port=8888 (28 April 1997).
```

Subsequent References to the Same Source

If you cite more than one book (or article, etc.) by the same author, any second or later reference only needs three hyphens in place of the author's name.

```
Countryman, Edward. Americans. New York: Hill and Wang,
    1996.
---. People in Revolution. New York: W. W. Norton & Com-
    pany, 1987.
```

Common Abbreviations Used in Footnotes, Bibliographies, Catalogs, and Reference Books

anon.	anonymous
app.	appendix
art.	article (plural, arts.)
b.	born
bk.	book (plural, bks.)
bull.	bulletin
c.	copyright
ca.	*circa*, about, approximately. Used with approximate dates, e.g., "ca. 1804."
cf.	*confer*, compare. Used only when the writer wishes the reader to compare two or more works.
ch. or chap.	chapter (plural, chaps.)

col.	column (plural, cols.)
comp.	compiler (plural, comps.)
d.	died
diss.	dissertation
ed.	edition, editor (plural eds.)
e.g.	*exempli gratia,* for example
enl.	enlarged
et al.	*et alia,* and others
et seq.	*et sequens,* and the following
fac.	facsimile
fig.	figure (plural, figs.)
ibid.	*ibidem,* in the same place
id.	*idem,* the same (person)
i.e.	*id est,* that is
ill.	illustrated, illustration
infra	below (referring to a later point in the work)
l. or ll.	line(s)
loc. cit.	*loco citato,* in the place cited (referring to the same passage cited in an immediately previous footnote)
MS	manuscript (plural, MSS)
n.	note, footnote (plural, nn.)
n.d.	no date (of publication is given)
no.	number (plural, nos.)
n.p.	no place (of publication) or no publisher (is given)
n.s.	new series
o.p.	out of print
op. cit.	*opere citato,* in the work cited
o.s.	old series
p.	page (plural, pp.)
par.	paragraph (plural, pars.)
passim	here and there (throughout the work cited)
pseud.	pseudonym
pt.	part (plural, pts.)
q.v.	*quod vide,* which see
rev.	revised
sc.	scene
sic	so, thus (enclosed in brackets to indicate an error or unusual statement in a quotation)
supp.	supplement (plural, supps.)
supra	above (referring to an earlier point in the work)
trans.	translator
viz.	*videlicet,* namely
v. or vol.	volume (plural, vols.)
vs.	*versus,* against

Glossary

Archive: A place in which public records or historical documents are preserved.

Atlas: A bound collection of maps, often including illustrations, informative tables, or textual matter.

Bibliography: A list, often with descriptive or critical notes, of works relating to a particular subject, period, or author; in student papers, a list of the works referred to or consulted.

Biography: A written history of a person's life.

Book review: An essay that comments on a particular work or a series of works on a single subject.

Call number: A combination of characters assigned to a library book to indicate its place on a shelf.

Catalog: A complete listing of items, such as books, arranged systematically with descriptive details. *See also* Library catalog.

CD-ROM: A compact disc capable of containing a large amount of data that is read by a computer.

Chart: A visual display of quantitative information. Common examples are bar charts and pie charts.

Cheating: *See* Plagiarism.

Citation: A reference to a source of information used in preparing a written assignment; usually takes the form of a footnote/endnote. *See also* Documentation.

Cyclical school: School of historical thought that believes history repeats itself. According to this school, essential forces of nature and human nature are changeless, causing past patterns of events to repeat themselves endlessly.

Database: A large collection of data organized for rapid search and retrieval (as by a computer).

Dissertation: An extended, usually written, treatment of a subject; specifically one submitted for a doctorate.

Documentation: The use of historical or other evidence to support a statement or argument; usually takes the form of footnotes/endnotes or material such as pictures, graphs, tables, or copies of documents.

Draft: A preliminary sketch, outline, or version of an essay or paper.

Ellipsis: In a long quotation, the omission of words that are not necessary to the point being made; also, the punctuation (. . .) that appears in place of the omitted words.

Encyclopedia: A work that contains information on all branches of knowledge or that comprehensively treats a particular branch of knowledge; usually comprised of articles arranged alphabetically by subject.

Endnote: A note of reference, explanation, or comment placed at the end of an essay or paper. *See also* Documentation.

Evidence: *See* Primary source; Secondary source.

Essay exam: A test that requires a complete, well-organized written answer on a particular topic.

Footnote: A note of reference, explanation, or comment placed below the text on a printed page. *See also* Documentation.

Graph: A precise drawing, usually taking the form of a series of points and lines that make visual the numerical changes in the relationship between two or more things.

Historian: A student or writer of history, especially one who produces a scholarly synthesis; a writer or compiler of a chronicle.

Historical novel: A work of fiction based on actual events and people.

Historiography: The study of changes in the methods, interpretations, and conclusions of historians over time.

Identification question: A test question requiring the identification of a person, place, object, or event and an explanation of its importance in history.

Interlibrary loan: The loaning of a book by one library to another.

Internet: A worldwide network of computers that can transfer information back and forth.

Journal: A daily newspaper; a periodical dealing with matters of current interest.

Keyword: A significant word from a title or topic used to search electronic catalogs for works on a particular subject.

Library catalog: A system that organizes all the holdings of a library; most are now electronic and can usually be searched by title, author, or keyword.

Library stacks: Shelves on which a library's books and journals are stored.

Microfiche: A sheet of microfilm containing pages of printed matter in reduced form.

Microfilm: A film bearing a photographic record on a reduced scale of printed or other graphic matter.

Monograph: A scholarly study of a specific topic.

Multiple choice exam: A test made up of questions with several possible answers, one of which is the correct or best answer.

Note cards: Small pieces of paper ($3'' \times 5''$ or $4'' \times 6''$) that are convenient for notes and the indexing of those notes when researching.

Objective exam: A test made up of factual questions for which there is only one correct answer for each question.

Online catalog: An electronic catalog that enables the user to search the holdings of a library, and possibly other libraries and databases, from a computer.

Paraphrase: A restatement of a passage, idea, or work giving the meaning in another form. Paraphrases of original work, like direct quotations, require proper documentation. *See also* Plagiarism.

Periodical: A publication with a fixed interval between issues.

Plagiarism: To steal and present the ideas or words of another as one's own; to use material without crediting its source; to present as new and original an idea or product derived from an existing source. Plagiarism is a serious act of academic dishonesty. *See also* Paraphrase; Quotation.

Primary source: Firsthand evidence that records the words of someone who participated in or witnessed the events described or of someone who received his or her information from direct participants.

Progressive school: School of historical thought that believes human history illustrates neither endless cycles nor divine intervention but continual progress. According to this school, the situation of humanity is constantly improving.

Providential school: School of historical thought that believes that the course of history is determined by God and that the flow of historical events represents struggles between forces of good and evil.

Quotation: A statement that repeats exactly the words of a source. Such a statement must be enclosed within quotation marks and properly documented. *See also* Plagiarism.

Reference book: A work, such as a dictionary or encyclopedia, containing useful facts or information.

Research bibliography: A list of sources that may be needed to research a topic/theme for a formal paper; includes publication information and location of the materials.

Research outline: A list of the parts of your topic/theme that need to be researched and a tentative ordering of these parts.

Research paper: A formal writing assignment on a specific theme that requires the reading and synthesis of primary and secondary sources; also requires documentation such as footnotes/endnotes and a bibliography.

Revise: To look over again in order to correct or improve; to make a new, amended, improved, or up-to-date version of an essay or paper.

Rough draft: First version of a written assignment which is polished and revised in later drafts.

Search engine: On the Internet, a service that allows the user to locate World Wide Web sites, usually by keyword or subject.

Secondary source: Records the findings of someone who did not observe a historical event but investigated primary evidence.

Short answer exam: Test that requires brief written answers to factual questions.

Stacks: *See* Library Stacks.

Statistics: A branch of mathematics dealing with the collection, analysis, interpretation, and presentation of numerical data; a collection of quantitative data.

Subject bibliographies: Lists of books, articles, and other material according to subject.

Subject headings: Terms used in catalogs, such as the *Library of Congress Subject Headings*, to describe the contents of a library's materials.

Table: A systematic arrangement of data, usually in rows and columns for ready reference; a condensed enumeration.

Take-home exams: Tests usually consisting of one or more short essays that are prepared outside of class.

Textbook: Often the principal reading in an introductory course; usually supplemented by other, more specialized materials.

Theme: A narrow part of a topic that you have chosen or been assigned for research. A theme sets limits on the area to be investigated and also suggests the kinds of questions that will be answered and the points that will be made.

Topic: A subject chosen or assigned for research.

Web browser: Software that interprets hypertext markup language (HTML) and displays embedded graphics and multimedia; allows the user to view World Wide Web sites.

Word processing: The production of typewritten documents, such as course assignments, by computer programs that allow great flexibility in editing.

World Wide Web: Part of the Internet that uses hypertext markup language (HTML) to connect texts, including images and sound, by means of embedded links.

Writing outline: Framework for a research paper that lists thoughts and ideas in an organized manner and acts as a guide for writing the rough draft of a formal paper.

Yearbook: A book published yearly containing a report or summary of statistics or facts.

Index